Alfred Owen Legge

The Growth of the Temporal Power of the Papacy

A historical review with observations upon the Council of the Vatican

Alfred Owen Legge

The Growth of the Temporal Power of the Papacy
A historical review with observations upon the Council of the Vatican

ISBN/EAN: 9783337424039

Printed in Europe, USA, Canada, Australia, Japan

Cover: Foto ©ninafisch / pixelio.de

More available books at **www.hansebooks.com**

THE GROWTH

OF

THE TEMPORAL POWER

OF THE

PAPACY

A HISTORICAL REVIEW, WITH OBSERVATIONS

UPON THE 'COUNCIL OF THE VATICAN'

BY

ALFRED OWEN LEGGE

'PASSIAMO PRESTO, E SULLA PUNTA DEI PIEDI, QUEL MACCHIO DI FIMO E DI SANGUE CHE SI CHIAMA PAPATO.'—*Guerrazzi.*

London

MACMILLAN AND CO.

1870

[*All rights reserved*]

OXFORD:
BY T. COMBE, M.A., E. B. GARDNER, E. P. HALL, AND H. LATHAM, M. A.,
PRINTERS TO THE UNIVERSITY.

TO

MY MOTHER,

THE TEACHER OF MY YOUTH,

THE TRIED AND FAITHFUL COUNSELLOR

OF RIPER YEARS,

I DEDICATE

WITH PROFOUND AND REVERENT LOVE

MY FIRST ESSAY

IN LITERATURE.

PREFACE.

THE present volume has no pretensions to be a History of the Papacy. That great subject, as a whole, has been ably dealt with by numerous writers; the *separate aspect* which is here presented, and which possesses a special interest at the present time, has not, so far as I am aware, received that adequate but concise treatment which I have felt to be a want in popular literature. With great diffidence I have ventured to attempt to fill this gap.

The reader will therefore not find here much that he would naturally look for in a History of the Papacy. That history, prolific in characters uniting with every degree of intellectual power the most degrading vices or the most sublime piety, has been the subject of occasional side glimpses; the main object proposed being to present, in a succinct form, the processes by which the primogenial simplicity and unworldliness of the early Christian Church have been exchanged, under the fatal influence of a worldly ambition, for a corrupt and idolatrous faith, a temporal sovereignty, and a lordship over the human conscience which grows with the advancing years.

I do not affect to be unacquainted with what early or modern writers have contributed to history on this subject. Here and there I have drawn freely upon these valuable resources. But in every case where the conclusions of other writers have been accepted I have, where unacknowledged in the usual way, attempted to express opinions so adopted in phraseology of my own, and claim the credit at least of independent thought and a fair amount of industrious research. Materials for my work have been gathered from various sources, most of them readily accessible. I desire, however, to make special acknowledgment of the courteous assistance which I have received on several occasions from the gentlemen in attendance at the Reading Room of the British Museum. Notwithstanding this valuable assistance, I have found not a little of the labour of my work to consist in extensive reading, which has only been ascertained to be useless after the labour has been performed.

It is with a feeling of diffidence, approaching to awe, that I now offer the results of my reading to the public. A careful endeavour to avoid diffuseness in the narration of familiar passages of history has consciously exposed me to the danger of superficiality. In so far as this danger has been avoided, the directness and compression at which I have aimed will, I believe, be appreciated in this intensely practical age.

The rapid march of events in connection with the so-called Œcumenical Council might induce me to modify some of the opinions expressed respecting this remarkable phenomenon; but where the scene changes so unexpectedly from day to day, I have felt it imprudent to postpone the publication for the sake of a more confident exposition of what is, after all, a subsidiary incident of my narrative. The question of the Fall of the Papacy is indeed one of the very deepest import; but though it may be precipitated by the event which Pope Pius IX believes ordained of God for its full development and glory, the real causes of its decay have been long in operation, and can neither be eradicated nor greatly aggravated by the foregone conclusions of an assembly, however august, without freedom of debate or power of administration, and sworn to ratify the decisions of him who 'alone receives the plenitude of power neither from the Apostles, nor from Councils, but immediately from Christ!'

A. O. L.

FAKENHAM GROVE, PATRICROFT,
    March 19, 1870.

TABLE OF CONTENTS.

CHAPTER I.

THE subject stated. Dual nature of government. Temporal sovereignty coveted by the Pontiffs. On the titles 'Pope' and 'Pontiff.' Abolition of the right of popular election of the Roman Pontiff. Foundation of the Christian Church in Rome. Relics of St. Peter. The title and office of Bishop. And of Clergy. Origin of the Surplice. Renunciation of secular avocations by the Clergy. The Primacy of St. Peter unknown to the early Church. The Bishops of Rome advance their claims to supremacy. Spread of Christianity. Baptism of Constantine. The first Christian Church a *Basilica*. Gifts and legacies to the State religion receive legal sanction. The Church enriched at the cost of right and justice. Ulterior objects of the Bishops of Rome in the acquisition of landed estates. Struggle for supremacy between the rival Churches of Rome, Alexandria, and Constantinople. Traditional hankering after territorial sovereignty revived in Gregory the Great. Decaying power of the Byzantine Empire in Italy. Recognition of the supremacy of the Roman Pontiff by the Emperor Phocas. The Inconoclastic Controversy. Gregory II withdraws his allegiance from the Emperor, and is elected by the Romans to be their temporal ruler. Enters into alliance with the Frankish Kings. Pepin subdues the Lombards and transfers the conquered territories to the successors of St. Peter. Papal prerogatives imperfectly defined. The alleged donations of Constantine . . . . p. 1

CHAPTER II.

The political influence of the Pontiff extended on the assumption by Charlemagne of the Imperial dignity. The Synod of Frankfort. The Decretal Epistles. Calamities supervening upon the dismemberment of the Empire. Degradation of the Papacy. Otho the Great employs measures to secure his legitimate control over the election of the Roman Pontiff. Commencement of the struggle between the Empire and the Papacy. Deposition of John XII. Conflicting claims of the Emperor and the Pope. Effects upon the Papacy of the destruction of the Carlovingian Dynasty. John XVI contests with Hugh Capet the superiority of the Pope over a Council. Dissensions in Rome. Discordant claims of Pope and Emperor. Hildebrand resolves to free the Popedom from its subordination to the Empire. Persuades Leo IX to submit the validity of his claim to the Tiara to the free decision of the

Romans. Effects an alliance with the Goths. Transfers the right of Papal election to the College of Cardinals. Elected Pope. Henry IV takes umbrage at the election of Hildebrand. Grounds of hostility between the Emperor and the Pope. The Celibacy of the Clergy. The right of Investiture. Results of the contest. Death of Gregory VII. Summary of his services to the Papacy. The Countess Matilda. Urban II, A.D. 1088. Cripples the power of the Emperor in Italy . . p. 28

CHAPTER III.

Urban II and the Crusades. Urban continues the controversy respecting the right of Investiture. Calixtus III. The Concordat of Worms. Issue of the controversy. The territorial sovereignty of the Popes called in question. Adrian IV. The development of the spiritual Power of the Papacy synchronizes with the decay of the temporal Power. Renewal of the struggle with the Empire. Triumph of Pope Alexander III. Condition of the Papacy at the accession of Innocent III. His imperious policy, and its effects upon the status of the political Papacy. Innocent III was the practical founder of the Papal States. Disputed succession to the Imperial throne. Innocent excommunicates the Emperor Otho. Death of Innocent. Establishment of the Inquisition. The prolonged struggle for supremacy destructive of the power alike of Pope and Emperor. Rudolph elected Emperor, A.D. 1273. His policy towards Rome. Surrenders the disputed bequests of the Countess Matilda. New era in the history of Papal claims. Independence of the Empire acquired by the Papacy destructive of the ancient and imposing theory of Church and State. The free Republics of Italy a thorn in the side of the Papacy. Schism of the Eastern Church. Disorders in Rome. Quadruple struggle for the sovereignty of Rome. The administrative system of the Papal Court. Guelphs and Ghibellines. The Power of the Papacy extended by the recognition of its right of arbitrament in the feuds by which Italy was torn. Curious complications attending the elevation of Prince Charles to the Sicilian throne. The 14th and 15th centuries undistinguished in the political annals of the Papacy . . . . p. 47

CHAPTER IV.

Character of Boniface VIII. His quarrel with Philip IV. Benedict XI, A.D. 1303. His death by poison. Philip IV secures the election of Bernard de Got, who assumes the title of Clement V. His subserviency to Philip. Transfer of the Papal residence to Avignon. Clement grants Philip a tithe of the Church property in France. The contest for supremacy revived on the accession of Henry VII. Growing power of the Church. The Diet at Frankfort, A.D. 1338, disallows her presumptuous claims. Consequences of the abandonment of Rome by the Popes. Gregory VI returns to Rome, A.D. 1376. St. Catherine of Sienna. Character of the Pontiffs of the 14th century. Insurrection in Rome on the death of Gregory XI. State of the city. Contrasted with Imperial Rome. The populace demand the election of an Italian Pontiff. Urban VI. Clement VII, Anti-Pope. Commencement of the Great Schism. Distraction of Christendom. The dawn of light . p. 65

CHAPTER V.

The 15th century a transition period. Impatience of Europe at the prolonged Schism. Council of Pisa. Three rival Popes. Council of Constance, A.D. 1414. Purpose of Sigismund in convening the Council. Its imperfect realization. Widespread infidelity. Immorality of the Clergy. The Church brought back under one Head. Character of Martin V. Declares the supremacy of the Pope over a Council. Enters Rome in triumph, A.D. 1421. The imperious assumptions of Martin re-open the controversy respecting the Papal supremacy over a General Council. The Council of Basle, A.D. 1431, asserts the supremacy of a Council. Deposition of Eugenius IV. Eugenius summons a rival Council at Ferrara. And transfers it to Florence. The Byzantine Emperor declares in favour of the Council of Florence Disingenuous conduct of the Pope. Altercations with the Greek Clergy. Equivocal union of the Eastern and Western Churches. Universal recognition of the supremacy of the Roman Pontiff. Proceedings of the Council of Basle. The Tiara offered to Amadeus the Ex-Duke of Savoy. Who takes the title of Felix V. The last Schism. Felix V. resigns the Tiara. The Schism healed. Pretensions of the Pontiffs. Exaltation of the Papacy under Nicholas V. Failure of the Council of Basle to promote ecclesiastical reforms. The Pontiffs of the 15th century . . . . p. 80

CHAPTER VI.

Decrepitude of the Papacy. The Church presents the only medium for intellectual distinction. Rising resentment of her lordship over the human conscience. Julius II, A.D. 1503, resuscitates the waning glory of the Papacy. His absorbing patriotism. Political complications. The Council of Pisa. The Holy League. The Council of the Lateran. Reconciliation of Julius with Louis XII. The League of Cambray. Vicissitudes of the Venetian Republic. The treachery of Julius towards Alfonso, Duke of Ferrara. Complex character of the Pontiff . p. 98

CHAPTER VII.

Leo X, A.D. 1513. His ambitious projects, Popularity with the Romans. Charles V abolishes the practice of rendering homage to the Pontiff. The Reformation. The nepotism of the Popes the chief hindrance to the consolidation of the Papal Power. Unfavourable influence upon the national aspirations of the division of Italy into numerous petty States. Decline of the Imperial authority in Italy. Inherent weakness of the Papacy. Clement VII glories in the humiliation of Italy. Spread of the Reformed Faith. The Holy Alliance. The Sack of Rome. The Treaty of Cambray. Coronation of Charles V. The temporal sovereignty of the Pope confirmed. Disputes concerning Parma and Placentia. Italy again the theatre of War. Paul IV refuses to recognise the succession of Ferdinand to the Imperial throne. Supports the French in attacking Naples. Ambitious projects of the Guizes. Alva at the Gates of Rome. Blind superstition of Philip II. He falters at the threatened exercise of the spiritual Powers of the Church. Restores the Cities taken from the Pontiff. Treaty of Cateau Cambresis, A.D. 1559. The Massacre of St. Bartholomew. Sixtus V a great temporal Pope. His public works. And foreign policy. The liberty of Italy extinguished. Decline of the Papal supremacy in Europe. Sixtus V mainly concerned for the aggrandizement of the spiritual power of the Papacy. The Papacy not susceptible of reform . . p. 111

CHAPTER VIII.

The annals of the Papacy during the seventeenth century barren of political interest. Urban VIII, A.D. 1623-1644. His objection to the Spanish marriage. Seeks the conversion of James I to the Catholic faith. Threatening attitude of Spain and France. Richelieu in alliance with the Huguenots. His treachery. Negotiates a peace with Spain. Urban VIII unites the two Powers in a league against England. The projected invasion. Buckingham commands the English Squadron. His Assassination. Consequences to the Huguenots. The Duc de Nevers succeeds to the Crown of Mantua. Intriguing policy of Urban VIII. The Thirty Years' War. Resuscitation of the struggle for supremacy between the Empire and the Papacy. Pusillanimity of the leading actors in this drama. Causes which led to the overthrow of the preposterous claims of the Papacy. The Italian policy of Urban and its results. His melancholy end. The Peace of Westphalia. Continued decay of Papal power. The Gallican Church asserts its independence of Rome. Indifference of Europe to the Papal Agony. The Peace of Utrecht. The Quadruple Alliance. Limitation of the power of Austria in Italy. Paramount influence of France in the States of the Church. Benedict XIV. Clement XIV. Contrasted characteristics of the Pontiffs and the secular rulers of Europe at the close of the eighteenth century. Voltaire. p. 132

CHAPTER IX.

The purpose of Napoleon in encouraging the spirit of revolt in the Papal States. He threatens the overthrow of the Papal power. Obliges Pius VI to purchase an ignominious peace. Dismemberment of the Papal States and occupation of Rome by a French army. Further humiliation of the Papacy. Pius VI taken prisoner. A Republic proclaimed in Rome. Death of Pius VI, A.D. 1799. The French driven from Rome. Election of Pius VII. Brighter prospects. Napoleon resolves upon the restoration of a national religion in France. The ideas of 'religion' entertained by the First Consul. Negotiations with Rome. The Concordat. The Gallican Church, in its servility to Napoleon, forfeits its vaunted liberties. Napoleon compels the Pope to sequestrate the sees of the Bishops who rejected the civil constitution of the French clergy. The way thus prepared for the extension of Ultramontanism. Elation of the Pontiff at the conversion of France. Napoleon commences preparations for his Coronation. Cardinal Consalvi opposes the solicitations of Napoleon for the presence of the Pontiff. Napoleon is too powerful to be thwarted. His ideas concerning the proper relation of the Church to the State. The Coronation, December 2, 1804. Illusions of the Pontiff. Disingenuous conduct of the Emperor. Asserts his supremacy as Emperor of Rome. Threatens to deprive the Pope of his temporal sovereignty. Dignified attitude of Pius VII. The forces of the Emperor beleaguer Rome. Napoleon's reasons for postponing the occupation of Rome. Formal annexation of the States of the Church to the French Empire. Arrest of the Pontiff . . . . p. 150

CHAPTER X.

Napoleon offers Pius VII the appurtenances of a Court in the south of France. The Pope, declining to hold intercourse with the sacrilegious monarch, is removed to Savona. And thence to Fontainebleau. Rome is declared the second city of the French Empire. The object of Napoleon in despoiling the Papacy of its temporal dominions. Universal sympathy extended to the Pontiff. Effects of his rigorous treatment. The Pope induced to sign the Concordat, whereby he formally renounced his claims to temporal sovereignty. Napoleon's triumph. Pius VII retracts his assent. The Emperor proposes his liberation. Napoleon's downfall and abdication. Protestant Powers instrumental in the reinstatement of the Pope in the territorial sovereignty. Enthusiastic reception of the Pontiff in Italy. His conciliatory disposition. Restoration of the Papal territory. Grasping spirit of the Papacy exemplified in the demands of Pius VII. Puerile demonstrations against the French in Rome and Piedmont. Hatred of Napoleon shared by the allied Sovereigns and the petty rulers of Italy. Hence the restoration of the political Papacy. Restoration of the Order of the Jesuits. And of the Holy Office of the Inquisition. The States of the Church. Extension of the power of Austria fatal to Italian freedom. Unlamented decline of Papal power. Pius VII unequal to the emergencies of the times . . p. 167

CHAPTER XI.

State of society in the Papal States under the recent Popes. Fatuitous obstinacy of Gregory XVI in rejecting the counsel of the great Powers. Disaffection of his subjects and consequent disorganization of society. Election of Pius IX. A reforming Pontiff. Enthusiasm of the Romans. The Priest before the King. The Council of State. Illusions dispelled. Alienation of the advanced Liberals. The 'Moderates' adhere to the Pontiff. Piux IX a traitor to Italian freedom. Cardinal Antonelli. Count Rossi. Flight of the Pope. The Republic proclaimed in Rome. Rivalry for the honour of reinstating the Pope. The proffered assistance of Piedmont declined. The distracted condition of Austria affords Louis Napoleon the opportunity of securing the honour to France. Excesses of Republican Demagogues at Leghorn. Antonelli's antipathy to French intervention. General Oudinot disembarks his troops at Civita Vecchia. Enters Rome on 29th of June, 1849. Return of Pius IX to Rome. Disaffection of the people. Dependence of the Popedom upon France. Growth of the Kingdom of Italy. Schemes of Napoleon powerless against the contagion of the national sentiment. Invasion of the States of the Church. Garibaldi's lofty patriotism. Annexation of the States of the Church to the Italian Kingdom. Aspromonte. The Government of Pius IX wanting in all the elements of popularity. Government by Ecclesiastics an anachronism in the nineteenth century. Incompatible with the freedom and unity of Italy. Results of twenty years' struggle with the Revolution. The temporal sovereignty not conducive to the dignity of the Holy See, or to the interests of Catholic Christendom . . . . p. 182

CHAPTER XII.

Injurious effects of the French occupation of Rome. The Pontifical Sovereignty dependent upon French protection. Probable effects of the loss of the temporal Power upon the Popedom itself. Increase of the Papal armaments. The Œcumenical Council. The inordinate pretensions of the Papacy exhibit the danger to the peace and unity of Italy involved in its prolonged existence as a temporal Power. The tenacious grasp of temporal Sovereignty threatens the destruction of the Papacy. Napoleon declared the temporal Power to be fatal to religion. M. Rouher's 'Never.' Pius IX deposed by the French. Louis Napoleon anxious to withdraw from the embarrassing position consequent upon French intervention. Hostility of the Papacy to the enfranchisement of the human mind. Its influence extended by its intolerant presumptions. Based on the accepted principle of authority. Illustrated in the position of Dr. Newman. And in the servility of the Catholic press. Characteristics of the Roman Church. Credulousness of the Roman Catholic laity. Increasing influence of the Papacy. How explained. Romanism attractive to the morbid and the sentimental. The sufferings of Pius IX have awakened a universal sympathy. Excesses of sympathy. 'Pius the Great.' The growth of Papal assumptions. Their probable effect upon the Papacy. The Council. Objects of Pius IX in convening a General Council. The 'brief and compendious rule.' Infallibility claimed by Pius IX when elected Pope. And after his restoration in 1849. Why, then, is a Council necessary to declare it? Characteristics of the past Councils of the Church . . . . . . p. 198

CHAPTER XIII.

Considerations upon the Council. Its constitution. Devoid of organic continuity with its predecessors. The early Councils. First recognition of the infallibility of General Councils. Convened by the Emperors. Co-equal rights of the Pope and the Episcopate. The Council of Nicea. The attitude assumed by Constantine. The first Council of Constantinople. The Councils of Ephesus and Chalcedon. The Quinisextine Council. The second Council of Nicea. The first seven Councils summoned by the Emperors. Gradual usurpation of the right by the Pope of Rome. The Council of Lyons. The second Council of Constantinople. The Council of the Vatican not Œcumenical.

Essential conditions of Œcumenicity. An Œcumenical Council 'has become a chimera.' Protestants not invited. The invitations to the Eastern Church. The verdict of posterity. Attitude assumed by the lay Catholic Powers. Organizing of the Pope's opposition. The protest of Austria against the 21 Canons. Count Daru's despatch. The French claim to representation in the Council. Antonelli's reply. Unanticipated protraction of the Council. Motives assigned for its convocation. Their inadequateness—how explained. The theory of Pius IX. Proceedings of the Council veiled in secresy. Parties in the Council. Threatened secession. The preponderance of Italian bishops a ground of protest. Analysis of the Council as a representative assembly. Is the opposition 'melting like snow in the glance of Pio Nono?' Anticipated docility of the Fathers not realized. Means adopted to commit the bishops beforehand to the dogma of Papal infallibility. Early indications of divergent opinions. And of resolute opposition. Undaunted firmness of the Pope. Measures adopted for the suppression of the opposition. The Anti-Infallibility address. Protest of German and Hungarian bishops. One-half of the members of the Roman Catholic Church represented by the opposition. Irritation of the Pontiff. Desperate attempts of the Infalliblists to silence the opposition and recover lost ground. The Catholic world placed on the defensive . . . . p. 212

CHAPTER XIV.

Range of observations proposed. Unlimited pretensions of the Roman *Curia*. Opinion of the *Civiltà Cattolica* upon the validity of civil laws contrary to the decrees of the Council. The dogma of the Temporal Power. Its definition improbable. Its discussion a strategical art of the *Curia*. The connection between the Temporal and Spiritual Estate 'prescribed by the law of God.' The assumption of the Virgin. The Syllabus. Remonstrances of Louis Napoleon. Duple reply of Rome. The alleged consistency of the Pope in adhering to the principles avowed in 1846. Will France withdraw her claims to representation in the Council? The *Tablet* on the claims of France. The propositions of the Syllabus designed to secure to the Ultramontanes the retention of their present power. Papal Infallibility. Reason assigned for its definition. Spirit of independence developing in the Council and in Catholic countries. Delusive promises of freedom of debate. The Abbé Laborde. New regulations. The Schema *Constitutionis de Ecclesia Christi*. The 21 Canons. Upon whom do the curses of the Church descend? The lay Sovereigns of Europe, whilst conceding liberal constitutions, cannot countenance Roman intolerance. Article of the Schema defining Infallibility. Infallibility not a new doctrine in the Roman Church. A fundamental question. Having a political as well as a religious aspect. The alleged necessity of a Council to propound dogmas suggests the *fallibility* of the head of the Church. Infallibility involves supremacy. Fallibility *versus* Infallibility. France and Austria opposed to the fanatical pretensions of the Ultramontanes. Will Italy regain her capital? Effects of the supremacy involved in Infallibility. Objects of the Council re-stated. 'Terrible Revolutions' predicted by the *Civiltà Cattolica*. The dogma of Papal Infallibility fraught with danger to the Church. How received in Spain. In Switzerland. In Germany. Dr. Sepp's address to the Vatican Council. Father Hyacinthe's letter. The protest of Count Montalembert. The fascinating influence of this doctrine. The impulse given by the Council to the spirit of inquiry. The probable effect upon Christendom of a dogma disannulling the decrees of earlier Councils. Abrogation of the famous canon, *Quod semper etc.* Illimitable spiritual power of an infallible Pontiff. Severe testing of the fabric of the Roman Catholic Church. The teachings of Popery. The response of Christendom to the Papal challenge. Insufficiency of the reasons assigned in the Syllabus for the convocation of a General Council. Characteristics of Pius IX. Archbishop Manning's definition of 'modern civilization.' The principles of authority and of the right of private judgment in conflict. Triumph of light over darkness . . . . . . p. 254

THE TEMPORAL POWER OF THE PAPACY.

CHAPTER I.

THE temporal power of the Roman Church is at the present time a subject of engrossing interest to every thoughtful mind. Viewed either as an Italian or as a religious question, it involves principles which demand the attention alike of the politician and the Christian in every land, and which passing events surround with a special interest.

I propose briefly to trace the development of that power through the ages in which the Church has been successively subject to the Roman Emperors, the Ostrogoth kings of Italy, the Eastern Roman Emperors, and lastly to France.

Everywhere, and in all time, history exhibits communities of men, living under the constant influence of two orders of things. These, whether we call them civil and ecclesiastical, human and divine, political and religious, or Church and State, are just the expression of man's own dual nature, and are as inseparable as body and soul. Inseparable, and yet distinct, they each exercise a beneficent influence upon the other, and a combined and potent effect upon society, in proportion as the distinct mission of each, and its harmonious but independent modes of operation, are clearly recognized. Such is not the theory of the Roman Church. Trampling upon the eternal law of love, of which it claims to be the infallible exponent, this Church has struggled through long ages, and with untiring energy, for the acquisition and retention of political power, which it has with equal consistency perverted into spiritual despotism.

For a thousand years the temporal has been associated with the spiritual power of the Papacy, and, since the arrogant assertion of Hildebrand, 'The Pope is the sun, the Emperor the moon which shines with borrowed light,' it has remained, though not unchallenged, a cardinal feature of Papal rule. Allied to the spiritual power of the Pontiff, it is held to have conferred a dignity and lustre upon the Court of Rome to which no secular power could aspire, and to have justified the exclamation attributed to a successor of Hildebrand, 'How profitable hath this fable of Christ been unto us.'

Of the titles Pope and Pontiff, by which the supreme head of the Roman Catholic Church is usually designated, it may be remarked that, until the time of Gregory VII, the title of Pope, 'Papa,' was given to all bishops alike. This title, which, amongst other fantastical explanations, has been derived from 'Poppœa,' from the proverbially short life of each Pope; from 'Pa,' for *pater*; or again, 'Pa' (Paul), and 'Pe' (Peter); from 'Papos' (keeper); and 'Pappas' (chief slave)[1], signified then, as it does still in our own language, Father, and was applied indifferently to every teacher. Gradually the title came to be applied specially to bishops, and as in process of time

---

[1] Dean Stanley's 'Eastern Church.'

it grew yet more restricted in its signification, if not in its use, the bishop to whom it was pre-eminently applied was not the bishop of Rome, but, as we shall presently see, of Alexandria. The Patriarchs of the Eastern Church retained this title until near the close of the eleventh century; that is, for as long a period as it has since been specially applied to the Pope of Rome. It was not until A.D. 1076, that Gregory VII decreed that it should be thenceforward ascribed to none but the Roman 'Papa,' prefixing at the same time a 'sanctus,' whence came the modern style 'His Holiness the Pope,' though the word then signified nothing more than 'Reverend,' and is thus preserved in the English Church, in the title 'Most Reverend Father in God.'

In the Eastern Church, the same title, 'Papa' (*Pater patrum*), was employed to designate the Primate. Down to the time of Heraclas, A.D. 230, the Bishop of Alexandria, being the sole Egyptian bishop, was called 'Abba' (Father), and his clergy 'Elders.' From his time more bishops were created, who then received the title of Abba, and consequently 'Papa,' 'that strange and universal mixture of familiar endearment and of reverential awe, extended in a general sense to all Greek Presbyters and all Latin Bishops, was the special address which, long before the names of Patriarch or of Archbishop, was given to the head of the Alexandrian Church [1].' It is curious to note that in the Roman Church the word, in its original signification—Father—continues, as at the first, to be applied to all holding the office of teacher or priest; whilst its Syriac equivalent, 'Abba,' now applied to the heads of monastic

[1] Dean Stanley's 'Eastern Church.'

institutions, has never been appropriated by the Bishop of Rome.

The title 'Pontiff,' derived, not from the Jewish High Priest, but from the Roman Emperors, carries us back to those days of 'muscular Christianity' when work, which conduced to the public weal, was intimately associated with religion. The 'Pontifex Maximus' was a high Pagan dignitary who lived in a public residence at the north-east corner of the Palatine, the chief of the College of Pontiffs, or 'Bridgebuilders;' and the Bishop of Rome received, through the emperors, the title of 'Pontifex,' because entrusted, amongst other duties, with the construction and repair of bridges. Thus Milton, picturing Satan as building a bridge over chaos to get to this planet, calls it 'a work pontifical[1].' Under the old Roman constitution, everything pertaining to religion was placed under the jurisdiction of the College of Augurs, an institution which the Cæsars took almost entirely into their own hands; Augustus and his successors to the time of Constantine, as Presidents of the College, assuming the title of Pontifex Maximus. The duties of the office were to conduct all public sacrifices; to inflict the punishment of death by scourging upon any who insulted the Vestal Virgins; to preside at the assemblies and games; to witness the religious ceremonies of marriage; and to arrange the calendar[2]. Thus the very name which expresses the

---

[1] Dr. Griesinger gives *posse et facere*—to do and to be able—as the derivation of this title, and adds that the ancient Romans had a kind of ministry of public worship, the president of which was entitled Pontifex Maximus. In either case the Christian Popes assumed the heathen title without any compunction as to its origin.

[2] Dean Stanley.

highest ecclesiastical character of the Roman Pontiff, exhibits the secular origin of his primacy.

Until the close of the ninth century the Popes were elected by the people. The popular right of election was abolished by Hildebrand, who transferred it to the College of Cardinals, less numerous then than now, although the number varied with the will of the Pontiff, until Sixtus V limited it, as Ranke informs us, to seventy; 'as Moses chose seventy elders from the whole nation, to take council with them;' or perhaps, as affirmed by other Roman Catholic historians, that being the number of Christ's disciples.

The Christian Church in Rome was founded by the Apostle Paul during his two years' imprisonment in that city. It is unnecessary to enter into the controversy respecting the claims of the Apostle Peter to this honour; for, however strongly tradition may affirm the claim, the fact of his ever having *visited* Rome rests upon tradition alone. It is, at least, very singular that no reference is made to an event of so much importance to those who claim to be regarded as his spiritual successors, either in the Acts of the Apostles, which record so many of his journeys, or in any of the Christian writers of the first two centuries. The only passage in the writings of this Apostle from which the fact can be deduced[1], would identify the seat of the Papacy as the spiritual Babylon,—a means of proof

---

[1] 1 Peter v. 13. It is a curious fact that both Protestant and Roman Catholic partizans have insisted that 'Babylon,' whence St. Peter dates his first Epistle, was only a metaphorical name for the metropolis of heathendom; the former from a wish to identify the Roman Church with the Babylon of Revelation; the latter in order to establish the connection between the Roman Church and the Apostle to whom our Lord committed the keys.

upon which the Roman controversialist would probably not insist. Many relics of this Apostle are still shown, and receive the adoration of the faithful in Rome, such as the chains he wore during his incarceration; a portion of his fishing-net, originally believed to have been kept in the cloisters at Westminster; his bones and teeth; his toe-nails, which at one time were so abundant it is said they would have filled a sack; the pillar upon which he suffered martyrdom; and, to complete the catalogue, one of his bulls is still extant! His head also,—we must suppose whole and entire, since it is *the head*, and not a fraction of it, which is adored in each fane,—reposes, encased in silver, at St. Peter's, St. John's of Lateran, and again at St. Praxedes[1]. Less absurd are these than many of the innumerable relics of the saints which enrich every church in Rome; such as the chemise of the Holy Virgin, the swaddling-clothes of our Lord Jesus Christ, and the three thorns of the crown of thorns, which close inspection has shown to be made of iron; and less revolting than 'the phial full of milk of the most blessed Virgin Mary;' and again, 'a phial full of the precious blood of our Lord Jesus Christ.' Until the

---

[1] With the exception of St. Matthew and St. Thomas, all the Apostles, with many of the first Christian martyrs, have left behind them at least two bodies, which are preserved and venerated in divers parts of Christendom. 'Sainct Matthew and Sainct Thomas,' says Calvin, 'have remayned the most poorest.' After his crucifixion, the remains of St. Peter are said to have been placed in the catacombs of the Vatican, whence they were afterwards transferred to the church of St. Sylvester. In the middle of the fourth century the body was divided, one-half being remitted to its original resting-place, and the other deposited in the church of *S. Paolo fuori le Mura*.

latter part of the seventh century the seat used by the chief of the Apostles was conspicuous amongst these relics; but unfortunately, in 1662, the chair needed repair, when, on the removal of the outer covering, an elaborately carved image of the Labours of Hercules was discovered, revealing the truth, unwelcome as it was unexpected, that it had been made in honour of a heathen divinity! Notwithstanding this exposure, the faithful still view, with awe-stricken reverence, the indent in the rock against which one of the soldiers, whilst conducting the Apostle to his dungeon, struck his head, proving it the sterner stuff. The impression is guarded by an iron grating, above which is the appropriate inscription—*prodigio*. The marble slab upon which, as an altar, St. Peter said mass, and another bearing the impress of the Saviour's feet, and commemorating the alleged fact of his having arrested the Apostle in his attempted flight from Rome, apparently fail to suggest the enquiry whether the Roman highways were indeed paved with marble (which the Romans did not adopt in their architecture until after the fall of Sicily), or, if so, why the imprint of a footstep remains, where all the traffic of old Rome has failed to leave a trace behind.

The President, or Chief Elder of the Church, early received the title of *Episcopus*. This title, however illustrious, and consequently coveted, invested him with no peculiar prerogative, but was employed simply to distinguish him from his colleagues in office. Its nearest anti-type in the present age is, perhaps, to be found amongst the Dissenters of this country—as in the 'Chairman' of the Congregational Union; the 'Moderator' of the Presbyterian Synod; or the 'President' of the Wesleyan Conference. The office, however, was in all probability a permanent one. This we infer from the title, 'Angel of the Church,' employed in the Apocalyptic letters. We shall presently see that this broad ground of the Christian equality of all the chief pastors of the Church, was not lost sight of until the close of the sixth century, when a bishop, canonized by the Roman Church, cited the words of Christ to show the impiety of a claim to supremacy, or to the possession of authority transmitted from St. Peter,—a figment not referred to in the canons of the earlier councils, or in the writings of the early Christian centuries. The co-equality of the early Christian Churches, and of their chief pastors, is unimpeachably evidenced in that invaluable document, the first Epistle of St. Clement to the Corinthians, A.D. 70. The opening paragraph, 'The Church of God at Rome, to the Church of God at Corinth,' frankly recognizes the fact, as yet unquestioned, of perfect equality. St. Clement attempts to exercise no authority, nor to assert any degree of superiority, and 'most singularly for a Roman bishop, in speaking of St. Peter and St. Paul, he names St. Peter first, indeed, but passes briefly over him, to enlarge with far more emphasis and exaltation upon St. Paul,— as if St. Paul had really been the principal founder of the Roman Church, and St. Peter merely his associate [1].'

The Chief Elder of the Church at Rome, upon whom a merely honorary precedence had been conferred, not one of peculiar privilege—much less of universal jurisdiction—soon came to be regarded with distinguished reverence by the provincial communities. And, indeed,

[1] See Appendix to Lord Lindsay's 'Œcumenicity and the Church of England.'

the honour was a perilous one, and the men who sufficiently prized the service of the Church to accept it, were, during the first two centuries, worthy of the reverence which was voluntarily accorded them, but which, as time advanced, they did not hesitate by deliberate and strenuous efforts to court, and upon occasion to demand. Such reverence seriously endangered the spiritual equality which distinguished the members of the new faith. And so it came to pass, that the honour voluntarily accorded to individual bishops for their piety, virtues, and courage, was, by degrees, claimed as properly due to the episcopal office itself; until, in the third century, the claim of the bishops to be regarded as God's peculiar priesthood or portion—κλῆρος—as distinguished from the common people—λαὸς—secured to them the distinctive title of *clergy*. A distinctive dress was also adopted, and its use enforced under a penalty of a month's confinement, on a diet of bread and water. Probably, however, the dress, like that of the Friends in our own country, became distinctive only inasmuch as it was permanent, and did not accommodate itself to an ever-changing fashion; for the white gown, which has always been the ordinary dress of the Popes, was, in fact, the common costume of the early Christians—the common classical dress of all ranks in Roman society. To this costume 'the early Christians adhered with their usual tenacity, partly to indicate their cheerful, festive character, as distinct from mourners, who went in black; partly to mark their separation from the peculiar black dress of the philosophical sects, with which they were often confounded[1].' In this, and as Dean Stanley

[1] Dean Stanley.

has shown [1], in a vast variety of customs, some of them of great interest in their bearing upon the religious controversies of the present day, the Pope alone preserves the practices of primitive Christianity, which have perished on all sides of him. The introduction of the tonsure was probably not anterior to the sixth century. Before the close of the third century, secular avocations were wholly renounced, and, whilst the severance between the clergy and the laity became every year more distinctly marked, tokens of respect toward the former were not only voluntarily accorded, but positively required by ecclesiastical law [2].

The Chief Elder of the Church at Rome claimed special dignity from the position of that city as the metropolis of the civilized world; from the fact of its alleged Apostolic foundation, and of its being the mother church of nearly all the provincial communities.

The figment of Apostolic descent was, as we have already seen, the invention of a later era. No such claim to supremacy was affirmed by the Roman Presbyter, or *Episcopus*, in the ante-Nicene period. However early the tradition of the martyrdom of St. Peter at Rome may have been received, it is certain that the churches of the first four centuries were ignorant of his alleged primacy, and authority over the other Apostles, and likewise of the transmission of that authority to his successors.

The simplicity of the Bishops of Rome was corrupted by their increasing authority; the pride of precedence early begot a lust for power, and they suffered no opportunity for asserting their supremacy to pass unim-

---

[1] 'Good Words,' 1868.
[2] Riddle's 'History of the Papacy.'

proved. So early as the close of the second century, in a controversy respecting the day upon which Easter should be observed, Victor, then Bishop of Rome, threatened to refuse to hold communion with those Churches of Asia which proclaimed the duty of celebrating the mystery of the Resurrection of our Lord only on the day of the Lord. He did, in fact, publish letters declaring the heterodoxy of all such. Yielding, however, to the unanimous desire of the Asian bishops, and the eloquent pleading of Irenæus,—whose character as a peace-maker so well answered to his name,—that he would not occasion schism in the Church of Christ upon a subject respecting which Polycarp, who himself had observed the sacrament with the Apostle John, had left the Church a conspicuous example of toleration, he withdrew them [1]. The failure of his unworthy efforts, whilst it evinces the rising spirit of the Papacy, establishes the fact that at this time the Bishop of Rome was not regarded as the universal head of the Church.

The unity of the Empire favoured the spread of Christianity, and the persecution of its early professors, who went everywhere preaching the word, secured its extension, and had already conferred upon it a firm organization. The constancy of faith, and the purity of life, which marked the adherents to Christianity, contrasting with the superstitions and abominations of Paganism, gradually brought the latter into contempt. Constantine professed himself a Christian, and as the Emperors had always presided over the Pagan system, and had found it an important engine of State, the same patronage was now transferred to Christianity [2].

The conversion to Christianity of the Emperor Con-

---

[1] Eusebius. [2] 'Compend. of Univ. Hist.,' Jarrold and Sons.

stantine marked an important era in the history of the Christian Church. Although prompted by motives of policy, rather than by religious conviction, or a genuine moral sympathy, his baptism at the hands of Sylvester, the then bishop of the Church of Rome, was fraught with momentous consequences. 'Many judge of Constantine,' says Niebuhr, 'by too severe a standard, because they regard him as a Christian; but I cannot look upon him in that light. The religion which he had in his head must have been a strange jumble indeed ... He was a superstitious man, and mixed up his Christian religion with all kinds of absurd superstitions and opinions. When certain Oriental writers call him " equal to the Apostles," they do not know what they are saying, and to speak of him as a saint is a profanation of the word.' Constantine himself appears to have been sufficiently alive to the fact. Believing that complete purification could only be once obtained through baptism, he deferred the ceremony which should give him a right to the continuance of that prosperity in a future life which he had enjoyed in the present, to the last moment that was consistent with perfect security [1]. It was the settled policy of Constantine to make the service of the Church more profitable than that of the State. He accordingly showed a singular fertility of resource in devising means whereby men of rank and influence were induced to enter the Church as a profession. It is worthy of notice, in passing, that the introduction of lights in the Christian worship is attributable to Constantine. Originally they were no part of the ceremonial—no 'essential' representation

---

[1] 'History of the Intellectual Development of Europe,' by Dr. J. W. Draper, 2 vols. 8vo.

of doctrine. The display of lights was a heathen custom, and was adopted by Constantine, not as an emblem, but for the purpose of attracting the heathen to the Christian worship.

Through the influence of courtly example and patronage, the despised sect now became rich and powerful. No patriarch had as yet enjoyed more than an honorary supremacy, and the right of the Emperor, in virtue of his office as Pontifex Maximus, to intermeddle in religious affairs was readily conceded. The clergy, 'preaching the duty of passive obedience now, as it had been preached in the days of Nero and Diocletian, were well pleased to see him preside in councils, issue edicts against heresy, and testify, even by arbitrary measures, his zeal for the advancement of the faith and the overthrow of Pagan rites [1].'

Constantine, by his own munificence, enabled the Christians to restore their edifices, which had been destroyed during the persecution under Diocletian, and the property of many heathen temples was made over to the Church. Not a few of the existing churches in Rome claim the first Christian Emperor for their founder. The most distinguished of these is St. Peter's, the site of which tradition affirms to be the spot on which the Apostle suffered martyrdom. The Lateran, an imperial palace, was also granted to the Christians as an episcopal residence,—the first 'patrimony of St. Peter's.' It is a significant fact that the origin of the Papal power, which has always relied for support upon the weapons of this world, was thus purely secular. The first church was not a temple, but a 'Basilica,'— a Roman court of justice, accommodated to the pur-

[1] 'The Holy Roman Empire,' by James Bryce, B.C.L.

poses of Christian worship. 'If the Pope,' says Dean Stanley, 'were to be regarded only as the successor of St. Peter, his chief original seat would, of course, be in the Basilica of St. Peter, over the Apostle's grave. But this is not the case. St. Peter's Church, in regard to the Pope, is merely a chapel of gigantic proportions, attached to the later residence which the Pope opened under the Vatican Hill. His proper see and cathedral is the Basilica of St. John "in the Lateran," that is, in the Lateran palace, which was the real and only bequest of Constantine to the Roman Bishop... In it accordingly is the true Pontifical throne, on which are written the words *Hæc est papalis sedes et pontificalis.* Over its front is inscribed the decree Papal and Imperial, declaring it to be the mother and mistress of all churches. In it he takes possession of the See of Rome and of the government of the Pontifical States.'

By the celebrated edict of Constantine, A.D. 321, gifts and legacies to the State-religion received legal sanction. They immediately poured in abundantly from every quarter, begetting a thirst for wealth, which was constantly stimulated by the success of the artifices through which it was secured. We have the authority of one of the most prominent of contemporary clergymen in the English establishment, for stating that the reign of Constantine was the beginning of the decline of Christianity in spiritual things, quite as much as it was the beginning of its rise in temporal grandeur. An early ecclesiastical writer informs us that the Roman clergy 'made it their special business to be duly informed of any noble ladies, widows especially, who may be accessible to "pious influences," such ladies would then receive no lack of ecclesiastical visitors;

and if one of the good fathers greatly admired any of the household appurtenances, or pretty jewels of the mistress, what could she do but beg him to accept, in the name of the faith, the trifle which had found favour in his eyes.' Nor did the clergy scruple to commend to such as betrayed an unwillingness to part with their possessions, the example of the devout Christians who had shown themselves 'accessible to pious influences.'

'The ignorance and superstition of the times,' remarks the author of the 'Universal History,' already quoted, 'favoured the claims of the priesthood, and as the efficacy of gifts for the expiation of offences was a principle generally admitted in the Dark Ages, liberal donations of land and other property augmented their power and influence,' whilst they laid the foundation of the temporal sovereignty of the Popes. The property of orphans was shamefully tampered with, and no wealthy penitent was suffered to die in peace at Rome, until the Church was assured of a large share of his possessions. Thus, at the close of the fourth century, the Bishop of Rome 'lived in a dignity and pomp much more befitting a wealthy and luxurious earthly potentate, than a spiritual teacher and shepherd of souls. The choicest viands, the richest vestments, the rarest steeds for his chariots, a crowd of servile attendants to do his bidding; a bishop's staff summoned all these things into existence for the holder, whose court almost vied with the Emperor's own. We can scarcely be surprised that the governor of Rome, who was still attached to the old faith, replied when his conversion was attempted, "Make me bishop of Rome, I'll turn Christian directly[1]."' Contemporary writers concur

[1] 'The Mysteries of the Vatican,' by Dr. Theodore Griesinger.

in their testimony, that this wealth had been almost wholly procured through the devout offerings of the noble dames of Rome; or wrung from wealthy penitents on their death bed, by the exercise, on the part of the priesthood, of an arrogated authority, enforced by harrowing appeals to morbidly excited consciences. Therein lay the vital germ of Papal wealth. 'The Roman bishops enriched themselves at the cost of right and justice, by the hands of their female penitents, who, amid the luxury and immorality, of the fast collapsing Western Empire, had often a heavy list of sins to atone, and were but too ready to make their peace with heaven, when earth had no more pleasures to offer, by a liberal bribe to the Church.'

But a new ambition,—in comparison with which gold and costly jewels, and even ecclesiastical supremacy, however prized, were as nothing,—was already looming upon the horizon of the Roman Bishops. The patronage of the sovereigns, whose kingdoms were of this world, was a good thing; but the union, in the sacred person of the Bishop of Rome, of the representative upon earth of Him whose kingdom is not of this world, with royal prerogatives, and a temporal sovereignty, whose lustre, derived from the double source of spiritual and secular jurisdiction, should eclipse the glory of every other government upon earth, was an object worthier of ambition. From the middle of the fourth century, when *religion* had given place to *theology*, and Christendom was absorbed in controversies, the inevitable issue of the futile decisions of Councils, this object was persistently kept in view. The acquisition of lands was more eagerly sought, and there is abundant evidence that when these were not attainable either by gift or legacy, recourse was had to forged wills and fraudulent title-deeds. But these possessions remained *the private property* of the Church, and conferred no rights of temporal sovereignty. They were, however, valued for the influence which always attaches to the possession of landed estates, and which must at length become overwhelming when they are held by a corporation which may always receive, and can never alienate; which is always renewing itself, and can never die.

The history of this period is the record of the struggle for supremacy of the three great sees—of Rome, Alexandria, and Constantinople. In this contest Rome possessed all the advantages accruing from the prestige conferred by historical associations, and a precedence which was universally conceded; whilst the removal of the seat of empire to Constantinople had relieved her from that imperial observation and control to which the rival Churches, weakened, moreover, by their own intense rivalry, were more immediately exposed.

The supremacy of the Bishop of Rome, first, though unsuccessfully asserted, A.D. 109, in the controversy respecting Easter, appears to have been recognized in numerous appeals from distant Churches throughout the second and third centuries. Advantage was taken of the corruptions and dissensions which prevailed, to proceed from giving advice to interference in the arrangement of the affairs of those Churches, chiefly in Italy, which thus appealed to the authority of Rome. The Papacy, it has been well said, 'is a worm which breeds in spiritual corruption, and fattens upon Christianity when turning to decay.'

The supremacy, so pertinaciously asserted, was not suffered to remain unimpugned. At the Council of Carthage, A.D. 254, St. Cyprian boldly affirmed that the precedence conceded to the Roman Bishop, on account of the political position of his see, did not imply the recognition of any authority over Christians out of his own diocese. 'None of us,' he said, 'ought to set himself up as a bishop of bishops, or pretend tyrannically to restrain his colleagues.' By degrees, however, Rome emerged from this equality. Hitherto the bishops of Rome had not aspired to the exercise of either of the three powers—the legislative, the administrative, nor the judicial—which are the proper attributes of sovereignty. The first opportunity for attempting to assert the latter was afforded by the Council of Sardica, A.D. 343. In their zeal for carrying their point against the favourers of Arian tenets, the bishops were willing to sacrifice even their own independence, and invested the Pope, Julius, with the character of universal umpire or judge [1], authorized 'to appoint judges for a bishop; in the second instance to hear the cause on the spot, with the assistance of a Roman legate, and, in the event of a further appeal, to pronounce sentence himself [2].' Both the Eastern and the African Churches, however, protested against 'this arrogant claim,' nor had it any practical effect, until the fabrication of the Isidorian Decretals imparted to it an important and dangerous significance.

The controversies which rent the Church during the fifth century were constantly referred to the arbitration of the Roman See. It was in vain that, at the Council

---

[1] Riddle's 'History of the Papacy.'
[2] 'The Pope and the Council,' by Janus.

of Chalcedon, a canon was passed to the effect that the supremacy of the Roman See was not in right of its descent from St. Peter, but because it was the bishopric of an imperial city. The Church which teaches the infallibility of the decisions of Councils, and pronounces them binding upon the conscience of Christendom, hesitated not to refuse her recognition of the validity of a canon hostile to her pretensions; and her supremacy became more and more distinct.

The divisions between the Eastern and Western Churches, arising out of matters essentially frivolous, often placed the Popes in an embarrassing position. Their power and wealth continued to increase, notwithstanding; and at the close of the sixth century the Pope was the richest landowner in the Peninsula. Appealing to the undefined traditions of antiquity, to the religious superstitions of the age, and to the unquestionably great services which the bishops had rendered, in the protection of Rome from successive barbarian invasions, the Pontiffs contrived to increase their influence, and to invest it with a superstitious awe.

The imperious mind of Gregory (the Great), a man of no ordinary gifts, and the last true Roman Pastor, chafed under the humiliating vassalage in which he stood to the decaying Byzantine Empire. 'He craved the long-coveted possession of sovereignty, which he believed to be within his grasp, if he dare but put forth his hand and seize the prize. To Gregory, however, we can appeal for an authoritative refutation of those Roman Catholic historians who, in their zeal to establish the original supremacy of the Roman See, affirm that it was generally recognized at a much earlier date. In the year 588 the Patriarch of Constantinople claimed for himself and his See a pre-eminence both in power and holiness. In reply, Gregory published a vigorous protest, in which these significant words occur,—'This I declare with confidence, that whoso designates himself "Universal Pastor," or, in the pride of his heart, consents to be so named, he is the forerunner of Anti-Christ [1].' Again, quoting the words of Christ, 'Call no man your father on earth,' he adds,—' What then, dearest brother, will you say in that terrible trial of the coming Judge, when you have sought to be called by the world not only Father, but General Father?'

The determined resistance of Gregory to the pretensions of the See of Constantinople has, by some historians, been assigned to a jealous fostering of the generally recognized supremacy of his own See. In this view I find it impossible to concur. The moderation of his pretensions in the exercise of his spiritual functions contrasts strangely with his ambitious schemes for exalting the Papal office by the union of temporal power with his spiritual jurisdiction. But the fact is there, attested by unimpeachable evidence running through the thirteen years of his anxious and active Pontificate. 'Peter, the prince of the Apostles,' he says, 'never assumed to be universal bishop. O tempora! O mores! In consideration of the primacy of Peter, that title was offered to the Bishop of Rome by the synod of Chalcedon; but be it far from every Christian heart to admit of a title so blasphemous.' Again, in a letter to the Patriarch of Alexandria, this Pontiff, whom the Church has signally honoured by according to him the title of 'GREAT,' and the honour of canonization, made use of these words, which we commend to the Infalliblists now assembled

---

[1] 'The Eighteen Christian Centuries,' by Rev. J. White.

in Rome,—'You say that you have obeyed my commands. Pray do not use such expressions. *I issue no commands.* I know myself and you; you are my brother, and *I only recommend what seems to me* good for the Church. You give me the title of Universal Bishop, which dishonours me in diminishing the dignity of the order to which I belong. You know it was offered to my predecessors by the Council, but none of them would accept it.' It must, however, be admitted that in the exercise of the spiritual jurisdiction which he conceived to belong to his See, 'in virtue of the authority of the prince of the Apostles, Peter,' Gregory not unfrequently infringed the moderation of his claims. His Pontificate was distinguished for the promotion of ecclesiastical rites and ceremonies; for the enforcement, with a strictness amounting to severity, of ecclesiastical discipline; and pre-eminently for his missionary spirit, in illustration of which the mission of Augustine to this country will suggest itself to the reader.

The greater part of the Peninsula was at this time subject to the Byzantine Empire, and was governed by Exarchs from Constantinople. Their position was invidious. Deriving little assistance from the power which they represented, and which, after a succession of feeble monarchs, was tottering to its fall, they were constantly exposed to the danger of aggression on the part of their vigorous neighbours, the Lombards. This position of affairs afforded Gregory the desired opportunity. He offered the Emperor both money and men to check the movement, already initiated by the Lombard king, to unite all Italy under his sceptre; the condition imposed being that Gregory, now styled the Pope, should be invested with *the full legal jurisdiction* of his landed possessions, and with the right of presentation to all civil offices within the patrimony of the Church. His death, A.D. 604, occurred whilst the negotiations were in progress. In the same year, Phocas was raised to the imperial dignity by an insurrection in the army. Without committing himself to a recognition of the claims of the late Pontiff to civil jurisdiction within the territories now belonging to the Church, he acknowledged those of Sabinian, the successor of Gregory, to ecclesiastical supremacy. Henceforward the Bishops of Rome were regarded as, beyond dispute, the ultimate depositories of authority concerning all matters and persons ecclesiastical—a position long coveted and still alleged to have been divinely bestowed. History, however, points to the man, whom she also describes as 'a monster of vice,' as the bestower of this pretended supremacy, and of 'the diadem of gold,' the first in order of the three crowns.

The iconoclastic strife brought matters to a crisis. The worship of images had become so prevalent that the Emperor Leo attempted its forcible suppression. Gregory the Second strenuously supported the idolatrous practice, and, in 727, withdrew his allegiance from the Emperor, whilst the Romans unanimously elected him their temporal as well as spiritual ruler. The die was now cast. No Pontiff heretofore had headed a purely political movement; but Gregory boldly dissolved the ties which bound him to the Emperor; and the prize for which the Roman Bishops had longed, and vainly diplomatized, for four hundred years, was grasped. The triumph did not afford unmixed satisfaction. The exasperated Emperor retaliated by violently wresting from the Papal See the rich patrimonies scattered over the Peninsula and Sicily, undeterred by the proud self-consciousness which inspired Gregory II to protest that, by all the nations of the West, he was regarded as a God upon earth. A more fatal result to the Church was the loss of that unity which had been so firmly secured. She had substituted for the pastoral superintendence of her First Elder, deliberating in council with his brethren of other Churches, the despotic rule of an absolute temporal sovereign, claiming privileges and rights alien to the spiritual interests of the Church—to its early traditions, and to the profound convictions of its most distinguished prelates.

Convinced of the folly and peril of leaning for support upon a power which had so often betrayed them, Gregory and his successors entered into alliances with the Frankish monarchs. With the most barefaced defiance of all political morality, Pope Zacharias, who succeeded to the chair of St. Peter, A.D. 741, sanctioned, for his own worldly advantage, the act of violence and usurpation by which Pepin appropriated the crown of Childeric. This was the first occasion upon which the Holy See had been invoked as an International Power; and it was an ill-omened employment of its newly-acquired rights. Pope Zacharias crowned Pepin king of the Franks, and the king proclaimed the successors of St. Peter sovereign Pontiffs, and lords of the city and territories of Rome. The Bishop of Rome became the sovereign of a temporal kingdom, which must henceforward be supported by the same methods and arts whereby secular governments are everywhere maintained. The complex organization of the Roman Curia was the work of ages, but it had its nucleus in that fatal act whereby the ecclesiastical and political administration of the Papacy became so intertwined that the harmonious working of the system was for ever at an end.

The Western Church was now freed from its subserviency to the Empire of the East; but now also began that connection between Rome and France, which has proved fruitful of so much misery, and which remains, after eleven centuries, the insoluble problem of European politics; whilst the prolongation of the French occupation is, in the present state of Italy, an insult to that renovated country. More than this, it is a danger to Europe, and a source of weakness to France, whose ruler thus proclaims his recantation of the noble principles in defence of which, in early youth, he took up arms and witnessed the heroic death of his brother fighting against a Pope for the liberties of Italy.

Zacharias was succeeded by Stephen II, who, through the aggressions of the Lombards, and the apparent indifference of Pepin, was in no small danger of losing all that his predecessor had acquired. Pepin, however, found it convenient to allay the misgivings which some tender consciences among his subjects entertained, concerning the legitimacy of his title to the Gallic crown. For this purpose he sought absolution from the Pope for his perjury to Childeric; undertaking in return to subdue the Lombards and secure the safety of Rome. This done, he returned to France, when the Lombards, under their King Aistulph, again marched upon Rome. Stephen despatched three embassies in succession, imploring Pepin to return and 'root out these lawless devils, the Lombards.' The last embassy carried an autograph letter from St. Peter, written expressly for this occasion, and which is still in existence, though we have no record of the manner of its conveyance from Paradise to the Pope. The letter, a fabrication, which for strangeness and audacity has never been exceeded, is written in Latin, and runs thus:—'Pepin, the princes his sons, the Frankish nobility, and the Frankish nation, in the name of the Holy Virgin, the thrones, dominions, and powers of heaven, in the name of the army of martyrs, of the Cherubim and Seraphim, of all the hosts gathered round the throne, and under threat of utter damnation, not to let his peculiar city Rome fall into the hands of the hell-brand Longobards.' There was little ground for apprehension of any critical examination of this extraordinary document at the warlike court of Pepin, who of course obeyed the behest. His army once more crossed the Alps, and repelled the encroachments of the Lombards; and true to the religious motives which had prompted him to undertake the expedition, he transferred the recovered territories to the successors of St. Peter. With his own hands Pepin deposited on the tomb of the Apostle the deed by which they were surrendered to him and his successors; thus establishing a valid claim to St. Peter's powerful intercession for the Divine forgiveness of his unjust seizure of the Frankish kingdom. A portion of southern Tuscany was also secured to the Church; and Pepin received from the Pope the title of 'Protector of Rome and of the Roman See.' But although Pepin laid the keys of the conquered towns upon the altar of St. Peter's, by which act, says Ranke, 'he laid the foundation of the whole temporal power of the Popes,' the latter could exercise no real authority in them. The revenues of the lands were theirs; the supreme authority over them was retained by the Frankish kings, and the limits between the Imperial and Papal authority were never very distinctly drawn.

It was long affirmed by the authorities of the Romish Church, that these territories were originally presented to the Roman Bishops by Constantine [1]. There was a time when to doubt this assertion was a grave theological error, only to be atoned by the severest penalties; and some of the earliest martyrs to Roman intolerance, were those whose heresy consisted in questioning the genuineness of Constantine's alleged donation. Even Dante believed the fable, and wrote in the bitterness of his noble, pious heart:—

> 'Ah! Constantine; to how much ill gave birth,
> Not thy conversion, but those rich domains
> That the first wealthy Pope received of thee!'

But this attempt to ante-date the temporal sovereignty of the Popes is now universally acknowledged to be opposed to historical fact [2]. The Christian Church,

---

[1] The famous 'Donation of Constantine' was a forgery concocted at Rome in the middle of the eighth century. 'The forgery,' says the author of 'The Pope and the Council,' 'betrayed its Roman authorship in every line; it is self-evident that a cleric of the Lateran Church was the composer. The document was obviously intended to be shown to the Frankish king, Pepin, and must have been compiled just before 754. Constantine relates in it how he served the Pope as his groom, and led his horse some distance. This induced Pepin to offer the Pope a homage, so foreign to Frankish ideas, and the Pope told him from the first that he expected, not a gift, but restitution from him and his Franks.' The object of this forgery was to establish the right of the Popes, as the successors of the Roman Cæsars, to the territory of all Italy.

[2] If the forthcoming Œcumenical Council executes the programme of which we have already the official intimation, it will undertake the correction of hitherto prevalent estimates of history,

however, had become essentially 'a kingdom of this world.' Its doctrines were corrupted; its worship was mere ceremonial; its ministers were a 'sacrificing priesthood,' and its chief elder a sovereign Pontiff. The Roman Church had become the Roman Court.

and it will again become heresy to question the alleged donation of Constantine.

CHAPTER II.

The assumption of the Imperial dignity by Charlemagne, and the re-establishment of the Western Empire, confirmed and extended the ecclesiastical supremacy and the political influence of the Roman Pontiff. The undisputed possession of territorial sovereignty was still delayed; the Bishops of Rome, in common with all other bishops, receiving confirmation in their office from the Emperor, who regarded them still in the light of subjects.

The infallibility of the Pope, in matters of faith, was far from being universally recognized, notwithstanding the reverential and even servile language in which it had long been the custom with all bishops to approach him. The support accorded by Gregory II and his successors to the doctrines of the second Nicene Council concerning image worship, had begotten a widespread aversion to the Pontiff's claims to infallible dictation, and a reluctance to acknowledge his supremacy over all the Churches of the West. The decrees of the second Council of Nicæa were condemned by the Synod convened by Charlemagne, at Frankfort, whose deliberations were conducted under the personal direction of the Emperor. Not only the worship, but even the veneration of images was prohibited; whilst the tone of superiority which Charlemagne affected over the Pope, and his despotic interference in ecclesiastical matters, secured him the pseudonyme of *Epis-*

copus episcoporum. But the Pope was now too powerful even to contemplate the possibility of a check in the progress which had been so rapidly made towards that universal dominion to which the Papacy steadily aspired. The ignorance which generally prevailed, and the consequent necessity of employing ecclesiastics in the highest secular offices, favoured resort to one of those stratagems which Rome has always so well known how, and when, to employ, in tightening her grasp upon the human conscience [1].

'Suddenly there appeared a professed collection of Epistles of Roman Bishops, from the time of the Apostles to the beginning of the seventh century, in which the doctrine was distinctly and forcibly laid down that the Roman Pontiff was the supreme head, lawgiver, and judge of the whole Church, without whose approbation and concurrence the acts of neither metropolitans nor councils could possess any validity. These ancient and venerable documents, said to have been collected in the seventh century by the celebrated Isidore, bishop of Seville, and now published under the title of "Decretal Epistles," but in reality very different from the

---

[1] From the middle of the fifth century the pretensions of the Papacy had been supported by a course of systematic fabrications. Of these, perhaps the most important (from the fact of its being afterwards incorporated in the Isidorian Decretals, and so lending to the latter the stamp of authority) was the interpolation of the original list of Roman bishops, which became the foundation of the *Liber Pontificalis*. The object of this forgery was to confirm existing legends of Roman martyrology, and of the Popes and Emperors, such as the baptism of Constantine; and to supply a basis for the belief, designed to be elevated into dogma, that the Popes, from St. Peter downwards, *had acted as legislators of the whole Church.*

collection under the name of that writer which had become known in the course of the eighth century,—appeared to possess an authority beyond the reach of cavil or of doubt; and that respect and submission to the Roman See which had hitherto been regarded by some as a matter of opinion, or as the necessary conclusion from certain premises, or which others had supposed to have been founded only in prescription, from long usage and ancient custom, was now proclaimed and accepted as involved in the very constitution of the Church from the beginning [1].'

The success of this forgery was complete, and had a lasting effect, far beyond what its author contemplated, upon the future history of the Papacy. It was the first step—palpably false and fraudulent—in that strange but complete transition from the catholicism of the Fathers to that of the modern Popes, and effectually changed the whole constitution and government of the Church. Here and there a voice was raised against the Decretals [2]; but the great authority of the Roman Pontiffs served to invest them with such a pomp of authenticity, that it was seldom any one dared to in-

[1] Riddle's 'History of the Papacy.'

[2] A singular illustration has been recently afforded in the work of Monseigneur Maret, 'Du Concile Général et de la Paix Religieuse,' of the permanent effects of these forgeries in giving a retrospective colouring and interpretation to the entire field of Christian antiquity, and to the evidence adduced, even by the moderated tones of Gallicanism, in support of the pretensions of Rome. Here is a prelate, honest enough to disavow the whole collection of forgeries and interpolations, who, notwithstanding, betrays an unconscious bias—the inevitable result of their enduring effect on the thought of Rome—towards the traditions of which they are the source, a profound attachment toward the disturbing theories which they have systematized.

sinuate a doubt of their genuineness, until the sixteenth century, when Erasmus demonstrated their spurious character. But notwithstanding the lapse of three centuries since their exposure, the honest but perilous doubt of the Protestant sceptic on the subject of miracles performed eighteen hundred years ago, is held as infamous, where an unreasoning adherence to a system whose very life is permeated with principles based upon fraud and chicanery, occasions little surprise and less censure.

Upon the dismemberment of the Empire, at the death of Louis le Debonnaire, a dark, anarchical period followed; perhaps the darkest in the annals of the Papacy. Contending factions of the nobles assumed to themselves the power of electing occupants for the chair of St. Peter, which had become their prey and plaything, whilst the Papal territory was reduced to utter insignificance.

During the first half of the ninth century the Papacy sank back into utter confusion and moral impotence. Three dissolute women, Theodora, and her daughters, Marogia and Theodora, contrived to bring the whole patrimony of St. Peter under their sway, and disposed of the tiara at their pleasure. Crimes, too odious to narrate, and before which murder pales, were perpetrated to gratify their lusts. Laymen of infamously notorious character filled the chair of the Apostles, which was bought and sold like a piece of merchandise. The Papal palace became a vast seraglio; the very churches echoed to obscene songs and bacchanal festivities. This degradation of the Papacy culminated in the person of John XII, son of Marogia, who, elevated to the Papal throne at the early age of eighteen, distinguished himself as the most profligate, if not the most guilty, of the infallible heads of the Church, who, agreeably to the theory of Isidore, confirmed by two Roman Synods, must be held to inherit innocence and sanctity from Peter[1]. Then it was that Otho the Great, from whom Beranger held the kingdom of Italy in fief, learning the true state of affairs in Rome, resolved to terminate so great a scandal by a more unequivocal exercise of his own authority, and of his legitimate control over the election of future Pontiffs. Invited by the Pope to come to his aid against Beranger, Otho undertook his expedition into Italy, with a view to obtain the real sovereignty of the country, and received the crown at the hands of the Pontiff. The jealousy of John was presently awakened, and he entered into traitorous alliance with the son of Beranger.

This contest between the Emperor and the Pope is worthy of notice, both as a curious episode in the history of the Papacy, and as the first in that long series of struggles between the two powers, which theoretically were but one, the World-Priest and the World-Monarch, claiming to represent upon earth the similitude of the Divine unity. John shut himself up in Rome, but not daring to encounter a siege, fled into the Campagna. The city was thus open to the occupation of Otho, who convened a council in St. Peter's to enquire into the character of the fugitive Pope, him-

---

[1] Two centuries later this holiness of all the Popes, of which he affirmed that he had personal experience, was made by Gregory VII the foundation of his claim to universal dominion. 'Every sovereign,' he said, 'however good before, becomes corrupted by the use of power, whereas every rightly-appointed Pope becomes a saint through the imputed merits of St. Peter.'

self presiding in the capacity of temporal head of the Church. Strange were the accusations which were brought against this 'Holy Father!' He had drunk the devil's health; had ordained a deacon in a stable; had put out the eyes of his spiritual father, Benedict; had invoked the help of Jupiter in throwing the dice; defiled the Pontifical palace by his vices; and, most heinous offence of all, was addicted to hunting! Otho despatched a summons to John to appear before the Council, and clear himself from this formidable array of accusations. His reply was sufficiently brief to quote in full. 'John the bishop, the servant of the servants of God, to all the bishops. We have heard tell that you wish to set up another Pope; if you do this, by Almighty God I will excommunicate you, so that you shall not have power to say the mass or to ordain no one.' Otho replied to this singular Apostolic epistle in a bantering reproof of the Pontiff's bad morals and bad Latin; but the messenger by whom his missive was despatched, failed to find the sporting Pontiff, who, undeterred by the scandal which the practice of his favourite vice had occasioned, was following the chase. Otho immediately demanded of the Council the condemnation of the Pope, and Leo VIII was elected to fill the Papal throne, which they had declared vacant. The Emperor now claimed an absolute veto upon Papal elections. He regarded the new Pope simply as the first in dignity amongst his subjects; 'the creature of his own will; the depository of an authority which must be exercised according to the discretion of his sovereign.' He obtained from Leo the distinct recognition of these claims.

After the death of Leo VIII the troubles of the

Papacy were redoubled. The Papal pretensions, however, to the right of disposing of the Imperial crown, were strengthened through its acceptance by Otho at the hands of John XII, and by the alleged necessity of recognizing the superiority of the Emperor over all other princes, as possessing authority conferred by God *through the instrumentality of the Pope*.

The destruction of the Carlovingian house, A.D. 987, left the territories of the Church a prey to the Italian princes. Of the twenty-four Popes who occupied the Apostolic throne during the century and a half which followed, two were murdered, five were driven into exile, four were deposed, and three resigned. Some attained the tiara by arms; some by money; others, again, by the influence of princely courtesans, whilst one, at least, was self-appointed. One of these heirs of St. Peter entered on his infallibility before he had attained his twelfth year. This was Benedict IX, who, a few years later, fell in love, and, in order to marry, sold the Popedom to the arch-priest John, who took the name of Gregory VI. Disappointed in his hopes of marriage, Benedict again claimed the tiara which he had just sold. Meanwhile, some of the nobles had elected a rival, who took the name of Sylvester III; and it is curious to observe that Hildebrand, and others of the high church party whose lives were to be spent in warring against simony, decided the claims of the three rival Popes by supporting him whose only right was that of purchase. Another Pontiff of this period received a *posthumous* sentence of deposition, his corpse being disinterred for the purpose! Another, Judas-like, received a bribe to recognize the Patriarch of Constantinople as universal bishop[1]. But the world would assuredly have condoned the simony involved in so useful an employment of his infallibility, if only the supremacy of the Church which he bartered had been transferred to the purer communion.

The Pontificate of John XVI acquired importance from the successful struggle in which that Pontiff was engaged with Hugh Capet, on the question of the Pope's jurisdiction over bishops. The Pope took his stand upon the authority of the forged Decretals, in which all matters relating to bishops were expressly reserved to the judgment of the Pontiff, whilst the French clergy contested the Papal claims, appealing to ancient canons, and to the practice of the Church during eight centuries, in favour of the co-extensive jurisdiction of a Council. John defended the rights of the Holy See against the king and the bishops of France. A second Council met at Rheims, and declared it to be a law of the Church that the office of a judge over bishops belonged to the Pope alone. The victory for the Papacy was a most important one. But whilst John thus succeeded in establishing his spiritual jurisdiction at home and abroad, the increasing power of the Roman aristocracy involved the Papacy in troubles from which it sought to escape by calling in the aid of the Emperor Otho III. . 'It was not,' says Dr. Dollinger, 'until Otho III appointed his cousin Bruno, and afterwards, A.D. 999, the celebrated Gerbert, as Popes, and protected them by an armed force, that the Papacy could once more obtain and exercise its influence and authority in ecclesiastical affairs[2].'

[1] 'Essays on Ecclesiastical Biography,' by Sir James Stephen.
[2] 'The Church and the Churches,' by Dr. Dollinger.

A long period of dissension and anarchy followed, during which the Papacy lost much of its dignity; whilst a succession of Pontiffs emulated the vices and enormities of John XII and the Popes of the ninth century. The Papal chair was often vacant. 'It seemed,' says a modern writer, 'as if the cardinals wanted to show the world by a rare irony how easily the Church could get on without him from whom, in the new theory, all her authority was derived.' Southern Tuscany was lost; and nearly the whole of the Papal territory fell into the hands of contending factions. The wide and undefined claims of the Popes and the Emperors were adhered to with equal tenacity by either party. These claims were mutually destructive, and involved principles so entirely adverse, that all compromise was impossible. The idea of compromise was indeed eschewed by Pope and Emperor alike.

Throughout five successive pontificates (A.D. 1048–1083) the master-mind of Hildebrand, 'the Pope-maker[1],' continued to direct the affairs of the Papal See. During this period the influence of the clergy was greatly increased, and the ecclesiastical power of the Popes was carried to its height. It was the settled policy of this ambitious diplomatist to consolidate the secular sovereignty of the Pope, to make the Roman See independent of the Empire, and to increase the power of the clergy. The convulsions which shook the Empire during the minority of Henry IV favoured his projects. The Papacy was now as closely allied with the German Emperors as it had ever been with the Emperors of Rome, or the successors of Charlemagne.

---

[1] *Domnus Domni Papæ* was the nickname applied to Hildebrand in the time of Alexander II, his fifth nominee.

Hildebrand resolved to free the Popedom from this political subordination, and soon found means for the attainment of his object.

Leo IX, after assuming the Pontificate at Worms, passed through France with the title and insignia of his office, until, arriving at Clugny, he made the acquaintance of the distinguished monk, whose willing vassal he was thenceforth to be. Hildebrand easily persuaded the Pope of the impiety and degradation involved in receiving the Pontifical office at the hands of a layman, albeit that layman was the Emperor. He also induced him to make a public declaration that he could not regard the nomination as valid until it was endorsed by the free election of the Romans. Rejoicing in this aggrandizement of the Papacy at the expense of the Imperial authority, Hildebrand accompanied the new Pope to Rome, where he was duly elected.

Thus one most important principle was established. Before we proceed to notice the development of the plans which Hildebrand had now matured for the exaltation of the ecclesiastical power of the Pontiffs, we must glance briefly, and in its chronological sequence, at perhaps the most important service which he rendered to the purely secular authority of the Holy See. For a period of half a century, the Goths, who had originally come from France at the invitation of the Italian nobles, to root out the Greeks and Saracens, had been a thorn in the side of the Papacy. In 1053, Leo IX, who had taken the field against them in person, was taken prisoner, and compelled to recognize their right to those possessions of the Church which they had already seized[1]. The far-reaching mind of Hildebrand per-

---

[1] Riddle's 'History of the Papacy.'

ceived the danger to the temporal power, arising from the incessant disputes which followed, and he resolved to effect an alliance with the formidable foe. Nicholas II now filled the Papal chair, and, by the advice of Hildebrand, he formally invested Robert Guiscard, the Norman chief, with Apulia and Calabria, *as a fief of the Roman See*, with the title of Duke, and also with Sicily, then in the possession of the Saracens.

'By this arrangement Guiscard recognized the Pope as his feudal chief, and undertook to pay a yearly tribute to the Roman see, and to defend it against all its enemies, upon the demand of the Pope. The Pontiff had thus gained a titular supremacy over the Romans; and, besides this, he had consolidated a power in Italy which he might advantageously employ as a check upon either the nobles and towns of Italy, or the forces of the Empire, as occasion should require [1].'

Hildebrand now turned his attention to further efforts for the stability and extension of the dominion of the Holy See, by securing its greater independence of the Emperor. Hitherto the occupant of the chair of St. Peter had been elected by the Roman nobility, the people also having at least a nominal share in the election; whilst the Emperor claimed the right of confirming or putting a veto upon their choice. The election was always made in the presence of Imperial commissioners. Thus the Popes were little better than the vassals of the Emperors, who, of late, had even claimed to exercise the right of sole nomination. In proportion as the Papacy increased in power and dignity, this right became invested with a grandeur which constituted it the most prized of the imperial pre-

[1] Riddle's 'History of the Papacy.'

rogatives. The voice of the clergy was almost wholly excluded in a Papal election, and the power of the Emperor interposed an effectual barrier in the way of that universal dominion towards which the Papacy was steadily progressing.

'It was doubtless with a view to obviate these ill consequences that Nicholas II published a decree, which he had caused to be confirmed by a Roman Council in 1059, to the effect that in future neither the nobility nor the people should take any part in the election of a Pope, but that the right of election should belong properly to the clergy alone, who, however, should exercise this right not altogether in a mass, but only by means of their representatives. He thus constituted a college of electors, consisting of the chief and most influential of the Roman clergy, who, under the name of cardinals, had, for some time past, taken a leading part in the affairs of the Church [1].'

As a salve to the Imperial dignity, it was provided that the Emperors should exercise the ancient right of confirming the election, 'if they should have previously sought and obtained it from the Holy See;' a privilege for which an Emperor was quite unlikely to sue. The success of this bold innovation was destined to be soon put to the test, and it resulted in the triumph of Hildebrand, and the freedom of the Papacy.

Nicholas died in 1061, and the Roman nobles declared themselves in favour of receiving a Pope at the hands of the Empress, who was now Regent, rather than from the cardinals. Two Popes were consequently elected; but political events, supposed to have been brought about by the secret machinations of Hilde-

[1] Riddle's 'History of the Papacy.'

brand, favoured his plans. Hanno, Archbishop of Cologne, who had become the guardian of the young Emperor, declared himself in favour of Alexander, the nominee of Hildebrand, who, in 1062, was recognized as Pope.

Hildebrand, who was now Cardinal-Archdeacon, had more than once an opportunity of himself stepping into the Papal chair. The conviction that he could best serve the interests of the Church by securing the election of suitable men, induced him to sacrifice his personal interests. Certain it is that his power in Rome was so great that no intrigues on his part were requisite to secure the Papal dignity[1]. When, on the death of Alexander II, his election took place, he acquiesced with a reluctance which it is impossible to regard as feigned, however much he triumphed in witnessing the complete success of his new regulations concerning Papal elections. 'When he heard it,' says Ranke, 'the venerable Archdeacon was sore afraid, and rushed to the pulpit, wishing to quiet the people. But Hugh the White prevented him, and thus addressed the people: "Men and brethren, ye know how that from the days of our lord, Pope Leo, this Hildebrand it is who has exalted the Holy Roman Church, and has freed the city; wherefore, since we have none better, nor one like unto him, whom we can choose for the Roman Pontificate, we have chosen this man, one ordained in our Church, known unto you and unto us, and in all things approved." And when the cardinals, bishops, . . . and the clergy of lower rank had, as the custom is, shouted together, "St. Peter has chosen Gregory Pope," he was

---

[1] Niebuhr.

seized upon and drawn along by the people, and against his will was enthroned at St. Peter ad Vincula.'

Hildebrand was elevated to the Papal throne about the same time that the Emperor, Henry IV, began to exercise his Imperial rights.

It was but natural that Henry should resent the insult which he conceived to have been offered to the Imperial crown by the election of Hildebrand, now Gregory VII. For this opposition Gregory was prepared. But he possessed the tact to avoid a contest, and obtained from the Emperor a formal recognition of his election, choosing, from motives of policy, to allow once more the exercise of this disputed right.

Gregory was now at liberty to devote all his energies to the accomplishment of the great objects of his life; —the deliverance of the Roman See from all secular control, and the prosecution of the ecclesiastical reforms already initiated at his instance.

Before his election he had boldly intimated to the Emperor that, as Pope, he must infallibly assume a hostile relation to him. This hostility was mainly directed to the accomplishment of three objects, with the simple enumeration of which I must content myself. These were, the celibacy of the clergy; the destruction of the monster evil of simony; and the great contest respecting investiture.

The success which attended his bold denunciation of the Emperor, and the King of France, for the open and organized traffic in ecclesiastical offices that disgraced their respective courts, and cast discredit upon the Roman See, and the craven submission of these sovereigns, encouraged him to proceed with a high hand to the decisive measures which he had matured in his long monastic contemplations. By the introduction of celibacy, which he rendered compulsory, in spite of the most formidable opposition, and of the tears and imprecations of those whom he forced to break the tenderest of all ties; in spite also of a canon of the Church [1], which threatened with excommunication all persons who should declare a married priest disqualified for the performance of divine offices, he succeeded in converting the whole body of the clergy into a kind of monastic order. By providing that no clerical office should, in future, be conferred by a layman, under penalty of excommunication [2], he transferred the allegiance of the clergy from the Emperor to the Pope.

The real question at issue in this controversy respecting investiture, was the limits of the power of the Roman See, whose ordinances Gregory determined to enforce against all sovereigns who disputed them [3].

---

[1] Passed at the Council of Gangra, in the fourth century, and incorporated in all collections of canon law.

[2] Ranke.

[3] Gregory borrowed one main pillar of his system from the False Decretals. Isidore had made Pope Julius (about A.D. 338) write to the Eastern bishops: 'The Church of Rome, by a singular privilege, has the right of opening and shutting the gates of heaven to whom she will.' On this Gregory built his scheme of dominion. How should not he be able to judge on earth, on whose will hung the salvation or damnation of men? The passage was made into a special decree or chapter in the new codes. The typical formula of binding and loosing had become an inexhaustible treasure-chamber of rights and claims. The Gregorians used it as a charm to put them in possession of everything worth having. If Gregory, who was notoriously the first to undertake dethroning kings, wanted to depose the German Emperor, he said, 'To me is given power to bind and loose on earth and in heaven.' Were subjects to be absolved from their

The Emperors were no less determined in the assertion of their right to exercise control over the hierarchy. The strife was mortal. The ends sought by both the antagonists were unattainable. It was not until this fact had been forced upon them by sufferings as sad as they were unnecessary, that the real question, only then reduced within the bounds of its apparent dimensions, rendered an accommodation possible. Meanwhile, the long and haughty contest upon which Gregory VII had entered with the Imperial power, plunged both the leading actors in the drama into the extreme of misery and degradation. The Pope, before whom the mightiest prince of Christendom had been humiliated to the last degree; who, himself enjoying the luxuries of the Countess Matilda's castle at Canosa, had kept the royal penitent standing barefoot on the snow for three days and nights, until satisfied with the completeness of his own triumph and the irretrievable disgrace with which the crown, so abased, was overwhelmed;—the proud Pontiff, who had so sternly asserted the absolute superiority of the spiritual over the secular power, died in exile at Salerno, A.D. 1085, exclaiming, 'I have loved justice, and hated iniquity, therefore I die in exile!' Twenty years later, the Emperor, after a long reign, extending over half a century, died of a broken heart, the prisoner of his own son.

---

oaths of allegiance?—which he was also the first to attempt,—he did it by virtue of his power to loose. Did he want to dispose of other people's property? he declared, as at his Roman synod of 1080, 'We desire to show the world that we can give or take away, at our will, kingdoms, duchies, earldoms, in a word, the possessions of all men; for we can bind and loose.'—' The Pope and the Council,' by Janus.

But although his end was ignominious, and the means by which he sought to attain the great objects of his life were unworthy of admiration, Hildebrand's genius and courage, his services to the cause of civilization,—perhaps even to that of true religion, and certainly of the Roman Church, the lofty claims of whose hierarchy he so effectually established,—are unquestionable. 'He found the Papacy,' says Sir James Stephen [1], 'dependent on the Empire; he sustained her by alliances almost commensurate with the Italian peninsula. He found the Papacy electoral by the Roman people and clergy; he left it electoral by a college of Papal nomination. He found the Emperor the virtual patron of the Holy See; he wrested that power from his hands. He found the secular clergy the allies and dependents of the secular power; he converted them into the inalienable auxiliaries of his own. He found the higher ecclesiastics in servitude to the temporal sovereigns; he delivered them from that yoke to subjugate them to the Roman Tiara. He found the patronage of the Church the mere desecrated spoil and merchandise of princes; he reduced it within the dominion of the supreme Pontiff.'

As a Pope, Hildebrand stands alone. Strength of will, combined with exalted genius, have characterized few in the long succession of Roman Pontiffs. Arrogance and ambition have been the characteristics of many. But in either trait Hildebrand was, is, and will remain unequalled. Believing himself called of God to the accomplishment of a great work, he performed it with a zeal, inspired by a devout sense of responsibility,

---

[1] 'Essays on Ecclesiastical Biography,' by Sir James Stephen.

which was all the more admirable by reason of the cautious and far-sighted *policy* by which it was regulated.

The limits of this narrative forbid the attempt at anything beyond a passing reference to the romantic story of the Countess Matilda, the bold and successful supporter of all the pretensions of the most arrogant and ambitious of Pontiffs. She twice obtained the sanction of Gregory VII to a divorce from uncongenial marriages, in order that, with undivided energy, and with all the influence which her unequalled wealth, as the possessor of the richest territories in Italy, secured to her, she might devote herself to the furtherance of his ambitious projects. Her indomitable spirit enabled her to wield the sword of justice in behalf of the Church, not metaphorically only, in the tribunal, but with masculine energy as a warrior on the battle-field. In a voluptuous and superstitious age she lived austerely, and subdued her tastes for the devotional abstractions of the cloister, that she might consecrate herself wholly to the duties of her chosen vocation. It would be interesting to trace the history of her bequest to the Church of those rich Italian possessions [1], which became the subject of so much virulent contention during a period of fifty years, at the expiration of which they passed into the possession of the Emperor. It is impossible to deny the apparent justice of the Imperial claim to these territories, which were held by Matilda

---

[1] 'Her great domains comprised the Duchy of Tuscany, extending along the Tuscan sea to within a few miles of the city of Rome, and including Perugia and Imola within its limits; on the north it embraced the Duchy of Modena, to which had been added the district of Parma; while in the south with these territories she united the Duchy of Spoleto, and the Marquisate of Ancona.'—Butt's 'History of Italy.'

under feudal tenure, and consequently without power of alienation. After the lapse of a century they again reverted to the Church, together with other territories for which forged deeds of gift, bearing date four centuries back, were produced by the unscrupulous and cunning Innocent III. But with this history our narrative is not concerned.

After the death of Gregory VII, two successive Pontiffs of his own nomination were chosen to fill the vacant See. These were Victor III, who died after a brief Pontificate, and Urban II, who succeeded him in 1088. By a double stroke of policy this Pontiff effectually crippled the power of the Emperor in Italy. Persuading the Countess Matilda to marry the son of the Duke of Bavaria, whose enormous wealth and influence were by stipulation employed to harass the Emperor, and by instigating Conrad, the Emperor's only son, to rebellion against his father, he placed Henry IV in a position in which his whole and undivided energies were absorbed in the struggle to secure his German dominions. It would be difficult to overrate the importance of the service thus rendered to the Papacy in the height of its contest with the Imperial power, by a Pontiff whose self-confidence was a source of equal power as the greater genius of a Hildebrand.

'For they can conquer who believe they can[1].'

[1] Virgil.

CHAPTER III.

It was impossible that so astute a man as Urban II (A.D. 1088-99) should fail to perceive the opportunity presented by the prevailing fanaticism of the age for directing it to the accomplishment of quite other ends than those upon which it was immediately set. He only pursued the policy of Gregory VII, of whom he was in every respect a fitting successor, in encouraging the mad enthusiasm of Christendom for effecting the deliverance of the Holy Land from its infidel possessors; — a religious sentiment which, hostile to the opponent of ecclesiastical claims, became a powerful accessory to the Holy See, which had blessed the project [1]. The leadership in the holy wars of necessity devolved on the Popes.

Urban's first employment of the prestige which he thus secured, was the assumption of a more imperious bearing towards the crowned heads of Europe, concerning the disputed right of investiture, than had been adopted even by Gregory VII. His haughty rebuke,

---

[1] 'A Council was called at Clermont, by Pope Urban II, A.D. 1095, with a view to the recovery of the Holy Land; and the princes of Europe eagerly undertook the enterprise. . . . An armed force of *six hundred thousand*, commanded by Godfrey de Bouillon, was reduced to a tenth part of its number before reaching Jerusalem; but succeeded in taking the city A.D. 1099. Palestine was afterwards subdued, but the conquest was not permanent.'—'Compendium of Universal History,' Jarrold and Sons.

and threatened excommunication of William the Conqueror, will be familiar to every reader of English history.

For twenty years after the death of the original actors in this drama, the contest continued between the Emperors and the Pope, with varying success.

In the person of Calixtus III, the Papal chair was filled by a man lacking the high moral qualities and administrative tact of Gregory or of Urban. The nobles and bishops concurred in demanding a reconciliation, and Calixtus, too feeble in resources to parry the ill will of the clergy, as his great predecessors had done, by diverting it into another and a counter channel, acceded to the celebrated concordat at Worms. The vital principle of the controversy was surrendered, by this Council, on the miserable compromise that the Emperor should exercise the right of investiture with the sceptre only, and not with the crozier and ring.

The long assertion of the high Papal pretensions was attended, however, with one result, which the Emperor, in his triumph, was powerless to avert. The repeated and successful exercise of the spiritual powers of the Church, and especially of the terrible power of excommunication, more formidable now than ever, had surrounded the Papal throne with an awful dignity and power, which availed to compensate the loss of influence involved in the surrender of the right of investiture. It was clearly impolitic to jeopardize this awful power by the prolongation of a struggle, from which even a Hildebrand might have shrunk.

During the ensuing century Republican institutions made such progress in Italy that the civil power, both of the Popes and Emperors, became greatly curtailed.

The Popes were frequently obliged to flee from Rome, and their right to the exercise of any other than a purely spiritual authority was boldly canvassed [1]. In North Italy daring heretics arose, who proclaimed that, in becoming territorial lords the Popes had forsaken the principles of the Christian religion. Foremost amongst these was Arnold of Brescia, who declared that 'neither bishop, priest, nor monk could be saved if clogged, the former with regal or lordly power, the latter with worldly wealth or goods.' He shortly afterwards expiated at the stake the offence of an alliance with the Emperor.

Adrian IV (A.D. 1154–59), a poor English scholar, whose abilities had raised him to the highest dignity of the Church, succeeded, by fomenting the jealousy which the Emperor entertained towards the Romans, in recovering undisputed possession of Rome, but was powerless to prevent the devastation of the surrounding territory by the King of Italy. The disputes between the Pontiff and the Emperor had now degenerated into mere punctilios, such as the duty of the Emperor to hold the stirrup of his Holiness when dismounting from his horse; and that of the Pope to refrain from *double entendre* in his correspondence with the Emperor. Yet—and would that Rome would learn the lesson to-day—this period of the decadence of the temporal

---

[1] It is a curious fact that in the twelfth century one of the famous maxims of Gregory VII, ascribing personal holiness to every rightly-elected Pope, was suffered to drop. 'There was danger of the want of holiness suggesting the invalidity of the election; and therefore the decretal books, while upholding the rest of Gregory's postulates, were silent about this.'—'The Pope and the Council,' by Janus.

power of the Roman See, was that of its most exalted spiritual power, and of the acquisition of an influence, in other countries, far surpassing that of which it had been despoiled in Italy; whilst the right to dispense crowns was never so little questioned as now, when the spiritual head of the Church claimed no right to wield the sceptre of a temporal kingdom. We need not go beyond the history of our own country for confirmation of these assertions respecting the ideas of the Papacy which characterized the age. In regard to the first, it is sufficient to mention the name of Beckett; and as regards the second, the very charter of the English possession of Ireland proceeds on the assumption 'that all islands which are illuminated by Christ the Sun of Righteousness are a portion of the patrimony of St. Peter and the Holy Roman Church[1].' In asking for Ireland as a gift from the Pope, Henry II deliberately recognized the superiority which the Pontiffs claimed over all Kings, and their power of dispensing crowns, his own not excepted. Innocent IV declared his readiness to abandon the Donation of Constantine, upon which his predecessors based their claims to sovereignty, which he maintained was derived directly from Christ, and extended to the entire world, and all that it contained. Secular power was only to be tolerated, as secular princes avowedly exercised it, by commission from the Pope.

The alliance between the Emperor and the Pope, sealed by the blood of Arnold, was of short duration. 'By the grace of God,' said Frederick, 'I am Emperor of Rome. If Rome be entirely withdrawn from my authority the Empire is an empty name.' And

---

[1] Bull of Pope Adrian IV.

Adrian was fain to appeal for protection to those very republicans of Brescia and Milan of whom he had been the cruel oppressor. His sudden death alone prevented the fulmination of a bull of excommunication against Frederick, who, to meet the injurious and insulting claims of the Pontiffs to the possession of a supreme power, whose sanctity eclipsed that of the purely secular, added the epithet 'Holy' to the accustomed title 'Roman Empire.'

The schism which ensued upon the death of Adrian produced a more momentous conflict, in which the rival of the Pontiff nominated by Frederick (Alexander III) won a signal triumph over the Emperor. The victorious armies of Frederick had been decimated by the fevers of Rome. The Lombard cities, whose arms the Pope had blessed, rallied to the summons of Alexander. The strife was full of peril, when, by the mediation of the Doge of Venice, the Pope and the Emperor were induced to meet at St. Mark's. A slab of red marble still marks the spot upon which Frederick knelt in humble submission to the Pontiff, who raised him, with tears of joy, and imprinted upon his forehead the kiss of peace. Frederick thus withdrew from the contest to which his life had been devoted—his rivalry with the Pontiff for the chief place in Christendom.

At the close of the twelfth century the Popes had no settled territory in Italy. But in the person of Innocent III, who entered upon his Pontificate in the full vigour of manhood, a restorer was at hand, who proved no exception to the common rule, that, to a man of enterprizing spirit, opportunities will always present themselves for the exercise of his talents. Nor did he suffer the grass to grow beneath his feet. On the first day of his Pontificate he invested the Prefect of Rome with the insignia of his office, and compelled him to take the customary oath of allegiance to himself, rather than to the Emperor. Thus, by one well-timed, well-directed blow, he shattered the only remaining link which connected the Imperial sovereignty with Rome. Innocent III was the first Pontiff to lay down the theory, so often repeated by his successors, that, in the punishment of offences against the civil law, the Pope has the power to interpose with his judgment and annul the decisions of the civil tribunal. His entire Pontificate was characterized by the same imperious policy. Of this we have an illustration in the rebuke which he administered to the Tuscan States, which, whilst pledging themselves to the support of the Papal See, and to the recognition of no Emperor who was not approved by the Pope, at the same time recognized the supremacy of the Imperial power. Innocent reminded these reactionists that there were two great lights in the social heaven, having their seat in Italy, the lesser of which, the Imperial authority, received its light from the greater, the Papal See.

Innocent III successfully asserted his claim to the patrimony of St. Peter, and to all that was included in the donation of Matilda. Southern Tuscany again reverted to the Church, and the Pontiff obtained from the Emperor the recognition of his claim to the absolute sovereignty of the city and territories of Rome. This crafty and ambitious man, possessing all the daring, but lacking all the dignity of Gregory VII, was practically the founder of the Papal States, the cities of which, now weary of the German yoke, hastened to recognize and welcome his authority.

Events in Germany having brought upon the stage two competitors for the Imperial crown, Innocent determined to assume the right which Adrian III had vainly asserted, of nominating the Emperor. With that insinuating craftiness of which he was so great a master, he claimed, not the absolute right of nomination, but the right and duty of assisting the electors in such a state of affairs as the present, when they were unable to perform the functions which, he allowed it to be supposed, he regarded as their inherent right. The competitors for the vacant throne were Philip, brother of the late Emperor Henry VI, and Otho, formerly Duke of Saxony and Bavaria. The craftiness of Innocent led him into the fatal error of delaying too long to recognize the claims of either candidate. Philip made the most splendid overtures for his support, the very offer of which was a gain to the Papacy. But whilst Innocent coquetted with Philip, hoping to secure equally valuable concessions from Otho, his plans were frustrated by the assassination of the former. Otho was fully aware how little he was indebted to Innocent III for the adherence which he now secured, and opportunities for the manifestation of the malevolence which he entertained towards the Pontiff soon presented themselves. He seized the castles and fortresses which Innocent had recently annexed to the patrimony of St. Peter, conferred the Duchy of Spoleto upon one of his German nobles, and despoiled the Church of some portion of the inheritance of the Countess Matilda.

Innocent, now determined to compass the Emperor's fall, fulminated against him a sevenfold bull of excommunication, and, by means of emissaries in Germany, created a rising in which the King of Bohemia, the Duke of Bavaria, and other princes, both lay and ecclesiastical, took part in favour of the pretensions to the Imperial crown of Frederick, the young son of the Emperor Henry VI, whom, five years earlier, he had employed measures to exclude, in favour of the rivals, Philip and Otho. Innocent died, however, A.D. 1218, before the complete overthrow of his adversary was accomplished. The tremendous influence which the Papacy had now acquired again finds striking illustration in the history of our own country. The dispute between Innocent and King John, respecting the election of Stephen Langton to the See of Canterbury, terminated in the excommunication and complete humiliation of the King, who unconditionally surrendered his crown, with all the insignia of royalty, to the Roman legate, that he might receive them back as the free gift of the Pope, and hold his kingdom thenceforward as a fief of the Roman See. The subsequent absolution of the King from the oaths he had sworn at Runnymede, and the advice tendered him to annul the charter he had so reluctantly conceded, are matters familiar to the readers of English history.

Innocent III was the first Pontiff who employed armed forces for the suppression of heresy, and to him the Papacy is indebted for one of its most powerful engines of propagandism,—the Inquisition; designed to put an end, not only to all public teaching, but to private thought. The unprotesting acquiescence of Europe in the imposition of the abominable code of the Inquisition affords humiliating and signal proof of the unlimited and arbitrary power exercised by the Popes. Their claim to sovereign dominion of life and death over all Christians was no idle vaunt. Every departure from the teaching of the Church was now made punishable by death in its most appalling form, viz. by fire. The object proposed by Innocent in the establishment of the Inquisition, and pursued by every succeeding Pope for three centuries, was the complete uprooting of every difference of belief. Hence there ceased to be any distinction between heresies. It sufficed that a man differed in any respect from the common way of life of the multitude to attach to him the charge of heresy. 'The earlier laws of the Roman Emperors had distinguished between heresies, and only imposed severe penalties on some on account of their moral enormity, but this distinction was given up after the time of Lucius III, A.D. 1184. Complete apostacy from the Christian faith, or a difference on some minor point, was all the same. Either was heresy, and to be punished by death [1].

It was during the Pontificate of Innocent III that the most important attempts were made to recover the holy places from the Turks; for Innocent, as treasurer of the crusades, and as generalissimo of the Christian forces, was quite alive to the opportunity which this European folly presented for the aggrandizement of the Papacy; and it is not surprising that he was the most strenuous patron of the movement. It is said that of the immense wealth which poured into his coffers from all quarters, not a little remained there; whilst he augmented the revenues of the State by retaining certain taxes levied at first for the purpose of carrying on the holy war [2]. The principles which governed his

---

[1] 'The Pope and the Council,' by Janus.
[2] 'British Quarterly Review,' vol. xiv.

actions found apt expression in the maxim which he proudly adopted, that 'the Pope, in virtue of the plenitude of his power, might dispense even with rights.' For a period of fifty years, and through a succession of short Pontificates, the Roman See being more than once vacant, the contests between Pope and Emperor continued; the grounds of quarrel being generally frivolous, often absurd, whilst the result was prejudicial to the power of each.

Rudolph, the founder of the Hapsburg dynasty, was elected to fill the Imperial throne, A.D. 1273. The misery which their Italian possessions, and ecclesiastical quarrels, had entailed upon his predecessors, determined him to pursue a policy of non-intervention with regard to Rome. By a formal deed he resigned all pretension to the territories claimed by the Church, and to the long-disputed bequests of the Countess Matilda. It is said that in his horror of coming into collision with the power which had consumed so many German kings, he unintentionally surrendered by this deed territories belonging to the kingdom of Italy, to which the Papal See could show no title[1]. This grant comprised all those districts which at the commencement of the Pontificate of Pius IX formed the States of the Church, and by a subsequent compact, Corsica, Sardinia, and Sicily were included in the original grant.

From this point begins a new era in the history of the Papal claims. The Papacy had acquired a signal triumph in its establishment of the independence of the Emperor, but it clearly severed the links which had made the Holy Roman Church and the Holy Roman

---

[1] Butt's 'History of Italy.'

Empire one and the same thing in two aspects, a mystic dualism, corresponding to the two natures of its founder. 'As divine and eternal, its head is the Pope, to whom souls have been entrusted; as human and temporal, the Emperor, commissioned to rule men's. bodies and acts.' Such was the theory of the Holy Roman Empire; the self-consistent scheme of the union of Church and State. But the Emperor and the Pope were the champions of opposite systems, and the Papal independence, which was the result of their frequent collisions, severed the links which bound together the world-monarchy and the world-religion. Thus 'the very triumphs in which the Papal power asserted its separate and distinct sovereignty, were the destruction of that venerable polity by which its framers intended that all the Western world should be united in one great confederation of Church and State. When the Emperor resigned all power in Rome, the Holy Roman Empire survived only as a name[1].'

> 'Men are we, and must grieve when even the name
> Of that which once was great has passed away!'

Although the Pontiffs were now free from all competition with the Imperial power, their sovereignty was little more than nominal. The republics continued free, and the feudal lords not only retained their virtual sovereignty, but in some instances obtained a confirmation of it, as the price of their recognition of the supremacy of the Pope.

The power of the Church in relation to the State was visibly declining. In the conflicts in which the Pope and the Emperor were soon again involved, and in

[1] Butt's 'History of Italy.'

the contest for supremacy between the Greek and the Roman Churches, much that had been gained by Innocent was again lost. The Roman people had come to regard the Pontiff as merely their titular sovereign; and although the temporal authority of the Pontiffs varied according to their personal character, their sovereign power was brought within the narrowest limits, whilst the schism between the rival Churches became permanent. The struggle for the gradual recovery of power was, though intermittent, long and embittered. By slow degrees it was accomplished, but not until the insatiable ambition of the Pontiffs had weaned from them the respect and the willing obedience of their subjects, and greatly impaired the Papal authority in its most essential particulars. The whole secular and religious literature of Europe grew intensely hostile to the Papacy. What used to be called the Roman Church had become the Roman court. Enlightened men had long foreseen the change, and lifted up their warning voice in vain. Shade of Hildebrand! the fatal power with which you endowed the Church has transformed her into a mass of corruption, selling the souls of the elect for the sake of filthy lucre. The simony against which you warred is now exalted in high places, so that 'the little finger of the *curia* presses more heavily on the Church than ever the arm of Kings!' The hatred and contempt of the world troubled not those who were secure in the service of such a power, neither were they moved by such strange prophecies as that of the highly honoured St. Hildegard, who, as early as A.D. 1170, had uttered the following remarkable prediction of the Popes, which is preserved in the collections of Baluze and Mansi:—'They seize upon us, like ravening beasts, with their power of binding and loosing, and through them the whole Church is withered. They desire to subjugate the kingdoms of the world, but the nations will rise against them and the too rich and haughty clergy, whose property they will reduce to its right limits. The pride of the Popes, who no longer observe any religion, will be brought low; Rome and its immediate neighbourhood will alone be left to them, partly in consequence of wars, partly by the common agreement of the States.'

The court of Rome, corrupt from its cradle, and insusceptible of reform, was strong in proportion as the ignorance of the people was great. In its new conflicts with the Empire, ending in that arrangement which Catholic historians have called, with a mixture of pathos and irony, 'the Seventy Years' Captivity,' it learned that the ignorance engendered by superstition is not illimitable.

The authority claimed by the Emperor was not the only, nor indeed the most formidable, obstacle against which the Popes had to contend. The people of Rome manifested a growing dislike both to Papal and Imperial rule, and a preference, which upon occasion they did not fail to avow, for a republican form of government. And yet more formidable was the antagonism of a proud, restless, and ferocious nobility, many of whom boasted of their lineal descent from the great families of antiquity. Commanding the services of numerous and disorderly bands of retainers, they waged incessant warfare against each other, and against the constituted authorities. Taking possession of the ancient monuments of Rome, such as the Mausoleum of Adrian, the Colosseum, and the theatres, which Popes and Emperors alike suffered to fall into unregretted decay, they converted them into strong fortresses, which enabled them to defy the supremacy claimed by the Papal and Imperial powers.

Four influences were now contending for mastery at Rome—the Empire, the Pope, the feudal Barons, and the Republicans. True, the long-disputed claim of the Pontiff to the sovereignty of Rome had been conceded by the Emperor; but the Popes, being unable to control either the lawless violence of the nobles, or the republican independence of the city, it was but too likely that plausible pretexts would be found for the renewal of Imperial intervention. The Roman Constitution itself, fixed by a charter of Celestine III, A.D. 1191, recognized the existence of Republican institutions, and thus afforded ground for investing such interposition with at least a show of legality. The 'Senate' of Rome had conferred their authority upon one individual, under the title of Senator, who, like the Podesta of other towns, was armed with almost dictatorial powers. We have seen that Innocent III obliged the Senator to take the oath of allegiance to himself rather than to the Emperor. Since the death of Innocent, the Republican institutions had maintained their authority independent of that of the Pope, and there was nothing to hinder the investiture of the Emperor himself with the office of Senator, thereby securing him a legal right to exercise his power in the capital of Christendom. The election of Charles of Anjou to the office of Senator removed this source of danger, but it neither curbed the republican spirit nor checked the disorders to which the city was a prey.

It will be convenient, at this point, to glance briefly

at the administrative system of the Papal court, as constituted in the thirteenth century. The sacred college was composed of three orders of cardinals; cardinal deacons, cardinal priests, and cardinal bishops. The first of these were, originally, seven in number (afterwards increased to fourteen), their number and the duties of their office answering to the Apostolic institution. The cardinal priests were the chief priests of the principal churches in Rome, and enjoyed the same rank as the cardinal deacons, with whom, in early times, they formed the presbytery of the Bishop of Rome. In the ninth century the highest order of cardinals, the cardinal bishop, was created. Originally these were the bishops of the seven dioceses nearest to Rome, but in course of time the number was greatly extended, and the bishops of distant, and even of foreign Sees, were admitted to the order. These three orders of cardinals constituted the Pope's Privy Council, and, with other high ecclesiastics, who assisted in the executive administration, formed the Roman *curia*. Laymen were not wholly excluded. Amongst the large number of Papal officers,—especially in the cumbersome machinery for the administration of justice, composed of three separate courts, one only of which was limited to cardinals of the Church, under the personal presidency of the Pontiff,—we occasionally find subordinate departments presided over by a layman. From the executive government the laity were wholly excluded. The Papal treasury was enriched by a traffic in those minor offices which were open to laymen, and which conferred the importance—divested of the responsibility of power which alone constitutes the value of office to the statesman—attaching to a member of the Roman *curia.* Such was the court of Rome. Its head an infallible priest; his advisers all ecclesiastics, partaking the characteristics of the ecclesiastics of the times, ignorant, haughty, selfish; pledged to the rooting out of all independence of thought, of all civil liberty. And against it was arrayed the equal pride and obstinacy of the nobles; the growing ambition and restless activity of the Republicans; the crushing power of the Empire.

A conspicuous feature of the annals of the Papacy during the thirteenth century is the famous dispute between the Guelphs and the Ghibellines, the latter the supporters of the Emperor, the former[1] contending for the independence and supremacy of the Church. The effects of the evil spirit of discord thus engendered, may be traced in the history of this period in every state, and in every city, of Italy. The merits of these feuds are, for the most part, so involved, that the task of seeking to unravel them would be tedious and vain. Contemporary historians, in their endeavours to elucidate them, betray, in their mutual criminations, their own strong prejudices, and consequent untrustworthiness. The scenes of turbulence to which these feuds gave rise, whether occasioned by differences as to the forms of government, or by more contemptible but not less mischievous causes, had an important bearing upon

[1] The party names of Guelph and Ghibelline had been known in Italy at a much earlier date. The Ghibellines were the Imperial nobles, the aristocracy of the social body. The body of the people were Guelphs, who, when the civil and ecclesiastical powers were in antagonism, named themselves after the party professing attachment to the Church, only because the Papacy was in opposition to the Empire. See 'Trollope's History of the Commonwealth of Florence.'

the extension of the Papal authority; the Pope being often appealed to as arbiter; and although only a temporary compromise might thus be effected, the recognition of the right of Papal intervention was an element of power, to which Rome was not indifferent.

The elevation of the house of Anjou to the Sicilian throne was an inestimable advantage to the Papacy, the most formidable danger to the independence of which lay in the union of the kingdom of Naples with the Imperial crown. The influence of the Guelph party was now transferred to the royal family of France, who speedily acquired a predominant influence in the Peninsula. But the Sicilian prince, who was Senator of Rome, aspired also to become her master; and although his ambitious projects were defeated, the triumph which the Pope had achieved in wresting the Sicilian crown from the Emperor was attended with disastrous consequences to the Papacy itself. An attempt was made, by the extensive nomination of cardinals, which Charles was able to accomplish, to bring the Pontificate exclusively into French hands. Opposed, however, to the projects of this Franco-Guelphine alliance, was a powerful party closely allied with the leading families of Rome. The election of Boniface VIII, A.D. 1294 (of whom it has been said that he was 'the last of the Popes,' in that sense in which Brutus and Cassius were the last of the Romans), who was sworn to uphold the temporal and spiritual supremacy of the Roman See, and to rescue the Papacy from the entanglements in which it was becoming involved, brought this Roman party, who were entirely hostile to France, into alliance with the patriotic Guelphs. The consequent confusion in ecclesiastical disputes was great; but the deliverance of the Papacy from the troubles and dangers inseparable from the threatened French domination, was an incalculable boon.

From this period, to the close of the fifteenth century, a long and undistinguished interval occurs. It was, indeed, an age of advancement; and though uninteresting as regards the development of the Papal power, was in many respects highly brilliant. Whilst the discovery of printing gave, throughout Europe, a tremendous impulse to intellectual cultivation, Italy displayed an intellectual superiority unequalled since the overthrow of the Roman Empire; but, says Hallam[1], 'Her political history presents a labyrinth of petty facts so obscure and of so little influence as not to arrest the attention, so intricate and incapable of classification as to leave only confusion in the memory. The general events that are worthy of notice, and give a character to this long period, are the establishment of small tyrannies upon the ruins of Republican government in most of the cities, the gradual rise of three considerable states, Milan, Florence, and Venice, the naval and commercial rivalry between the last city and Genoa, the final acquisition by the Popes of their present territorial sovereignty, and the revolution in the kingdom of Naples under the lines of Anjou and Aragon.'

[1] 'History of the Middle Ages,' vol. i.

CHAPTER IV.

THE ecclesiastical disputes, to which reference was made in the last chapter, were embittered by the personal quarrel between Philip IV of France and Pope Boniface VIII. This Pontiff, who in his mad ambition styled himself 'Pontiff and Emperor,' assumed the second crown of the Tiara; the third, completing the symbol of Pontifical dignity, as High Priest, Emperor, and King, being added twenty years later by John XXII. Boniface was in the habit of appearing in public bearing the sword in one hand and the keys of St. Peter in the other; nor did he scruple to declare that the Pope was exalted by God above monarchs and monarchies, held the first rank upon earth, and was gifted with miraculous power. His conclusion from these premises had at least the element of consistency. 'The secular authority,' he affirmed, 'was merely an emanation from the ecclesiastical; the double power of the Pope was *an article of faith*, and submission to the Roman Pontiff NECESSARY TO SALVATION.'

Had Boniface possessed the subtlety of Innocent III, he would have conducted his quarrel with the wary and cautious king with greater prudence. He chose the most objectionable instruments to support his arrogant assumptions at the French court, and the dictatorial and threatening tone which they adopted towards Philip entirely defeated the object of their mission. Not content with administering reproof to the King for the delinquencies of his past life, and haughtily demanding reformation for the future, Boniface now proceeded to convene a Council in Rome, charged with the duty of reforming all the abuses that existed in the court and kingdom of France [1]. To this Council the French clergy were summoned, and the King himself was cited to appear and answer the charges preferred against him. Herein Boniface plainly overstepped the limits of prudence. His motives are obvious. To have placed Philip at once under an interdict would have been a more congenial method of procedure to the imperious Pontiff. But the spiritual weapons of the Church had been too frequently employed by the later Popes, and often in circumstances in which it was impossible that they should be followed by their intended consequences. In the isolated instances in which they had been operative, they had occasioned inconveniencies so wholly disproportioned to the evils for which their chastisement was imposed, that the jealousy of governments and nations was aroused. Measures were everywhere devised to counteract their consequences. Excommunications and interdicts had begun to lose their force, and were, in fact, already regarded as mere formalities, dependent for their efficacy upon a concurring public opinion. No one was more cognizant of this fact than Boniface. Hence his resort to the expedient of a Council, the King's refusal to appear before which, and submit to the judgment of God and of the Pope, might involve him in a quarrel with his own subjects. The way would thus be prepared for an interdict which, deriving its force from the religious instinct of the nation, would be invested with all its primogenial

---

[1] Riddle's 'History of the Papacy.'

terrors. But Boniface had too much presumed upon the waning powers of the Papacy. Philip, determined to show the real strength of his opposition, immediately assembled a large parliament in Paris, who unanimously affirmed that in temporal matters they owed fealty to none but God and their King; and the French clergy were prohibited from attending the Council.

Diplomacy was not, in those days, characterized by the modern refinements which darken counsel; and Philip did not hesitate to rebuke the presumption of Boniface in such words as these,—'There were Kings in France before there were bishops, and he would rule within his realm in total disregard of what such a blinded, fraudulent, demoniacal pretender could say.' The quarrel had now become a mortal one. At the parliament which Philip had assembled in Paris, a series of resolutions were passed, denouncing the Pope as a heretic, simoniacal, corrupt, and a pretender. Boniface had already entered into a new alliance with the Emperor, whom he hoped to persuade into a declaration of war with France. Encouraged also by the devotion manifested by many of the French clergy,—no less than four archbishops, thirty-five bishops, and seven abbots having repaired to Rome in spite of the prohibition of Philip,—he took the only course open to him, and excommunicated the King. Philip forthwith confiscated the property of the recalcitrant bishops, and proceeded to summon a second assembly of the States General at Paris, which sanctioned the adoption of measures for convening a general Council that should have power to judge and depose the Pope. A proceeding at once so irregular and unprecedented can hardly have been seriously entertained by Philip. It has been suggested that his object was 'to take precaution against any act of the Pope in deposing himself, and absolving his subjects from their allegiance; a measure which he adopted in the form of an appeal to the projected Council, and to the new Pope whom that Council should elect,—an appeal which speedily received the adhesion of all communities and classes of men throughout the kingdom.'

The bull of excommunication was to have been published on the eighth of September. On the seventh the Pope was attacked by a troop of banditti, taken prisoner, and conveyed away on a miserable horse with his face to the tail. He was rescued and conveyed to Rome, only to be again seized and imprisoned. His death, the cause of which must ever remain a mystery, occurred within a month from the date of his first imprisonment.

Benedict XI, who succeeded Boniface, A.D. 1303, commenced his reign by fulminating threats against Philip, to which the King responded by distributing large sums of money amongst the cardinals. A strong French party was by this means established in the conclave; and Philip looked forward with confidence to the next vacancy of the Pontificate for the desired opportunity of bringing his long quarrel with the Holy See to a successful issue. It occurred sooner than was expected. One evening, whilst the Pope was at supper, a girl, closely veiled, presented a basket of figs. In an unguarded moment the Pontiff partook of them without the customary precaution of having them first tasted, and it is to be hoped that the King's pious wish, 'that he was in heaven,' was fulfilled, for, ere morning, the Pope was dead. Philip was prepared. He had secured from Bernard de Got, Archbishop of Bordeaux, a man low born, mean-spirited, and of dissolute life, a pledge of complete subserviency if he were elected Pontiff. A command was despatched to the servile conclave, and Bernard was elected, assuming the title of Clement V.

We have now reached one of the most important epochs in the history of the Papacy. The relationships subsisting between Clement V and the French King, and the momentous bearing of these upon the temporal power of the Papacy, are well described in the following passage which I quote from a work that is only too little known [1]:—'Of all the concessions to the demands of Philip which were made by Clement, at the very commencement of his Pontificate, the most comprehensive and important was that of enacting that the Papal residence should be fixed within the limits of France. By this means the King of France had the Pope completely in a state of dependence upon himself, and henceforward it became his policy, and that of his successors, not to work the complete overthrow of the Papal power, but to perpetuate and uphold it, so far as it could be made instrumental in favour of France; but the new Pontiff carefully concealed, as far as possible, his state of dependence on the French crown. His obligation to reside in France was kept for some time as a profound secret, even from the French party among the cardinals, and when the continuance of his sojourn in that country, during several successive years, began to give rise to suspicion, the circumstances of the times were pleaded in excuse, not without some effect. At first no particular place of residence was chosen, but

---

[1] 'The History of the Papacy to the Period of the Reformation,' by the Rev. J. E. Riddle, M.A. 2 vols. 8vo. Bentley, 1854.

Clement removed with his court from one town or monastery to another. At the end of about five years, however, the intentions of the Pontiff, and his real position with regard to Philip, could no longer be concealed, and Clement fixed his residence at Avignon, which was in the territory of the Count of Provence, and as part of the kingdom of Burgundy, was nominally under the protection of the German Emperor. Immediately upon his accession Clement granted Philip the tenth of all Church property in France for the space of five years; he also nominated ten French cardinals.'

During the nine years of his Pontificate Clement remained the obsequious tool of the unscrupulous King, whilst Italy, abandoned by both Emperor and Pope, fell a prey to disorders fomented by the contests between the Guelphs and the Ghibellines. Both Philip and Clement died A.D. 1314.

The new Emperor, Henry VII, had resolved upon recovering the ancient Imperial rights in Italy, and, in spite of the opposition of the Guelphs, prevailed upon the Pope to perform the ceremony of coronation. But as Henry advanced his claims, it soon became apparent that he would encounter the stern and uncompromising opposition of the Pontiff, who, after some parleying, pronounced against him the sentence of excommunication. The old contest for supremacy was thus resuscitated; but the early death of the Emperor terminated the struggle, and contributed to uphold the influence of the Holy See. Although the name survived, the Imperial power in Italy terminated with the life of Henry VII. The advantages to the Papal pretensions resulting from the struggle for supremacy which the Popes maintained against Louis of Bavaria, must be assigned to the effeminacy of the Emperor. The Popes still claimed the right of confirming Imperial elections, and of receiving upon his coronation an oath of fealty from the Emperor. The claim, however, was contested, and it was expressly disallowed by a Diet held at Frankfort in 1338, which established 'as a fundamental principle that the Imperial dignity depended upon God alone, and that whoever should be chosen by a majority of the electors became immediately both king and emperor, with all prerogatives of that station, and did not require the approbation of the Pope [1].'

For seventy years, during which Italy was torn by the contests of Guelphs and Ghibellines, of rival Popes and rival Emperors, the seat of the Papacy remained at Avignon, Rome being abandoned to the vicarial government of a legate, whose authority was merely titular. Seven Popes in succession reigned in this luxurious, but dissolute and corrupt retreat, until A.D. 1376, when the promise, often repeated and long delayed, was fulfilled, and Gregory XI returned to Rome. Nine years earlier, Urban V, instigated by the indignation of Europe at the abandonment of the tomb of St. Peter, had, to the great joy of the Romans, transferred the Papal court to Rome. Since the days of Adrian IV, no such recognition of the supremacy of the Roman Pontiff had been exacted, as was then accorded by the Emperor Charles IV, whom the astonished citizens beheld in solemn procession leading the Pope's horse from the Castle of St. Angelo to the church of St. Peter's. But Urban V cared less for the

[1] Hallam's 'Middle Ages.'

exaltation of the Papacy than for his own sensual indulgence. After remaining in Rome hardly more than two years, he declared, to the utter astonishment of his subjects, that 'regard to the general good of the Church rendered it his duty to return to France.' The people were incensed;—the old Ghibelline sect, which, forty years earlier, had been instrumental in elevating Louis of Bavaria to the Imperial throne, and procuring the deposition of John XXII,—reappeared, strengthened by recruits from every province and town in the Pontifical States. In Rome they encountered only the feeblest opposition, the French legates having called into existence a formidable combination hostile to the power of the Church.

It was to suppress these disorders, and in obedience to the summons—' In the name of God '— of St. Catherine of Sienna, that Gregory XI returned to Rome in 1376. This extraordinary fanatic, the fame of whose sanctity was coextensive with the profession of the Christian faith, had performed a pilgrimage on foot from Florence to Avignon, that she might personally plead with the Pope, and entreat him to restore peace to troubled Italy, by again taking possession of his See. The narration by this simple, pious woman, of the atrocities which were being perpetrated in Italy in his name, and the reproaches of some of the bishops by whom her suit was sustained, appear to have touched the conscience of Gregory. In spite of the opposition of the cardinals, to whom the prospect of exchanging the licence of the Papal court at Avignon, for the sterner morals and more arduous duties of Rome, was anything but acceptable, Gregory set out for Italy. As he sailed up the Tiber he was greeted with enthusiasm; but the Romans, mindful of the brief sojourn of Urban V in his capital, received him with indifference. Their distrust was well founded, for it was only the sudden death of the Pontiff in 1378 that prevented his emulating the example of Urban and returning to Avignon. The mission of St. Catherine, however, had been successful. The Pope had been restored to Rome; there too he had died; and there, in accordance with immemorial custom, the conclave must assemble to elect his successor.

In forsaking an Imperial city, the source of all their claims to sovereign authority, for a foreign provincial town, the Pontiffs had exchanged supremacy for subordination. And this was done at a time when the Imperial power was least able, and least disposed, to contest the claim, in asserting which so many of the representatives upon earth of the Prince of Peace had expended, without compunction, the blood and treasure of their subjects. As the power of the Pontiffs was crippled, their characteristic vices were unfolded. Haughtiness, greed, and sensuality polluted the Papal chair; whilst Europe smiled contemptuously at assumptions which were simply ludicrous in the person of the captive at Avignon. It should, however, be borne in mind that, however much the transfer of the Papal court to Avignon was the act of the French King; however much its prolonged sojourn there corroborates the testimony of history to the dissolute characters of the Pontiffs, who practised, there, vices which would not be tolerated in Rome; or reflects upon the courage and fidelity of the chief shepherd of the Church upon earth, in pusillanimously forsaking the post of duty and of difficulty, for the luxury and ease of a secure and profligate retreat; it was in no small degree attributable to the freedom it enjoyed from the contending factions which, in Rome, had constantly disturbed its serenity, and endangered the recognition of its authority. In one respect, at least, the world was a gainer by the result, for the Papacy never did, and never will, recover the hold which it lost upon the minds of men.

A universal insurrection ensued upon the death of Gregory XI. Almost every town in the Papal States rose to assert the freedom of the people from the tyranny of the French legates. In Rome anarchy reigned triumphant. Bereft of the wealth which, as the seat of the Pontifical court, Christendom had poured into its lap, the city had nothing to sustain its greatness. Piety attracted no pilgrims; nor did the museum of the world bring visitors, whose lives and persons were at the mercy of lawless violence. No industry there found a centre. The arts were not cultivated; and it is said that the population had dwindled to 17,000, whilst grass grew in the streets! And this was the Rome of the Cæsars! This, the once proud mistress of the world, whose *palaces*, under the Empire, were more numerous than its *inhabitants* under Gregory XI; whilst its amphitheatres, constructed to seat 80,000 and 100,000 spectators, were too limited to accommodate the crowds which thronged them, until the Circus Maximus, enlarged from time to time, to meet the requirements of the public, finally afforded accommodation to 385,000 spectators, or more than twenty times the number of the entire population of the city under Gregory XI. The extent of the population of Rome, under the Empire, has been a subject of much vexed controversy. The above-mentioned fact is in itself sufficiently suggestive of its enormous extent, and after a careful study of much that has been written on the subject, I hold it within the region of proof that, inclusive of both sexes, it must have reached and most probably exceeded 5,000,000 souls [1].

The contrast between Imperial Rome and the insignificant town under the priestly rule of a libertine Pope, with its mixture of licence and superstition, of pomp and humility, of luxury and fasting, of tyranny and subserviency, is too glaring to be easily realized. Ages since her glory had departed, and how utter was her degradation! In the fourteenth century, 'Rome,' says Ranke, 'was become a city of herdsmen; its inhabitants were not distinguishable from the peasants of the neighbouring country. The hills had long been abandoned, and the only part inhabited was the plain along the windings of the Tiber; there was no pavement in the narrow streets, and these were rendered yet darker by the balconies and the buttresses which propped one house against another; the cattle wandered about as in a village. From S. Silvestro to the Porta del Popola, all was garden and marsh, the haunt of flocks of wild ducks. The very memory of antiquity seemed almost effaced; the *Capitol* was become the *Goats' Hill* (Monte Caprino), the *Forum Romanum*, the *Cows' Field* (Campo Vaccino). The strangest legends were associated with the few remaining monuments.'

It is impossible to fix the precise date at which the site of the ancient city became deserted; but it is certain that early in the ninth century there were,

---

[1] An admirable *résumé* of this controversy is given by Mr. Story in an Appendix to the second volume of his 'Roba di Roma.'

within Rome itself, cultivated lands of considerable extent, a circumstance for which the calamities which befel the city during the sixth, seventh, and eighth centuries would account. 'An earthquake,' says Lord Broughton, 'shook the Forum of Peace for seven days in the year 408, but such were the convulsions of nature during the succeeding century that Gregory the Great naturally supposed the evils of which he had himself been the witness to be the principal cause of the ruin around him. To the earthquakes, tempests, and inundations, he attributed not only the depopulation of the city but the fall of her dwellings, *the crumbling of her bones*. The rise of the Tiber is specified as having overthrown many of the ancient edifices. Pestilence and famine within the walls, and the Lombards without, had reduced her to a wilderness, and it is to be believed that the population shrunk at that period from many spots never afterwards inhabited.' And again, 'A scarcity in the year 604, a violent earthquake a few years afterwards, a pestilence in or about the year 678, five tremendous inundations of the Tiber from 680 to 797, a second famine in the Pontificate of Pope Constantine, which continued for six-and-thirty months, a pestilence in the last year of the seventh century, and the assault of the Lombards for three months under Astolphus in 755,—these are the events which compose the Roman history of this unhappy period [1].'

The almost total demoralization of the Romans had not, however, wholly obscured the memory of their past greatness. The indications of national feelings and aspirations were faint and partial; their incapacity for self-government was notorious; but not less so was

[1] Lord Broughton's 'Visits to Italy,' 1816–1854. 2 vols.

their antipathy to foreign intervention, and pre-eminently to that of France.

On the demise of Gregory XI, the populace surrounded the palace in which the conclave was assembled to elect his successor, and clamoured, with threats and imprecations, for the election of a Roman, or at least an Italian Pope. They even menaced death to the cardinals if they did not immediately give them a Roman Pontiff. 'A Roman Pope! A Roman Pope!' was the cry to which the streets of Rome echoed throughout the night; whilst the tumult in the conclave, if less loud, was hardly less angry. 'If,' cried the excited populace, 'ye persist to do despite to Christ, if we have not a Roman Pope, we will hew these cardinals and Frenchmen in pieces [1].' French influence, however, was in the ascendant. Constrained by the threatening attitude of the Roman people, the electors did not, indeed, dare to nominate a Frenchman; but resorted to the artifice of fixing upon a *temporary Pontiff*, who promised not to avail himself of their nomination, and took, merely for form's sake, the title of Urban VI. But the new Pope, full of national sympathies, determined upon reducing the influence of France among the cardinals, and employed his first exercise of Apostolic authority in freeing himself from the oaths which he had taken. The astonished and affronted cardinals proceeded forthwith to the election of a rival from amongst themselves, on the plea that the election of Urban was invalid, having been effected under the pressure of intimidation. The Pontiff offered to submit the validity of his election to the decision of a General Council, but the cardinals, who were now

---

[1] Milman's 'Latin Christianity.'

protected at Anagné by the presence of French troops, declined all negotiation, and proceeded to elect Robert of Geneva, who assumed the title of Clement VII (Anti-Pope). France, Scotland, (then in alliance with France,) and Naples accepted the Frenchman, whose highest qualification for the tiara was that he was reputed a sagacious and experienced politician; whilst the greater part of Christendom, including England, adhered to his Italian rival [1].

Clement VII established his court at Avignon, whilst Urban VI remained in Rome. There was now therefore a Pope and an Anti-Pope. Thus commenced the great schism, which for eight-and-thirty years scandalized Europe. 'Two popes,' says Macaulay, 'each with a doubtful title, made all Europe ring with their mutual invectives and anathemas. Rome cried out against the corruptions of Avignon; and Avignon, with equal justice, recriminated on Rome. The plain Christian people, brought up in the belief that it was a sacred duty to be in communion with the head of the Church, were unable to discover, amidst conflicting testimonies and conflicting arguments, to which of the two worthless priests, who were cursing and reviling each other, the headship of the Church rightly belonged [2].' We are

---

[1] The qualifications which recommended the Cardinal of Geneva, were rather those of a successor to John Hawkwood or to a Duke of Milan, than of the Apostles. 'Extraordinary activity of body and endurance of fatigue, courage which would hazard his life to put down the intrusive Pope, sagacity and experience in the temporal affairs of the Church; high birth, through which he was allied with most of the royal and princely houses of Europe: of austerity, devotion, learning, charity, holiness, not a word.'—Dean Milman's 'Latin Christianity.'

[2] Macaulay's 'Miscellanies,' vol. ii.

told by Maroni that, in order to avoid the penalty of excommunication through rejecting the true Vicar of Christ, good catholics *reserved their obedience* for whichever was the canonical Pope!

Each Pontiff had his partizans in every country of Europe, and the bitterness thus engendered amongst courts and peoples, who cared little for either Pontiff, and were impatient of the growing scandal, soon begot a hatred of both; whilst, here and there, a dislike of the Popedom itself was awakened. The inextricable labyrinth in which the adherents of Papal infallibility were involved was insupportably perplexing. 'Their belief,' remark the authors of 'The Pope and the Council,' 'necessarily implied that the particular individual who is in sole possession of all truth, and bestows on the whole Church the certainty of its faith, must be always and undoubtingly acknowledged as such. There can as little be any uncertainty allowed about the person of the right Pope as about the books of Scripture. Yet every one at that period must at bottom have been aware that the mere accident of what country he lived in determined which Pope he adhered to, and that all he knew of his Pope's legitimacy was that half Christendom rejected it.'

The Papal supremacy was openly assailed by the Lollards, as a corruption of Christianity; and in England and Bohemia, though Wycliffe died early, and Huss and Jerome perished at the stake, the stream of light,

'————a rivulet, then a river,'

had begun to flow, which was destined, in the Providence of God, to grow with ever-increasing splendour, until all lands were enlightened by it.

CHAPTER V.

THE fifteenth century was a transition period both in the political and the religious history of Europe. It belongs neither to the Middle Ages nor to modern history. We cannot here trace the transition from the feudalism of the Middle Ages to the independent forms of monarchy which, as the century advanced, became established in Europe; but the fact should be borne in mind, as we come to consider the altered, and otherwise inexplicable, relationships of the Papacy to the secular powers, especially during that direful struggle for supremacy between France and Spain, which ended in the subjugation of Italy to the latter power.

It was a fortunate circumstance that no questions of religious dogma were involved in the schism which was wearying the patience of Christendom. But the importunate entreaties, and even threats, of the civil powers, and particularly that of France, failed to make any impression upon the obstinate selfishness of the rival Pontiffs. The abdication of both Popes, and a new election to the Papal throne, were the only means whereby peace could be restored to the Church. Of this, even the cardinals who had adhered with unbending obstinacy to their respective chiefs, at length became convinced. Wise in their generation, they recognized and controlled, as a means of securing harmony to the Church, that public opinion which, whilst believing in the necessity of its existence, insisted upon its purification, and clamoured for the limitation of Papal despotism. Hence originated the Council of Pisa, which, failing to command the universal recognition of Christendom, only embittered the schism by the introduction of a third pretender to the tiara.

The famous Council of Constance was brought together at the instance of the Emperor Sigismund, A.D. 1414, for the avowed purpose of healing the schism, of extirpating heresy, and of reforming the Church, in her head and in her members. This Council, which asserted itself to be under the direct inspiration of the Holy Ghost, continued its profitless labours for four years.

It was hard necessity only which had driven Pope John XXIII into a close alliance with the Emperor, who had determined to heal the schism by summoning a General Council from which it was at least possible that John[1] might emanate *a private man*. Such, however, was the hard but necessary condition of the powerful and all-important alliance. When, therefore, John XXIII had determined to submit to the inevitable Council, he firmly resolved not to trust himself within the dominions of the Emperor. His indignation was stirred when he learned that his commissioners had agreed with Sigismund to select the Imperial city of Constance for the meeting-place of the Council. He now determined to take the negotiations into his own hands, and arranged a personal interview with the Emperor at Lodi, trusting to his powers of persuasion to overcome the obduracy of Sigismund, and to win his

[1] 'The worst and most abused man to be found, when his badness had been thoroughly exposed in the Council at Constance.' —Justinger, 'Berner-Chronic.'

assent to the nomination of some Italian city, where the independence of the Council would be less secure. But although the discussion of this sore point was conducted with an ostentatious display of mutual respect, Sigismund was immovable in his decision. Imperial letters and a Papal bull were issued, summoning the General Council of Christendom to meet at Constance in the following year. The Pope and Emperor then proceeded together to Cremona, where an incident occurred which not only nearly prevented the meeting of the projected Council, but threatened also a tremendous crisis in the history of the Papacy. Fondoli, the lord of Cremona, who entertained his illustrious guests with sumptuous hospitality, conducted them to a lofty tower to survey the captivating prospect presented by the outspreading plains of Lombardy. Subsequently, upon his death-bed, Fondoli confessed the design, which he avowed that he bitterly repented having failed to carry into execution, of hurling both Pope and Emperor from the summit of the tower, thus securing for himself immortal fame[1].

It is unnecessary to follow, in their detail, the proceedings of this famous Council, which the writings of the late Dean of St. Paul's have familiarized to every reader of ecclesiastical history. The results may be thus summarized. They deposed two Popes and obliged a third to resign. By the deposition of John XXIII, and the election of Cardinal Otho di Colonna in his room, they brought the Church back under one head. They launched a fatal blow at the advancing tide of belief in Papal infallibility, by declaring, without a single dissentient voice, that in matters of faith the

[1] Milman's 'Latin Christianity.'

Pope is subject to the Council, which derives its authority immediately from Christ. They burned John Huss and Jerome of Prague, and condemned the writings of Wycliffe to the flames. But they ignominiously failed, as completely as the fathers who had assembled at Pisa, A.D. 1409, in their attempt to reform the Church, or to mitigate the corruptions of the times, which cried aloud for heaven's vengeance. In Italy the vices of the Church had produced a widespread atheism, in which the clergy and laity were alike participators. 'Scepticism was so general,' says Mr. Dyer, that 'the Council of Lateran thought it necessary to decree, in its eighth session, that the soul of man is not only immortal, but also distinct in each individual, and not a portion of one and the same soul. Erasmus knew of his own knowledge that at Rome the most horrible blasphemies were uttered by the priests, and sometimes in the very act of saying Mass; and he relates, among other things, an attempt made to prove to him, out of Pliny, that there is no difference between the souls of beasts and men. Such of the Italian ecclesiastics as were scholars prided themselves on the purity of their Latin style, which they were fearful of corrupting by a study of the Bible. They altered the language of Scripture to that of Livy or Cicero: Jehovah became Jupiter Optimus Maximus; Christ, Apollo or Æsculapius; the Virgin Mary, Diana. Cardinal John de Medici, afterwards Leo X, was not only a Platonist, but, if he had any religion at all, rather a pagan than a Christian, and he seems to have inoculated the Romans with his own opinions, for on the breaking out of a pestilence at Rome, during the Pontificate of his successor, Adrian, a bullock was sacrificed on the ancient Forum, with heathen rites, conducted by a Greek named Demetrius, to the great satisfaction of the people[1].' Hardly a writer of the fifteenth century fails to denounce the infidelity, ignorance, and profligacy of the ecclesiastics in every part of Christendom. 'In England the priests petitioned parliament, A.D. 1449, to be pardoned for all rapes committed before June *next*, as well as to be excused from all forfeitures for taking excessive salaries, provided they paid the King a noble (6*s.* 8*d.*) for every priest in the kingdom. The petition was granted, and the statute made accordingly. In A.D. 1455 the Archbishop of Canterbury issued an order denouncing the vices of his clergy, their gluttony, drunkenness, fornication, ignorance, pursuit of worldly lucre, &c. It appears from a decree of the eleventh session of the Council of Lateran, that some ecclesiastics derived an income from the stews; and Innocent VIII found it necessary to renew by a bull, published in April, A.D. 1488, the constitution of Pius II, forbidding priests to keep butcheries, taverns, gaming-houses, and brothels, and to be the go-betweens of courtesans[2].'

The Council of Pisa had resulted in the creation of three infallible heads of the Church, instead of two, and the abortive and simulative labours for reform of its successor at Constance, prepared the way for the Reformation.

The new Pope assumed the title of Martin V, and was recognized by all Europe. Martin was an accomplished man of the world. The Council soon discovered that, by electing a man of character, they had given themselves a master to whom it was less easy to dictate

---

[1] Dyer's 'Modern Europe,' vol. i.
[2] Ibid.

than to a John XXIII. Martin, by his firmness and decision, succeeded in rendering nugatory the measures which the Council had adopted for the reform of abuses. The Council was at the Pope's mercy. He dismissed the assembled Prelates with the bland assurance that their work was accomplished; but not until he had published a bull, which he caused to be read in the Council, declaring all appeal from a Pope to a Council unlawful and prohibited. Further, by the election of a Pontiff capable of reviving the waning reverence of Christendom, the Council of Constance, which had threatened to shake the Papal supremacy to its foundations, had really confirmed and strengthened its authority; and both the Emperor, who chafed under the consciousness that he had sunk to a subordinate position, and the assembled Prelates, who felt themselves baffled, and fallen under the incontestable supremacy of the Pope, were as anxious to be released from their irksome imprisonment, as Martin V was to release them[1].

After a slow progress through Italy, Martin entered Rome in triumph, A.D. 1421, as the absolute sovereign of the city, and quietly asserted all the unrevoked authority which had been conceded to Innocent III. The currency, which for three hundred years had borne the arms of the Senate, now displayed the effigy of the sovereign Pontiff. But the spirit of republicanism survived, and the Pope was not master of a single city in the Papal territory besides Rome. The doctrines of Huss had now obtained a firm footing in Germany; and the indignation which was felt at the perfidy of Sigismund, in violating the safe-conduct which had induced him to appear before the Council, intensified the de-

[1] Milman's 'Latin Christianity.'

mand for a final settlement of the great question at issue;—whether the long-endured and still agressive tyranny of Rome might not be overridden by the decisions of a General Council.

Throughout Christendom dissatisfaction was felt at the issue of the Council of Constance; and the assumption, by Martin V, of all the haughty demeanour and language of former Pontiffs; his interference in the disposal of wealthy benefices in Germany; his insulting usurpation of the undisputed primacy of the Archbishop of Canterbury, and vigorous efforts to suppress the growing spirit of independence in England; his denunciations of Henry V for his aggression on the Church, particularly in enforcing the Statute of Premunire, which subjected all persons bringing Papal bulls into the kingdom to perpetual imprisonment; by which 'execrable statute the King of England has so entirely usurped the spiritual jurisdiction, as if our Saviour had constituted him his vicar;'—these assumptions of the imperious Pontiff gave new energy to the cry for a final settlement of the question of Papal jurisdiction. Hence originated the famous Council of Basle, A.D. 1431, the last of the three great Councils of the fifteenth century, which, by reasserting the supremacy of the decisions of a General Council, even over a Pontiff, contributed the most powerful check to the usurpations of Rome. Martin V lived only to see the opening of the Council whose decrees were so fatal to his assumptions. A stroke of apoplexy introduced him to the majority before its deliberations had commenced.

The new Pope, Eugenius IV, of course dissented from a decree which endangered the recognition of his infallibility, and made him the creature of the Council, whose members, however, proceeded to enforce their decision by declaring his deposition.

Eugenius had summoned the Council sorely against his will, apprehending that negotiations might be opened with the Hussites, a growing disposition to which had been recently manifested; but the resolution of all sections of the Church, both lay and ecclesiastical, backed by the will of Sigismund, constrained him to compliance. Thrice he issued an edict of dismissal, 'on account of the fewness of those present,' threatening anathemas in the event of disobedience; but the reverend Fathers refused to disperse, alleging that they constituted the one true Œcumenical Council, whose powers had been already declared 'superior to the Pope.' Eugenius denounced the reverend Fathers as a Synagogue of Satan. The negotiations with the Greek Emperor respecting the reunion of the Churches afforded him the desired pretext for convening a rival Synod in Italy; he therefore declared that the Council sat only by his permission, and derived from him its limited authority, and determined to summon a rival Council at Ferrara. A Papal legate appeared at Basle to propose the removal of the Council to one of the great cities of Italy, of which the Pontiff offered the choice of seven. By a majority of two-thirds the Council rejected the proposal, well knowing that all hope of reforming the Church would be lost in a Council which, assembling on Italian soil, would be at once flooded with local bishops and the officials of the *curia*. Hence they were prepared to adopt the extremest measures, and received with indifference the protestations of Eugenius. The rival Council quickly assembled at Ferrara, and as the feud became more violent and irreconcilable, it was transferred, for greater convenience and security, to Florence. Here it declared that, 'It alone, inasmuch as it had been summoned by the Pope, constituted a true Œcumenical Council, whilst at Basle sat a beggarly mob, mere vulgar fellows from the lowest dregs of the clergy, apostates, blasphemers, rebels, men guilty of sacrilege, jailbirds, men who, without exception, deserved only to be hunted back to the devil, from whom they came.' The Council at Basle was nothing daunted by the insults and anathemas of its rival, which it returned with interest, and boldly declared Eugenius a simonist, perjurer, and irredeemable heretic; a firebrand of discord; a waster of the goods of the Church; a rebel against God. They cited Eugenius to appear before them at Basle, within sixty days, and answer for his acts. At the expiration of this term they declared the Pope contumacious, and, after some delay, in solemn convocation they pronounced his deposition[1].

The factitious importance with which the question of the union of the Eastern and Western Churches had become surrounded[2], afforded Eugenius a pretext for again insisting upon the selection of some Italian city as the seat of the Council. The Byzantine Emperor, John Palæologus, whose 'empire' now consisted of the city of Constantinople, was fain to accept the aid of the West at any price. In his hesitation whether to close with

[1] 'The Mysteries of the Vatican,' by Dr. Griesinger.
[2] It was the question of questions for Eugenius. 'If he could meet the efforts of the Synod of Basle by producing the testimony of the re-united Eastern Church on his side, it would greatly strengthen his case in the public opinion of the whole West.'—'The Pope and the Council.'

the emulous invitations of the Council or of the Pope, with both of whom he entered into negotiations, his sole consideration was to secure the most powerful ally against the Ottomans, who threatened to wrest from him the last vestige of the Empire. The Patriarch Joseph, though he yielded with reluctance to the principle of a foreign Council, and did not share the Emperor's illusion that the West would lay itself at his feet, elect him the successor of Sigismund, and thus bring about a reunion of the great Christian Commonwealth under one sovereign [1], concurred with him in the policy of accepting the invitation of the Pope, in preference to that of the Council. Joseph, however, nourished illusions of his own, which encouraged him in the difficult task of persuading the heads of his Church to enter into the dangerous enterprise. 'When the Eastern Emperor should behold the pomp of the Pope, the lowly deference paid to their ecclesiastical superiors by the great potentates of the West, he would take lessons of humility, and no longer mistake the relative dignity of the spiritual and temporal sovereign [2].'

The Greeks soon had occasion to suspect that Eugenius was more bent upon his own aggrandizement than upon the vaunted union of the Churches. The artful attempts which they witnessed to degrade the Patriarch from his absolute co-equality with the Pope, aroused their jealousy; and the concessions of the Patriarch, whom they conceived to be the tool of the Emperor, called forth their bitter reproaches. Some of the bishops contrived to effect their escape, and returned

---

[1] Milman's 'Latin Christianity.'
[2] 'Syropulus.' Quoted by Dean Milman.

to Constantinople, for which act of contumacy the indignant Patriarch commanded their suspension, and sent home orders that they should be 'soundly flogged.' Whilst these miserable disputes were raging, the Emperor was too much amused with his hunting to expedite their suppression. When, at length, the Council was formally opened, 'it was skilfully contrived that, while there was the most irreverent confusion amongst the Greeks, the Patriarch was treated with studied neglect, the Emperor himself with reluctant and parsimonious honours, the Pope maintained his serene dignity; all the homage paid to him was skilfully displayed [1].'

We must not linger over the theological discussions of the Council of Florence, which were long and furious. Before their conclusion, the Emperor Sigismund and the Patriarch Joseph had died. Eugenius survived to dictate his own terms. An act of union between the two Churches was agreed upon, and heaven and earth were summoned to rejoice over the event. But, like every attempt which the world has witnessed to impose uniformity of belief upon the minds of men, involving the subversion of the civil and religious liberties of the people, it was labour lost. The Patriarchal theory was wholly alien to the system of Rome, and every overture for union, during two centuries, had encountered the uncompromising hostility of the Greek hierarchy. The spirit which animated their response to John XXII's demand for their submission still survived. 'Thy plenary power over thy subjects,' they had said, 'we firmly believe; thine immeasurable pride we cannot endure, and thy greed

---

[1] Milman's 'Latin Christianity.'

we cannot satisfy. With thee is Satan, with us the Lord.' The act of union was indeed published with the most imposing solemnity in the cathedral of Florence, where now rested the remains of the Patriarch, whose remonstrant voice death had silenced. But it was a dead letter, the only abiding effect of which was a more bitter and radical estrangement between the rival Churches. 'The Emperor,' says Dean Milman, 'with the Greek clergy, returned to Venice, and, after a long and fatiguing navigation, to Constantinople, there to be received, not as the saviour of the Empire from the sword of the Turks, not as the wise and pious reconciler of religious dissension and the peacemaker of the Church, but as a traitor to his own imperial dignity, as a renegade and an apostate.'

The Council of Florence thus ended in an appreciable confirmation and extension of the power and dignity of the Pontiff. Again quoting Dean Milman, 'He, of all the successors of St. Peter, had beheld the Byzantine Emperor at his feet, had condescended to dictate terms of union to the Greeks, who had acknowledged the superior orthodoxy, the primacy of Rome. The splendid illusion was kept up by the appearance of ecclesiastical ambassadors—how commissioned, invested with what authority none knew, none now know—from the more remote and barbarous Churches of the East, from the uttermost parts of the Christian world. The Iberians, Armenians, the Maronites and Jacobites of Syria, the Chaldean Nestorians, the Ethiopians, successively rendered the homage of their allegiance to the one supreme head of Christendom [1].'

[1] Milman's 'Latin Christianity.'

This success of the Pope greatly intensified the hostility of the Council of Basle. Undeterred by the defection of the temporal princes, who shrank from the growing democratic tendencies of the Council, or by the tumultous altercations which disgraced its proceedings, they had already proclaimed the deposition of Eugenius. The Council was not unanimous in proceeding to this extreme measure, but such feeble opposition as was offered,

'A bitter and perplexed "What shall we do?"'

was quickly silenced, in this fashion: 'You do not know us Germans,' exclaimed the Archbishop of Aquileia, when this step was condemned by the Cardinal of Palermo. 'If you go on thus, you will hardly come off without broken heads.' The Council was now almost wholly composed of the clergy of inferior rank. Not one Spanish, and but one Italian, bishop remained to give a show of validity to its proceedings. Their places were filled by archdeacons, provosts, and priors, who were present to the number of four hundred. In place of the absent bishops, relics of famous saints were collected, and placed in the hall of Council. At this solemn appeal to the saints in bliss, we are told that 'a transport of profound devotion seized the assembly; they all burst into tears [1].' The edict for the deposition of Eugenius was soon after passed, and the Council, which contained only one legitimate elector, proceeded to the election of his successor.

A proposition was made to Amadeus, the ex-Duke of Savoy, to accept the questionable honour of the tiara. After some demur, the Duke signified his acquiescence.

[1] Dean Milman.

The difficulties which he had raised were not such as betokened a mind capable of dealing with the implacable hatred which would, of necessity, be aroused by the assumption of the functions of an Anti-Pope. The loss of his hermit's beard appears to have been the sacrifice most reluctantly made, and only assented to after his public appearance as Pope, when his ducal mind seems to have apprehended the unseemliness of the spectacle presented by a thick-bearded Pope, surrounded by a throng of closely-shaven ecclesiastics.

Schism was now once more established. Again, and for the last time, we see a Pope and an Anti-Pope hurling their spiritual thunders against each other. But we also see, what we have not seen before, the indifference of Christendom to the squabbles of two very commonplace Italian priests, aspirants to an office shorn, by its unworthy occupants, of the dignity and lustre with which the great Pontiffs of the bygone centuries had surrounded it.

> 'Oh! they are fled the light! those mighty spirits
> Lie rack'd up with their ashes in their urns,
> And not a spark of their eternal fire
> Glows in a present bosom [1].'

Schism, however, was an odious offence to Christendom, which resented with scornful reproaches these results of a system which was felt to be out of harmony with the spirit and the requirements of the age. The rival Popes might wage a warfare with the pen, and amuse or harass themselves, whilst they excited the disgust of Europe by their puerile hate and harmless anathemas. The days were for ever past when such

[1] Johnson.

a condition of things could occasion any apprehension for the peace of the world.

Amadeus assumed the title of Felix V. The fact of his being a layman, the father of a large family, and the rightful sovereign of one of the kingdoms of this world, being urged as favourable rather than disadvantageous to his election as Pope. One of the debaters in the Council which elected Amadeus to the Papal throne, clenched his arguments in favour of the union of the spiritual and temporal powers by a clumsy and imperfectly veiled apology for the profligate lives of the Pontiffs. It was, he maintained, an advantage to the State when the Pope had sons of his own, whose natural vocation it would be to resist the attacks of tyrants. In three days the ex-Duke received all the orders of the Church, and was ordained Priest, Bishop, and Sovereign-Pontiff. History thus records a Pope amongst the lineal ancestors of the present King of Italy.

Felix was denounced by Eugenius as a 'hell-dog' and 'Antichrist,' a 'golden calf' and a 'Mahomet;' and the Council at Basle as 'devils disguised as men,' who had set up the idol Moloch. The reader will observe that these Christian epithets were employed not by the Anti-Pope, who, having usurped the chair of the Apostles, had no infallibility to violate; they are the words of the canonical Pope, the successor of the Apostles, the Vicar of Christ. They have, therefore, an important bearing upon Christian ethics. The only Church in Christendom which claims to be infallible is chargeable, in the person of its supreme head, with the abrogation of St. Paul's injunction that a bishop must be 'of good behaviour, . . . patient, not a brawler.'

Felix V continued to discharge the functions of Pope for a period of ten years, when, in order to heal the schism, and restore peace to the Church, he resigned the Pontificate as voluntarily, and probably more gladly, than he had relinquished his ducal crown. This result was brought about by the new Emperor, Frederick III, who had been won over to the side of Eugenius, and, in March, A.D. 1446, proposed conditions for a reconciliation between the Pope and the Council, which the former, in substance, accepted.

Eugenius died in the following year, and Nicholas V, who succeeded him, immediately notified his assent to the terms of reconciliation. By this means the authority of the Pope was upheld against the Council of Basle, and a Concordat was concluded between Felix and Nicholas; the latter confirming in their offices the cardinals nominated by Felix, annulling the Papal censures against the Pope and the Council, and conceding the decrees of Basle as concerning promotions and appointments in Germany. At the same time the Pope maintained his right, when occasion should require, to act without regard to the provisions of the Concordat. His successor, Calixtus III, openly asserted the same claim, declaring to the Emperor that a Pope could not be bound by the terms of any compact, and that, in so far as he observed the Concordat, it must be regarded as a pure act of generosity and liberality on his part.

Nicholas V was now, as Pontiff, a great Italian potentate; and it was his ambition to lay the foundation of his power in the hearts of his people—in an honourable claim to the gratitude of Italy—and in this he succeeded. When Italy was distracted by intestine war, he kept no large army in his pay, and protested that he would never employ any arms but those of the Cross of Christ. Yet, not only did he preserve his own territories from aggression, but he became the pacificator of Italy. To secure to Italy that undisturbed peace which should be favourable to the moral influence of the Papacy, and to the cultivation of the arts, which he encouraged with lavish generosity, was the laudable ambition of Nicholas V. The Jubilee which occurred during his Pontificate, favoured his projects, as it also extended his fame. Pilgrims, from the highest ranks of society, swarmed into Rome from every country of Europe, and they carried back with them the praises of the Pontiff who, by his personal dignity, the munificence of his patronage of the arts, his irreproachable life, and his successful mediation in the conflicts to which Italy had been so long a prey, had resuscitated the majesty of the Roman Pontificate. It was the year of Jubilee, and the pleasing illusion was cherished that one virtuous and gifted Pontiff could re-establish, throughout Christendom, the waning power of the Papacy.

'Some there be that shadows kiss,
Such have but a shadow's bliss[1].'

In the matter of ecclesiastical reform, the Council of Basle effected no more than its predecessor at Constance. The abuses of the Papacy were more monstrous at the close of the fifteenth century than at any earlier period; whilst Pius II, in a bull bearing date A.D. 1460, condemned the principle sanctioned by both Councils, that a Council is superior to the Pope; and Julius II annulled altogether the decrees of the Council of Basle[2].

[1] Shakespeare.   [2] Riddle's 'History of the Papacy.'

I have already wandered, however, too far from the subject of this monograph, which is concerned only with the development of the temporal power of the Papacy, and must pass by that important era in the internal history of the Roman Church, in which the Papal monster who assumed the title of Alexander VI, and whose scandalous immorality and injustice aroused the horror of awakening Europe, held sway in Rome. These traits were not, indeed, monopolized by Alexander VI; but however much they may have characterized other Popes of his time, he occupies, in one respect at least, a unique position. Far from regarding the vicious practices of his predecessors as stains upon the Papal escutcheon, to be withdrawn from the public gaze, he practised them without attempt at concealment, and was the most notorious profligate of Europe. Discarding the conventional, if shallow, tribute to virtue, which led other Popes to term their offspring *nephews*, he openly acknowledged his children (of whom the famed and too severely censured Lucrezia Borgia was the youngest and most beloved), whose aggrandizement was the chief object of his solicitude; the end, for the attainment of which every species of crime was held permissible.

CHAPTER VI.

During the latter part of the fifteenth century there was no well-organized government in Rome. The character of the Popes had become degraded by the political strifes in which they were perpetually engaged. 'The veil woven by religious awe,' says Hallam, 'was rent asunder, and the features of ordinary ambition appeared without disguise.' The discovery was fatal to Papal authority. As, throughout Europe, the covetousness and profligacy of the clergy had lowered their character and influence, so the same qualities, more flagrantly exercised by their head, undermined the respect which was essential to the exercise of his temporal sovereignty. Towards the close of the fifteenth century, the profligacy of the Pontiffs, 'more notorious than could be paralleled in the darkest age that had preceded[1]', must be regarded as the foremost amongst those general causes which heralded the decrepitude of the Papacy.

Insignificant nobles and tyrants, hereditary governors of provinces, were able to set the temporal power of the Pope at defiance.

Throughout the two centuries which had elapsed since the death of Innocent III, the struggle on the part of the Church against the State had been concerning its immunities and property; its attempts to extend its

---

[1] Hallam's 'Middle Ages.'

legal jurisdiction in criminal matters; and especially to secure for ecclesiastics freedom from the jurisdiction of civil courts. It had undoubtedly acquired, both in its ecclesiastical and civil relations, a splendour and an appearance of strength greater than it had ever enjoyed before, notwithstanding the curtailment of its territorial possessions and power under the later Popes.

The human intellect had as yet dreamed of no road to distinction and power save through the medium of the Church. The historians, the poets, the philosophers of the fifteenth century, had their domicile in the cloister. Not only were the monks the canon lawyers, but, 'as far as it was known, or in use, the teachers and professors of the civil law[1].' Education was their exclusive privilege, jealously guarded, and extended over the whole domain of the human intellect. The Church, therefore, attracted to itself the intellect of the age. To an aspiring mind no other career was open. As the Church grew in wealth and power, the career which it offered to men gifted with intellectual capacity, vied with the tawdry honours of a decaying nobility; whilst to the younger sons of noble, and even princely families, and to the illegitimate offspring of Popes and kings, its service presented an irresistible attraction. Qualifications for their holy calling were not insisted upon according to nineteenth-century notions; though it is but just to remark that, in many cases, these aspirants to ecclesiastical distinction were characterized by high intellectual capacity, austere morals, and genuine piety. Where these traits were wanting, that which Rome valued more highly was secured. By drawing the religious teachers from every

[1] Dean Milman.

class, not excepting the highest, they were on equal terms with every class; by the inscription of famous names in the roll of her priesthood, the attachment of powerful families was secured, which thus 'welded together, as it were, the Church with the State [1].' There was not a kingdom in Europe in which education and public opinion were not moulded by ecclesiastics, bound in canonical obedience to the Pope at Rome. Their intellectual superiority and undisputed pre-eminence in the administration of secular affairs rendered them the indispensable coadjutors of the temporal sovereigns. It is not their intellectual superiority alone which accounts for this. 'It resulted,' says Dean Milman, 'from their almost exclusive possession of the universal European language, that they held and retained the administration of public affairs. No royal embassy was without its Prelate, even if the ambassadors were not all Prelates, for they only could converse freely together without mutual misunderstanding of their barbarous jargon, or the precarious aid of an interpreter. The Latin alone was as yet sufficiently precise and definite in its terms to form binding treaties; it was the one language current throughout Europe; it was of necessity that of all negotiations between distant kingdoms [2].'

Here and there we catch an ominous whisper of the rising moral indignation inspired by this universal lordship of the human conscience. The higher intellects of this age, the men who were the real leaders of European thought, sneered at those ceremonies and beliefs which, as princes or as prelates, they were paid

---

[1] Milman's 'Latin Christianity.' [2] Ibid.

to maintain[1]. A condition of things so shocking to the deep instincts of spiritual men, who mourned over the degeneracy of religion, emboldened those cries for reform which emanated from every corner of Christendom and found an echo even in the Vatican itself. The blind opposition of Rome to this moral sentiment was, indeed, the cause of her fall; but there is no greater proof of the power of the Papacy at the close of the fifteenth century, than the triumph she achieved in this universal sacerdotal domination. Throughout Christendom the vast fabric of the hierarchy stood unshaken.

Under the vigorous rule of Julius II, 'the warrior Pope' (A.D. 1503), the domains of the Church, which had been lost by his predecessors, were recovered; and the sovereignty of the Pontiff was established over all those territories which, down to the period of the French Revolution, constituted the States of the Church. The acquisition of the Legations, however, cannot be said to have extended the sovereignty of the Pontiff over these districts. The Pope contented himself with imposing a Legate, who occupied the highest place in the government, transmitting the revenues of the subject territory to Rome. The original power of the nobles, and the independent corporations of the cities and monasteries, remained unmolested. In the intoxication of his first success, Julius caused a medal to be struck, representing himself, with the tiara on his head and a whip in his hand, driving the French before him, and trampling under foot the escutcheon of the Valois. This fact, however commonplace, is interesting as affording an illustration of the character of the Pontiff who, with the vanity and ambition worthy of a Boniface,

---

[1] Forbes, Bishop of Brechin, 'On the XXXIX Articles.'

united a fiery and vindictive temper, of which the medal was emblematical.

It has been said of Julius, that nature made him a warrior, and destiny a priest. He himself saw no inconsistency in the union of the two professions in his own person. Believing himself divinely commissioned to effect the restoration and extension of the temporal dominion of the Church, he heroically devoted himself to its achievement, and succeeded. And if there is something shocking to modern ideas in the spectacle of a Christian priest, of threescore years and ten, armed with cuirass and helmet, leading his soldiers in person to an assault, sharing with them the hardships and dangers of a campaign, and dragging reluctant cardinals to his quarters, directly exposed to the fire of the enemy, we can at least admire the patriotism which was the source alike of his intrepidity and ambition, and should remember that he lived in an age when warlike skill and personal courage were considered as essential for a bishop, as we deem them to be for a commander of armies; when a Pope was held to be no more consistently engaged in offering Mass, than in leading an army against the enemies of the faith,—that is, of the Roman Church. To free his country from a foreign yoke was the dream of this valiant Pontiff's life, and in this he occupies a unique position in the long line of the occupants of St. Peter's chair. His indignation was stirred by the subversion of the Republican constitutions of Genoa and Tuscany. A cardinal having, on one occasion, remarked to him that the kingdom of Naples was always under the dominion of strangers, the irate Pontiff, striking his staff upon the ground, passionately exclaimed that, if heaven spared his life, he would soon free Naples from this reproach[1].

Always victorious in war, Julius used his success with moderation. Devoid of the nepotism which characterized the Pontiffs of his age, he remained constant to one idea, and fought to aggrandize, not himself, but the Church; conferring the blessings of good government upon the peoples whom he subjected to her rule. The continual changes in his alliances, with which he has been reproached, testify to his absorbing patriotism. He abandoned the alliance of France, of Venice, and of Spain, so soon as he thought that these powers offered any impediment to the success of his Italian projects[2]. His proud and intolerant spirit could endure even humiliation, in the cause of Italy. In the hope of detaching the Emperor Maximilian from his alliance with Louis XII, he submitted to the coarse insolence of the Bishop of Gurk, the Imperial envoy commissioned to open the abortive congress at Mantua, which was designed to secure the Italian conquests of the Emperor; a result, in the estimate of Julius, less injurious to the Papacy than the alliance of Germany and France. Although it was evident at the commencement of the negotiations that the differences between the Emperor and the Venetians on the one hand, and those of the Papacy with France and with the Duke of Ferrara on the other, were, at this stage, incapable of a peaceable solution, Julius was so bent upon effecting the humiliation of the French king, that he patiently endured the effrontery of the haughty

---

[1] 'Sismondi,' vol. ix.

[2] Van Praet's 'Essays on the Political History of the Fifteenth, Sixteenth, and Seventeenth Centuries.'

prelate, whose hatred of the Venetians inspired him with a determined antagonism to the Pontiff. The bait of a cardinal's hat was powerless to curb the insolence, or to sway the obstinacy, of the bishop. The projected congress failed, and hostilities were resumed. The alliance between Maximilian and Louis XII was cemented, and the Emperor dreamt of nothing less than restoring to himself and his successors all the prerogatives exercised by Charlemagne.

To the Bolognese, whose city, with the wide extent of territory over which its dominion extended, was one of the earliest conquests of Julius II, the Pontiff granted a constitution which secured to them, in harmony with submission to the Papal See, no inconsiderable degree of real independence. This they continued to enjoy down to the period of the French Revolution; though Bologna ceased henceforward to be reckoned amongst the sovereign states of Italy. The inconstant and ungrateful Bolognese were little mindful of these benefits. No sooner had Julius withdrawn from the city, after the collapse in the negotiations for the Congress of Mantua, than the citizens, with the peasants from the mountains, joined the French in an attack upon the Papal army, which they completely routed; whilst a colossal statue of the Pope—one of the finest works of Michael Angelo—was pulled down and destroyed with every mark of contempt [1].

In the last year of the Pontificate of Julius II, Louis XII of France, making common cause with the Emperor Maximilian I, summoned a General Council at Pisa, with the view of imposing a check upon the growing power of the Pontiff, and the inflated dignity

[1] Dyer's 'History of Europe.'

and influence with which he was surrounding the Papal See. Their efforts resulted in total failure; no more than half a dozen cardinals, two archbishops, and a few abbots comprising the assembly, which Louis himself characterized as a comedy. The illness of the Pope, at this time, inspired the erratic Emperor with the singular idea of becoming himself a candidate for the tiara. He assumed the Imperial title of Pontifex Maximus, and, by pawning the Imperial jewels, raised the sum of 300,000 ducats for distribution amongst the cardinals at the anticipated conclave. It is curious to observe how the princes of this period seemed to have exchanged parts: 'Maximilian wished to be a Pope and saint, and Louis XII was holding a Council; while the Pope himself, aping the name and deeds of the greatest of the Cæsars, and covering his white hairs with a helmet, led a body of old priests under the cannon's mouth [1].'

The Pope recovered, and the only important result of the Council of Pisa was the alliance, called the Holy League, concluded by the Pope, the King of Spain, and the Republic of Venice; with whom were afterwards associated the Emperor, and Henry VII of England. Its professed object was the protection of the Church from the sacrilegious attacks threatened by the Council of Pisa. The accession to the Holy League of the Emperor Maximilian I, after his defection from the French alliance, proved that the suspicions with which Louis XII had regarded its formation were well founded.

Julius II, apparently anticipating that the Council would command a larger measure of support from the French clergy, resolved to parry this blow at the Papal

[1] Dyer's 'Modern Europe.'

supremacy, by convening the rival Council of the Lateran; which, having the sanction of Papal authority, was of course regarded by the orthodox as the only genuine one. Before his death the Pontiff had the satisfaction of receiving not only the support of all the temporal powers, but that also of the Emperor himself, who abandoned the Council of his own creation.

Louis XII was already the victim of remorse for having taken up arms against the head of the Church, and was prepared to humiliate himself for the sake of peace. His submission only had the effect of firing the ambition of the Pontiff, who would be satisfied with nothing less than the expulsion of the French from Italy, and the ruin of the Duke of Ferrara.

Any notice of this remarkable Pope, which pretends to impartiality, would be incomplete and unveracious which failed to chronicle, with merited censure, the intriguing part which he played in the affair of the League of Cambray, and his subsequent treachery to Alfonso, its principal concocter. Here his characteristic moderation entirely forsook him; his patriotism was obscured in craft and lust of power. The principal object of the League was the dismemberment of the Republic of Venice. Romagna, including the important cities of Ravenna, Faenzi, and Rimini, were the share of the spoil apportioned to the Pontiff. It would occupy too much space to enter into the history of the struggle with the proud and valiant Republic. Anxious to avoid the calamity of war, the Venetians offered to surrender to Julius some portions of their possessions in Romagna. But the ambitious Pontiff was inflexible; and, single-handed, the Venetians entered into the conflict with the formidable alliance.

Misfortunes at home, and the tremendous power leagued for their destruction, soon brought them to the verge of ruin, and so overwhelmed them with dismay, that they were willing to surrender all those possessions which were coveted by the allies, if only the unmolested retention of Venice and the Lagunes were guaranteed to them [1]. On two occasions the Senate offered to give up the whole of Romagna to the Pope; whilst to Spain, and to the Emperor, they made overtures involving similar sacrifice.

The overbearing pride and insatiable ambition of the Pontiff proved the salvation of the Republic. As the war progressed, however, Julius gradually succeeded in recovering and establishing his rule in every city of the Romagna.

The jealousy of the Pope had been excited by the intimacy which existed between Alfonso, Duke of Ferrara, and the French king. A coolness ensued, which rapidly developed into animosity. Julius considered himself entitled to the gratitude of Alfonso, the only feudatory of the Church whom he had spared; and, unable to find a just cause of quarrel in his subserviency to Louis XII, he was at no loss to create one on another ground. He accordingly claimed, as the property of the Holy See, those castles in Romagna which Lucrezia Borgia had brought to Alfonso as her dowry [2]. Alfonso resisted these and other equally unjust demands. Louis XII in vain attempted to arrange an accommodation between his ally and the haughty

---

[1] An interesting narrative of this struggle is given by Mr. Gilbert in his recently published and most attractive biography of Lucrezia Borgia.

[2] Dyer's 'Modern Europe.'

Pontiff, who responded to these overtures by dismissing the ambassadors of the French king, as well as those of the duke, calling upon the latter to renounce his adherence to France.

When the French had been driven from Italy, and the League practically dissolved, the position of Alfonso became critical in the extreme. He well knew the fiery and vindictive temper of the Pontiff, and wisely resolved upon opening negotiations, with a view to a reconciliation. It was not his first attempt. On a former occasion he had employed the celebrated poet, Ludovico Ariosto, as envoy for this purpose. His reception by his Holiness is thus narrated by Mr. Gilbert:—'On his arrival at Ostia, where the Pope was then residing, he requested an audience with the Pontiff. His request was complied with, and Ariosto was ushered into the presence of his Holiness. He had scarcely been introduced to him when the Pope sternly told him immediately to leave his presence, or he would order him to be thrown out of the window[1].' On this occasion he selected as his ambassador, Fabrizio Colonna, an able general in the service of the Pope, who, at the siege of Ravenna, had fallen into Alfonso's hands as a prisoner of war. The respect and friendship which he had received at the hands of his victor had converted the quondam foe into a staunch admirer and friend. Insisting as the condition upon which his good offices should be given, that Alfonso should recognize the supremacy of the Pope, and consent to leave the cities of Romagna in his undisputed possession, Fabrizio proceeded to Rome. His mission appeared to

---

[2] 'Lucrezia Borgia,' by William Gilbert. Two vols. Hurst and Blackett.

be entirely successful, the Pontiff agreeing to a reconciliation upon the easy condition of Alfonso appearing at the Roman court, publicly expressing his regret for his offences, and promising obedience to the Church for the future. Alfonso accordingly appeared at Rome, threw himself at the feet of his Holiness, and expressed his contrition. Julius appeared moved by his submission, and expressed the satisfaction it afforded him. He then informed Alfonso that he had entrusted to a committee of six cardinals the duty of arranging the terms of a peace, and he had no doubt they could be easily and satisfactorily adjusted.

The Pontiff had presumed too far upon the penitence of his contrite foe. When the terms upon which the Holy Father was willing to extend his friendship to the humble suppliant were declared, they were instantly and indignantly repudiated. They may be briefly stated; and the arrogance which they display, combined with the perfidy which Julius was even then practising towards the man whom he received as an ally, constitute the darkest passage in his life. The city of Ferrara, with all the territory of the dukedom, were to be surrendered to the Church. Alfonso and his family were to retire into private life, pledging themselves never to return to Ferrara, which thenceforward was to be considered a Papal province!

Alfonso, after he had rejected these terms, without any pretence of deliberation, immediately commenced preparations for his return to Ferrara. Various pleas were urged for his not quitting Rome in such impetuous haste; and when the hour for his departure arrived, he found himself a prisoner,—his house surrounded with Papal guards. Nor was this all. On the day of his arrival in Rome, and before the negotiations with the Pope had commenced, a Pontifical army had entered his own territory, and was now rapidly approaching Ferrara, where the Duchess, better known as Lucrezia Borgia, was acting as Regent, in Alfonso's absence.

We cannot further follow the eventful history of Alfonso. The romantic story of his escape and return to Ferrara, by the aid of Fabrizio Colonna, is well told by Mr. Gilbert in his interesting work, to which reference has been already made. The episode claims allusion in this place in illustration of the character of this great Pontiff. It is an instance, of which history affords so many—the moral of which lies upon the surface—of the union, in the same character, of exalted genius, benevolence, and burning patriotism, with relentless enmity, meanness, and perfidy. 'A double-minded man is unstable in all his ways.'

It has been said of Julius II, that he was a Pontiff worthy of imperishable glory, had he worn any other crown than the tiara[1]. The proviso, we think, was unnecessary; for however his great idea of making the Papacy the instrument of Italian liberation[2] may be considered incompatible with the proper vocation of the Holy See, the Pontiff who possessed, in that age, the daring to conceive so lofty an enterprize, and made such stupendous efforts for its realization, established an unimpeachable claim to the gratitude and admiration of his countrymen throughout all time.

[1] Guicciardini.   [2] Dyer's 'Modern Europe.'

CHAPTER VII.

LEO X succeeded to the Pontificate A.D. 1513. His father, Lorenzo the Magnificent, by creed a Deist, had chosen the Church as a vocation for his son, with a view to the rich emoluments which it was in his power to secure to him. It is not improbable that the horizon of Lorenzo's paternal schemings was illumined by the hope of crowning his son's career by the acquisition of the tiara.

Through his father's influence with the French court and the reigning Popes, Leo, before the completion of his seventeenth year, enjoyed the revenues of six rectories, fifteen abbacies, one priory, and one archbishopric. He had not yet attained his thirty-eighth year when the same influence secured for him the coveted tiara.

Leo X shared the ambition, but was destitute of the patriotism, generosity, and personal courage, which distinguished his predecessors. Foiled in his endeavours to dissuade Louis XII (now in alliance with the Venetians, whom the arrogance of Maximilian had alienated from the Holy League) from his projected enterprize for the recovery of Milan, he entered into alliance with the Emperor, and formed the bold design of again driving the French out of Italy and of bringing the whole Peninsula under the authority of the Roman See. Seven years later, when, owing more to the hatred which the Milanese bore to the haughty and imperious French general, than to the valour of the Papal army, the French were compelled to evacuate Milan, Leo died from intoxication of joy at the French humiliation. Not, however, until he had witnessed the accomplishment of his darling project,—the recovery to the Church of Parma and Placentia which had been seized by Francis I on his conquest of Milan.

Extravagant eulogy has been expended upon this Pontiff as the munificent patron of the fine arts. But this patronage was far more that of the Pontiff than of the man. Rome has always taken care to turn to account her patronage of the fine arts to the inculcation of her doctrine and the increase of her power. The tones of Pius IX still linger on our ears when, at the opening of the Roman Exhibition, he spoke of religion as the inspirer of great works of art. Singling out three of the great art treasures of Rome, the Last Communion of St. Jerome, by Domenechino, the Moses of Michael Angelo, and St. Peter's, he said, 'It was religion which guided the pencil to which we owe the portraiture of the Great Doctor, it was religion which governed the chisel which put something divine into the head of the great Lawgiver of the people of God, and religion herself seems to have held the compass which traced the lines of the most magnificent temple in the world.' True; but so also says the Romish priest to the ignorant devotee to whom he points out the 'divine' frescoes of, let us say, the Campo Santo, Pisa. 'Here we have represented the most ghastly cartoons of Death, Judgment, Purgatory, and Hell; we behold angels and devils fighting for the souls of the departed, snakes devouring, fiends scorching, red-hot hooks tearing their flesh. Those on earth can, so say the priests, rescue their unfortunate relatives from this melancholy position by giving donations to their spiritual fathers, who will then pray for their escape. We read in the New Testament that the rich enter heaven with difficulty; but it is they, according to the Church of Rome, who enter easily, whilst the poor are virtually excluded[1].'

Though not unmindful of his Pontifical dignity and duties, and conspicuous for his munificence and liberal patronage of the fine arts, the political ambition of Leo X habitually subordinated these to his regal assumptions. Rome, under his government, was tranquil and prosperous. The impartial administration of justice promoted the happiness and security of the people, who, fully appreciating these blessings, decreed a perpetuation of their remembrance by erecting a statue to the Pontiff. But whilst it was the glory of Leo X thus to see the Imperial city advancing, under his sway, in dignity, in opulence, and in the culture of the arts, he failed to perceive that the foundations of the Papacy had been so severely shaken by the spirit of enquiry, aroused by the teachings of Wycliffe, Huss, and Luther, that, however great the charm of the Papal pretensions, as asserted by Julius II, respect for the Papacy in the minds of the people was a thing of the past.

In the hope of securing the homage of the Emperor, prescribed by long-established custom, Leo, though greatly chagrined at the election of Charles V, hastened to recognize an act which he had been powerless to avert. But Charles was already determined not to

---

[1] 'The Rule of the Monk,' by Garibaldi.

gratify the Pontiff's pretensions, and the practice was never afterwards followed.

The Anti-Papal stir which began to agitate Europe by reason of the corruptions of Christianity, and the pretensions of Papal Rome to make men purchase heaven with gold instead of virtue; the bold defiance of Luther at Wittemberg, when he pronounced that 'Enough' which instantly resounded throughout Europe; the rapid spread of the reformed doctrine in Switzerland,—all failed to convince Leo X of the danger which threatened the Papacy. His restless intriguing spirit clutched at two Italian towns, revelled in the abrogation of the liberties of the Gallican Church[1]— the attempt to recover which forms an amusing episode in the relations of Napoleon with the Papacy—and defied the spirit of revolt, which he neither understood nor feared. 'All the good that has ever been said of Leo X,' says Mr. Blunt, 'amounts to this, that he was a munificent patron of the arts, though his patronage was neither more nor less than the encouragement of Pagan instead of Christian art. He was as secular in his tastes as any Emperor of Rome, and his episcopal office was treated by him merely as one of the accidents of his position[2].'

[1] These liberties, which honourably distinguish the Gallican Church from other members of the Roman Communion, were based upon two maxims,—one that the Pope possessed no temporal authority, the other that his spiritual jurisdiction could only be exercised in conformity with such parts of the Canon Law as were received by the kingdom of France. It followed that Papal bulls were without validity in France, unless endorsed by the approbation of the King. See Hallam's 'Middle Ages,' vol. ii.

[2] 'The Reformation of the Church of England,' by the Rev. J. J. Blunt.

During the two succeeding centuries, the authority of the Popes gradually consolidated itself. One by one the cities and territories which Julius II had suffered to retain their independent government were brought into more complete subjection to the Holy See; some by intrigue; some by voluntary compact, induced by the prospect of good government; and others, again, by the extinction of the legitimate line of their ducal sovereigns, when the Pope claimed the reversion in his right as feudal lord. This claim was not always affirmed in the interests of the Church, much less in that of the people, whose allegiance to the rulers imposed upon them was given or withdrawn without so much as a thought of their being consulted.

The chief hindrance to the consolidation of the Papal power in these centuries, was that plague which had characterized the Popedom for ages—the nepotism of the Popes themselves, who made the Papacy subservient to the elevation of their kindred. Mingling in the dark conspiracies of the most corrupt age, they acquired new territories only to bestow them upon their own kinsmen at the expense of the Papal States. Ranke informs us that, in the fifteenth century, it was held to be a matter of conscience that a Pope should provide for his own family and promote their interests. In illustration of this he quotes a letter addressed by Lorenzo de Medici to Innocent VIII, in which, after some laudatory observations upon 'the retiring delicacy' evinced by his Holiness, he says, 'Zeal and duty lay it on my conscience to remind you that no man is immortal. Be the Pontiff as important as he may in his own person, he cannot make his dignity nor his importance hereditary; he cannot be said absolutely to possess anything but the honours and emoluments he has secured to his kindred.' It should, indeed, be borne in mind, that Lorenzo had given his own daughter in marriage to an illegitimate son of the Pope. But his letter, so far from being considered scandalous, was declared by the potentates of Italy to be replete with sound sense and honourable feeling[1].

The contest for the Empire of Germany between Charles V and Francis I had been terminated by the unanimous election of the former. The prostration and division of Italy had, for centuries past, been regarded by the Roman Pontiffs (with the notable exception of Julius II) as a first necessity for the proper exercise of Papal domination. Nothing could be more unfavourable to the development of any ideas of national independence than the nature of the petty governments, whether republican or otherwise, into which Italy was divided. Long deprivation of the habits of freedom had extinguished its very spirit, which survived only in the minds of a few. After the vicissitudes which marked that period of the Pontificate of Clement VII, antecedently to his reconciliation with the Emperor (effected by the treaty of Barcelona, June 29, A.D. 1529), this traditional policy of the Roman Pontiffs was adopted and unscrupulously pursued by this Pope; and never did Pontiff enjoy more secure and undisputed possession of his temporal power. His rule was detested, and the process by which its stability had been secured begat the abiding hatred of his subjects.

But Clement was no longer the helpless tool of in-

---

[1] Gilbert's 'Life of Lucrezia Borgia.'

constant allies, nor even of the unscrupulous and jealous Imperial government which, antecedently to the Spanish union, had been so uncompromisingly hostile to that aggrandizement of the temporal power, which had become the absorbing ambition of the occupants of the Papal throne. The Papal See had, now, become wholly independent of Imperial control. This was not owing to any vitality in the power or authority of the Pontiff, but to the jealousy with which the great European powers regarded the Italian policy of the Emperor, and to the decline of the Imperial authority which, previous to the election of Charles V, was reduced within the narrowest limits. The authority of the Papacy, though still sufficient to neutralize the reality of Imperial control, was equally diminished. The progress of the Reformation had shaken its influence throughout Europe, and its dependence upon the support of the secular governments was openly avowed.

Italy, now divided into small states, incapable of resisting the hostility of any great power, had lost even that vestige of liberty which she had enjoyed for two hundred years, and was prostrate beneath the deadly yoke of Spain. Her humiliation was the glory of the priest who claimed to represent upon earth, Him, whose mission it was 'to proclaim liberty to the captives and the opening of the prison to them that are bound!' But under the stillness of this prostration the germs of a new life were forming. Francis I was espousing the cause of the Protestants of Germany, whilst Henry VIII had pronounced the definitive separation of England from the supremacy of Rome. Charles V, alive to the dangers of a union of the Protestants with the King of France, vainly strove to effect a compromise which, under a specious show of concession, should be more fatal to the spread of the Reformation than the uncompromising resistance which, experience showed, only aggravated and strengthened the movement[1]. His projects failed, and the Emperor abandoned the hope of living at peace with the Reformers. The ambition of Clement VII to supplant, in Italy, the power to which he owed entirely his own elevation, induced him to enter into the project of a holy alliance whose avowed object it was to neutralize the power of the Emperor. The latter was indeed the sworn foe of the Reformers in Germany, whilst Francis had espoused their cause; but his humiliating defeat at Pavia, and the jealousy which was felt throughout Europe at his pretensions to interfere in the religious disputes of Germany, had corrected such heretical proclivities. A greater danger threatened the Papacy in the inordinate ambition and pretensions of the Emperor. It was important that the Holy League should obtain a decisive victory over the Imperialists. Once more the sovereign Pontiff vindicated his true apostolical descent in a ready appeal to the sword[2]; little anticipating that he himself would so soon experience the fulfilment of the judgment threatened to

---

[1] Van Praet's 'Essays on the Political History of the Fifteenth, Sixteenth, and Seventeenth Centuries.'

[2] 'And they said, Lord, behold, here are two swords. And he said unto them, It is enough.'—Luke xxii. 38.

'One of them which were with Jesus stretched out his hand and drew his sword, and struck a servant of the high priest's, and smote off his ear. Then said Jesus unto him, Put up thy sword into his place: for all they that take the sword shall perish with the sword.'—Matt. xxvi. 51, 52.

the rashness of the Apostle. France did not gain her anticipated victory. On the contrary, Rome was taken and sacked by the Imperial troops, and the Pontiff himself made prisoner.

Charles V was too astute a ruler to incur the risk of favouring the religious movement in Germany by prolonging a struggle with the Holy See, and he set the Pope at liberty after a brief confinement. Both parties were now anxious for peace, and the treaty of Cambray[1] at length delivered Italy from the devastation in which the long Franco-Spanish struggle for ascendency had plunged her; but without effecting any material alteration in the territorial arrangements.

In 1530, Charles received the Imperial crown at the hands of the same Pontiff, who, five years earlier, had attempted to form another Holy League to resist his ascendency. And now the sovereign Priest exulted at once in the new security in which he held his temporal power, and in the fatal blow inflicted upon Italian freedom. The Emperor still styled himself King of the Romans; but the reality was gone as completely as at the accession of the Tudor family, the claims of our own sovereigns to the title of Kings of France had lapsed. The Pope was the independent sovereign of the Roman States, and Charles V was the last of the German Emperors who went through the form of coronation either at Milan or at Rome.

The nepotism of Paul III (A.D. 1534–50) occasioned a renewal of the miseries which the French and Spanish contests had so long inflicted upon Italy. Paul had obtained the sanction of the Emperor to the alienation

---

[1] Called 'Paix des Dames' from its being signed by Louisa of Savoy, and Margaret of Austria, aunt of Charles V.

of the territories of Parma and Placentia (which, as we have seen, Leo X had devoted the energies of his life to recover to the Church) in favour of his natural son, Peter Luigi Farnese. The succeeding Pontiff disputed the claim of the new Duke of Parma, and endeavoured to resume the grant. The young duke appealed to France for protection. Before the dispute was settled Charles V had abdicated, and the Pontiff was himself an applicant for the alliance of France in an attempt to drive the Spanish power out of Italy. The dispute respecting Parma and Placentia was forgotten; but the young duke maintained his rights. For two centuries, and until the family became extinct, their hereditary succession was uninterrupted.

The Duke of Guise crossed the Alps with an army of 20,000 men, and for three years Italy was again devastated by the occupation of two gigantic foreign hosts.

We have only to note as an historical incident, having but a remote bearing upon our narrative, the assembling, during this Pontificate, of the Council of Trent. It was in December, A.D. 1545, when the Pope, who had long withstood the desires of the Emperor for the convocation of a General Council, believing that he had discovered indications of the intention of Charles V to exercise the ancient Imperial right of convocation, resolved to run no longer the dangers of delay. 'Then,' says Ranke[1], 'the old loiterer, Time, did at length bring the wished-for moment.' With the discussions of this Council, so long desired, twice dissolved, extending over a period of just eighteen years, and so utterly subservient to the Papacy, we have no concern. Discordant opinions met and combated at

[1] 'History of the Popes,' vol. i. p. 161.

Trent, but the real diplomatists of the Council were in Rome and at the courts of the lay sovereigns. The Pontiff in whose reign the Council closed (Pius IV) declared that the Papacy could no longer exist without the aid of temporal princes. Let him have the praise of being that Pontiff by whom 'the tendency of the hierarchy to oppose itself to the temporal sovereigns was deliberately and purposely abandoned[1].'

Paul IV (A.D. 1555-59), asserting the now almost obsolete pretensions of the Roman See, had refused to recognize the abdication of Charles V, declaring, in full Consistory, that he had no right to take such a step without the consent of the Holy See[2]. Philip II in vain attempted to overcome the obstinacy of the Pontiff, who refused to give audience to the ambassador commissioned to notify the accession of Ferdinand to the Imperial throne, and to solicit his coronation at the hands of the Pope. Ferdinand assumed the title of Roman Emperor Elect, and was recognized by all the crowned heads of Europe, excepting only the Roman Pontiff. This was the occasion of the discontinuance of the practice of Imperial coronations by the Pope, to which reference has been already made.

Paul IV was old enough to remember the freedom of Italy. He was in the habit of comparing the Italy of his youth to a well-tuned instrument, of which Naples, Milan, the Papal States, and Venice were the four strings[3]. Animated by a bitter hostility to Charles V, to whom he ascribed the successes of the Protestants, he adopted the policy of his predecessors with a view to deliver Italy from foreign dominion,

---

[1] Ranke. [2] Dyer's 'Modern Europe.' [3] Ibid.

and supported the French in an attack on the kingdom of Naples. But the Duke of Guise had objects of personal ambition in view, which he contrived to conceal from the Pontiff, and to which he was willing enough to postpone even the interests of France. As representative of the house of Anjou, he watched for the opportunity of asserting his own claim to the Neapolitan throne; whilst his brother, the Cardinal of Lorraine, aspired to the tiara. Paul IV was advanced in years, and as the probability of an early vacancy of the Pontifical throne appeared imminent, the Guises designed to facilitate the deliberations of the conclave by the presence of an overpowering French army[1].

Success attended the Spanish arms. The Duke of Alva penetrated to the very gates of Rome, and held the Pontiff in his power. But Paul IV well knew how to wield a power more terrible to the bigoted superstitious Philip II than 10,000 men of war.

In the bull, *Cum ex Apostolatus officio*, he boldly asserted his authority to depose every monarch, and hand over his country to foreign invasion. The following are a sample of the propositions which, 'out of the plenitude of his Apostolic power,' Paul IV, with the assent of his cardinals, defined in this famous bull:—

'The Pope, who, as "Pontifex Maximus," is God's representative on earth, has full authority and power over nations and kingdoms; he judges all, and can in this world be judged by none.'

'All princes and monarchs, as well as bishops, as soon as they fall into heresy and schism, *without the need of any legal formality*, are irrevocably deposed, deprived for ever of all rights of government, and incur sentence of

[1] Dyer's 'Modern Europe.'

death. In case of repentance, they are to be imprisoned in a monastery, and to do penance on bread and water for the remainder of their life.'

'None may venture to give any aid to an heretical or schismatical prince; *not even the mere services of common humanity;* any monarch who does so, forfeits his dominion and property, which lapse to princes obedient to the Pope.'

As a preliminary step the irate Pontiff, with a stroke of his pen, ordained the suspension of Divine worship in Spain, an act which bewildered the superstitious and irresolute monarch, and arrested the march of Alva. Whilst Philip wasted his time in consulting the theologians of Alcalà, Salamanca, and Valladolid upon the legitimacy of his campaign against the head of the Church, the Duke of Guise concentrated his forces upon Rome. His sudden recal to France by Henry II afforded Philip the opportunity of opening negotiations with the Pope. Paul IV insisted that Alva 'should repair to Rome to ask pardon in his own name, and that of his sovereign, for having invaded the patrimony of St. Peter, and to receive absolution for that crime.' The haughty Spaniard was forced to comply. At the threshold of the Vatican, Alva fell upon his knees and kissed, with real or simulated veneration, the foot of the bitterest and most inveterate foe of his sovereign and country[1].

Italy now ceased to be the chief theatre of war. Fortuitous circumstances had secured to the Papacy advantages which her arms, even when strengthened by the French alliance, were powerless to command. In the treaty of peace with Alva (Sept. 14, A.D. 1557) it

[1] Dyer's 'Modern Europe.'

was stipulated that the Spanish troops should be withdrawn from all the States of the Church, and that all places taken by Spain should be restored.

The treaty of Cateau Cambresis (A.D. 1559) restored the peace of Europe; and, during the remaining half of the sixteenth century, the history of the Papal See is devoid of political interest. Paul IV died congratulating the Church upon such a champion as Philip II, and upon such a bulwark as the Inquisition.

The only overt act of the Roman *curia* during this period which occasioned political ferment, was the publication, during the Pontificate of Pius V, of the bull *In Cœna Domini*. This famous bull, published with great solemnity, A.D. 1568, was the work of many successive Pontiffs. We do not look for beatitudes in a Papal bull, and assuredly they are not to be found here. Promulgated as a law binding upon Christendom throughout all the ages,—imposed upon all bishops and priests to be impressed in the Confessional upon the consciences of believers, and, for two hundred years, annually published in Rome upon Maundy Thursday,—this precious document bristles with anathemas reflecting the spirit of the system from which it emanated. It served at least one useful purpose, in demonstrating that in Catholic Europe there existed a limit to Papal encroachments. Sovereigns and parliaments forbade its publication. The French parliament ordained that all who promulgated the bull should be held guilty of high treason. Philip II forbade its introduction into Spain. Rudolph II protested against its publication in Germany. The bishops themselves opposed it in the Netherlands; whilst, two hundred years later, 'so rigid a Catholic as Maria Theresa' energetically repulsed a Papal decree which 'encroaches on the independence and sovereign rights of States in the imposition of taxes, the exercise of judicial authority, and the punishment of the crimes of clerics, by threatening with excommunication and anathema those who perform such acts *without special Papal permission*[1].'

The supreme care and duty of the Pontiffs of this period was the extirpation of heretics; a work in the prosecution of which they acquitted themselves right valiantly, pressing into their service fire and sword,—in short, every mode of assault which a corrupt and vindictive, a fierce and fanatical theocracy could bring to bear upon the vindication of the Roman Catholic faith against all assailants. This policy culminated in that most awful of all crimes that stain the page of history,—'that largest and most deadly manifestation of the evil passions of man's heart, that masterpiece of treachery and cruelty, that huge bath and mighty banquet of blood, which has never had, and never will have, fellow or rival, the Massacre of St. Bartholomew—the long and deliberately planned slaughter of 30,000 Protestants by fellow-countrymen with whom they had recently contracted amity, of subjects by a government that had lately and solemnly pledged them its protection, and of guests by hosts who had given a special invitation and afforded an ostentatious hospitality. This great work of aggressive and vengeful Romanism, in which all the conspicuous champions of the Roman Church concurred, which Philip II encouraged, which Catherine de Medici directed, at which Charles IX, Henry of Anjou, and Henry of Guise assisted, *received the benediction of the sovereign Pontiff*[2].'

[1] 'The Pope and the Gouncil,' by Janus.
[2] 'The Papal Drama,' by Thomas H. Gill.

The sixteenth century closed under the Pontificate of Sixtus V, a type of Pope not unlike him who first assumed the tiara,—a great temporal Pope, who, founding his power upon terror, clung to it as a heaven-bestowed trust, profoundly convinced that in all his undertakings he possessed the immediate favour of God[1]. The gigantic nature of his projects, in which he persuaded himself that, when his own resources failed, God would supplement them with legions of angels, commanded the admiration of Europe. There is but too much reason to believe that the indulgence of the iconoclastic tastes of Sixtus V has deprived Rome of many of the choice treasures of antiquity, in which he possessed neither the comprehension nor the sympathy to perceive anything but 'ugly antiquities.' Happily the vandalism which marked his passion for architectural pursuits was checked by the necessity of building as well as of levelling, and many of the sublime monuments of the Republic which had been destined to destruction, as 'ugly antiquities,' escaped. He designed to employ the enormous wealth, of which the extraordinary system of finance then in vogue at Rome gave him the control, in the execution of public works worthy of the city which, under his rule, once more assumed the aspect of the capital of the world. Most conspicuous amongst these were the colossal aqueducts by which he supplied the city with pure water. 'He brought the Aqua Martia from the Agro Colonna, a distance of two-and-twenty miles, to Rome: and this in defiance of all obstacles, carrying it partly underground and partly on lofty arches. How great was the satisfaction with which Sixtus beheld the first stream of

---

[1] Ranke.

this water pouring its bright wealth into his own vine-garden (vigna); still further did he then bear it onward to Santa Susanna, on the Quirinal. From his own name he called it the " Acqua Felice," and it was with no little self-complacency that he placed a statue by the fountain, representing Moses, who brings water, streaming from the rock, at the touch of his staff[1].' In this grand enterprize he declared to the architect that he designed to produce a work whose magnificence might compete with the glories of Imperial Rome, 'alarmed by no difficulty, and deterred by no cost.' Assuredly Sixtus V vindicated his claim to the title of *Pontiff*[2]. He governed with great ability, and revived the waning influence of Roman diplomacy. How he lent all the power of the Roman See to stir up the fierce democracy of France in its contest with Henry of Navarre; how, in his person, he assailed the principles of legitimacy, and, after citing Henry III to appear in person at the court of Rome, and answer for the murder of Cardinal Guise, he hurled against the nonconforming monarch a fierce bull of excommunication; how he frantically rejoiced in the subsequent assassination of Henry, attributing it to the immediate intervention of God that the king had been struck down by the hand of a poor monk; finally how, when Henry of Navarre, a Protestant, whom he had excommunicated, assumed the title of King of France, he was deterred only by his impatience of Spanish domination in Italy from helping to establish it in France,—these things are familiar to every reader of that sad but interesting episode in French history, the religious wars of the sixteenth century.

[1] Ranke.   [2] See page 4.

The liberty of Italy was now completely extinguished by her subjection to foreign domination. The authority of the Papacy, also, which for a brief interval seemed to have recovered much of the power it possessed in the eleventh and twelfth centuries, had fallen. Of this fact a significant illustration had been furnished early in the sixteenth century, in the resentment of Ferdinand II of Naples, at the pretensions of the Pontiff to interpose in his kingdom. The days were passed when the potentates of Europe trembled before that spiritual power which was able, when wielded by a Hildebrand or a Boniface, to repel the proudest pretensions, and baffle the haughtiest designs. Learning that a Papal messenger had brought a bull into his kingdom without the royal sanction, Ferdinand thus wrote to his Viceroy at Naples:—'We are equally surprised and displeased with you that you likewise have not resorted to violent means, and sent to the gallows the messenger who presented you with that brief. . . . You must use all possible diligence to seize the messenger if he be still in the same kingdom; if you can get hold of him, he must retract the presentation which he made you of the brief, and renounce it by a formal act, after which you will have him immediately hanged[1].' More than a century had elapsed since, in England, the promulgation of the Statute of Præmunire had called forth the bitter invectives of Martin V. But now almost every European government had passed similar laws in contempt of the pretensions of the Holy See.

Sixtus V, the Pope who 'kept the world in perpetual movement,' whilst entertaining exaggerated conceptions

[1] Letter of Ferdinand II to the Neapolitan Deputy. See Butt's 'History of Italy,' vol. i.

of the dignity of his position, was mainly concerned for the aggrandizement of the spiritual power of the Papacy. In the height of his contest with Henry IV, the victory which this Pontiff desired was the victory of Catholicism; the restoration of the universal supremacy of the Roman Church. When rebuking the Venetians for their congratulation of the heretical monarch on his accession, he thus addressed the Venetian ambassador:—'I beseech you to recall at least one step. The Catholic king has recalled many because we desired it, not from fear of us, *for our strength, as compared with his, is but as a fly compared with an elephant*; but he has done it from love, and *because it was the Pope who had spoken, the vicegerent of Christ, who prescribes the rule of faith to him, and to all others.*' And when, shortly afterwards, Monseigneur de Luxembourg, bearing a charge from the Catholic peers attached to Henry IV, was admitted to an interview with his Holiness, and expatiated upon the personal qualities, the courage and magnanimity of the king, 'the Pope,' says Ranke, 'was quite enchanted with this description. "In good truth," he exclaimed, " it repents me that I have excommunicated him." Luxembourg declared that his lord and king would render himself worthy of absolution; and, at the feet of his Holiness, would *return into the bosom of the Catholic Church*. "In that case," replied the Pope, " I will embrace and console him [1]."'

Sixtus was less concerned to assert his prerogatives as a temporal prince than to vindicate those of the neighbouring secular powers, whose privileges he sought to uphold and extend. He abolished entirely

---

[1] Ranke's 'History of the Popes,' vol. ii.

the Congregation taking cognizance of ecclesiastical jurisdiction in foreign countries, whose interposition had been the occasion of most of the disputes between the Holy See and the Empire. This voluntary concession of contested rights, however much it insulted the infallibility of his predecessors, was consistent with the whole scope of policy pursued by Sixtus V. How completely had the aspects of the Papacy changed when an arbitrary, impetuous, and powerful Pontiff could thus voluntarily divest himself of the trammels of secular power! 'He that abaseth himself shall be exalted.' Sixtus V enjoyed the fruits of his magnanimity. 'He received an autograph letter from the King of Spain, who informed him that he had commanded his ministers in Milan and Naples to receive the Papal ordinances with obedience no less implicit than that paid to his own. This moved the Pope even to tears, "That the most exalted monarch of the world should," as he said, "*so honour a poor monk*[1]."'

An important enactment of this Pontificate was the limitation of the number of cardinals to seventy, 'as Moses,' said Sixtus, 'chose seventy elders from among the whole nation, to take counsel with them.' He has also the credit of having fixed a high standard of personal character as the indispensable condition of admission to this high and sacred office. Men, they must be, 'of true distinction, of morals most exemplary, their words oracles, their whole being a model and rule of life and faith to all who behold them; the salt of the earth, the light set upon a candlestick[2].' Shades of Luther and Melancthon! see ye not in this Roman Church, presided over by a Chief Pastor of Apostolic

---

[1] Ranke, vol. i.   [2] 'Bullar,' quoted by Ranke.

humility; whose hierarchy, in theory at least, had attained so high a standard of purity and excellence; beloved at home, respected abroad; disentangling itself from political strifes and ambition; devoting itself to the reform of abuses, and to the advancement of religion,—see ye not here the signs, in which ye would not believe, of its Divine Seal as the true Catholic, Apostolic, and Infallible Church! The limits of this narrative do not admit of our examination into the principles upon which the Roman Church, at the close of the sixteenth century, contemplated the 'advancement of religion.' It must suffice us to state that the hopes, inspired by the character of Sixtus V, of a new era in the history of the Papacy, in which, abandoning the traditions of eight hundred years, it should vindicate its claims to the reverence and obedience of Christendom, as an essentially spiritual institution, whose purity and unworldliness certified its Divine origin and authority, were not destined to fulfilment.

CHAPTER VIII.

THE annals of the Papacy during the seventeenth century are interesting in their internal characteristics, as they are barren of political significance. Pontiffs of every variety of character occupied the Papal throne; but the moral weight of the Papacy was reduced to its lowest point. Baffled in their attempts to extend their Italian territory, the Popes wisely devoted themselves to energetic struggles against the spread of the Reformed faith, and to the enlargement of their spiritual dominion.

The long Pontificate of Urban VIII (A.D. 1623-44) is alone distinguished for its political importance. The part which this bold schemer played in the European complications which issued in the Thirty Years' War, was neither dignified nor successful. On his accession he confirmed the dispensation, granted by his predecessor, for the marriage of Prince Charles Stuart with the Infanta of Spain. Not, however, until guarantees had been secured from the heretical King of England, —who, to quote his own words, 'was not a monsieur who could shift his religion as easily as he could shift his shirt when he came in from tennis,'—for securing freedom for the exercise of religion to the Infanta and her household. Nor was this all. The Pontiff had set his heart upon the conversion of England[1]. One great

[1] See Gardiner's 'Prince Charles and the Spanish Marriage.'

objection urged against the proposed marriage, at the Court of Rome, was that it would bring about increased facilities of communication between England and Spain, which might be 'detrimental to the purity of religion' in the latter country. When, therefore, the marriage was conceded, the cardinals set themselves to secure that the increased communication between the two countries should be to the advantage of Roman Catholicism. Overtures were accordingly made to James I to induce him to emulate the courage and piety of Henry IV of France, and return to the bosom of the Roman Church; or at least to encourage the Prince of Wales to embrace the faith of Rome. But, finding that the king valued his crown and his religion above the Spanish union, they contented themselves with securing the repeal, or at least the suspension, of the penal laws against the Catholics, and exemption from secular jurisdiction to the ecclesiastics of the Infanta's household.

On the accession of Urban VIII, the two great Catholic powers were at open feud, each arming for the struggle which must result in the destruction of one or the other. The Emperor Ferdinand II, orthodox and victorious, was pledged to the rooting out of Protestantism from the Imperial dominions. The destinies of France were in the mighty grasp of Richelieu who, jealous of the preponderating power of the Emperor, had entered into that European combination which brought him, Cardinal of the Roman Church though he was, into alliance with the Huguenots. He was bent upon the destruction of the Spanish-Austrian power,—of that power to which the Papacy owed the Catholic reaction.

In March, A.D. 1626, Europe was startled by the intelligence that France had concluded a peace with Spain. The too-confiding Huguenots, whom Richelieu had employed for the furtherance of his own purposes, then discovered the perfidy to which their confidence had blinded them. Already had their betrayer negotiated with Spain measures for their destruction.

The dangers to Catholicism which Urban VIII had anticipated from the feud between the two great Catholic powers had now disappeared. The opportunity was favourable for the accomplishment of a design which the Pontiff had long entertained. This was none other than the formation of a league with the two powers for an attack upon England, 'to wrest the crown from a prince who, as a heretic before God, and regardless of his word before men, was altogether unworthy to wear it[1].' Ireland was the portion of booty which was to fall to the Holy See; but his Holiness was recommended 'to allow no word to transpire on the subject, lest it might appear that his suggestions had been actuated by worldly views.' It was not difficult to persuade either of the contracting powers of the feasibility and advantage of the scheme. The articles of the treaty were drawn up by Richelieu, and ratified April 20, A.D. 1627.

It was impossible that plans of such magnitude as were involved in a projected invasion of England should pass unobserved. Within three months from the signing of the treaty, the allies were themselves attacked by England. Buckingham, at the head of a magnificent fleet, appeared off the coasts of France in July, A.D. 1627. He summoned the Huguenots to arms.

[1] Ranke.

After some hesitation they responded to his call; but the war was conducted with little energy, and resulted in disaster to the Protestants. Thus, although thwarted in his designs against England, Urban had the satisfaction of witnessing the triumphs of Catholicism. The assassination of Buckingham left the destinies of the Huguenots in the hands of Richelieu who, in the following year, reopened negotiations with Spain for a combined attack upon England.

But events were already transpiring in Italy which affected the relationships of France and Spain, and once more brought the Pontiff, as an Italian prince, and as the head of Catholicism, into a prominent position. Vincenzo II, Duke of Mantua, had died without issue. His next of kin, the Duke de Nevers, was a Frenchman. Apprehension of the jealousy with which Austria and Spain might view the acquisition, by a Frenchman, of sovereignty in Upper Italy, induced Nevers to adopt a line of action which brought about the very evils from which he sought to escape. Before the death of Vincenzo, he proceeded secretly to Mantua and procured the old duke's recognition of his claims. One other step only appeared necessary to ensure to Nevers the peaceable possession of his crown. In a convent school at Mantua was a young girl, great-granddaughter of Philip II, the only remaining representative of the direct native line. A marriage with this princess was speedily arranged, and solemnized in the palace, before intelligence of Vincenzo's death reached Vienna or Madrid. This ill-advised procedure drew upon Nevers the vengeance of the two powers which he had vainly thought thus to elude, and, says Ranke, 'It will be readily admitted that they were calculated to exasperate and embitter these mighty sovereigns, whose pleasure it was to assume a character of religious as well as temporal majesty, to have a kinswoman married without their consent, nay, without their knowledge, and with a sort of violence; an important fief taken into possession without the slightest deference to the feudal sovereign [1]!'

The part which Urban VIII designed to take in these complications was soon made apparent. The marriage of the young duke with his cousin could only be completed by a Papal dispensation. 'The Pontiff granted this without having consulted the nearest kinsmen of the lady—Philip of Spain and the Emperor; and it was besides prepared precisely at the moment required [2].' As the proceedings of Austria grew more threatening, the Pope turned of his own accord to France. It was for this that Richelieu waited. He at once proceeded with alacrity to bring his boldest plans to bear against Spain and Austria, when thus invited by the Roman Pontiff. 'The king,' said Urban, 'might send an army into the field even before the reduction of La Rochelle was effected; an expedition for the assistance of Mantua would be quite as pleasing to God as the beleaguering of that chief bulwark of the Huguenots. Let the king only appear at Lyons and declare himself for the freedom of Italy, and the Pope on his part would not delay to bring his forces into action and unite himself with the king [3].'

Thus recommenced the war, in which nearly all Europe was speedily embroiled. The personal charac-

[1] Ranke's 'History of the Popes,' vol. ii.
[2] Ibid.
[3] 'Bethune's Despatches,' quoted by Ranke, vol. ii.

teristics of its leading actors, and the momentous interests at stake, constituted it one of the most interesting incidents of modern history. I am compelled to assume the reader's familiarity with the history of the gigantic struggle, and can here only glance at its bearings upon the temporal power of the Holy See.

It was inevitable that recollections of the ancient supremacy of the Emperors should be recalled, and that the secular rights of the Emperor, as opposed to those of the Holy See, should be insisted on. It might be expected that the interest of the war would centre in the respective heads of the two powers,—in the resuscitated, struggle for supremacy between the Papacy and the Empire,—and that, albeit the two leading powers of Catholic Christendom were opposed to each other in arms, the struggle would resolve itself into a religious war. It was far otherwise. We must look elsewhere, even to the champion of Protestantism, and to his strange ally, Richelieu, the consummate schemer, for the heroes upon whom the gaze of Europe was intently bent. Both Emperor and Pope were men of vacillating purpose, the slaves of expediency; and though obstinate, ambitious, and brave, incapable as generals,—mere charlatans in statesmanship. Thus Ferdinand, when he had conquered Mantua (and again, when his distinguished general Wallenstein, who had raised an army of 50,000 men[1], had defeated the King of Denmark, and held in check the practised warriors who had threatened the Emperor's overthrow in Germany), might have made himself master of Italy. On the former occasion he resigned the Duchy to Nevers,

---

[1] 'Compendium of Universal History.' Jarrold and Sons.

with the single condition of the empty formality that he should sue for pardon. On the latter, he yielded to the jealousy of his other generals, and to the importunity of the German princes, and deprived Wallenstein of his command. With the dismissal of this brave and able general who, on a suspicion of treason, the Emperor subsequently assassinated, his hopes of obtaining the mastery of Italy vanished.

Thus, too, the Pontiff—at war with that power by which the Catholic restoration had been most zealously promoted; in alliance at once with Gustavus Adolphus and with Richelieu, the most inveterate hater of the Protestants—found himself a promoter of political changes in direct opposition to the interests of the Church. Foreseeing the necessity of a change in the Papal policy, as the victorious Swedes swept over Bavaria, took Munich, and advanced towards the Italian borders, he yet refused to recognize the war as one of religion; bewailing that the Papal treasury was exhausted, and affirming that *he could do nothing*. 'The members of the *curia*,' says Ranke, 'and the inhabitants of Rome were amazed. "Amidst the conflagration of Catholic churches and monasteries,"—thus it was they expressed themselves,—"the Pope stands cold and rigid as ice. The King of Sweden has more zeal for his Lutheranism than the holy Father for the only true and saving Catholic faith[1]."' Yet so strangely perplexed was his policy that, whilst Urban thus incurred obloquy for his defection in the guardiancy of the interests of the Church, in theory he clung tenaciously to the last rag of his Pontifical claims, even such as were most palpably untenable. Thus, for instance, in the first

[1] Ranke, vol. ii.

attempt to negotiate a general peace, A.D. 1636, 'the hands of the legate were tied, precisely in regard to all those important points on which everything was absolutely depending¹.' It excites a smile to read that the legate was enjoined to oppose the restitution of the Palatinate to a non-Catholic prince! What the Pope effected was a demonstration of the impracticable character of the Popedom, and its divorcement from the living and actual interests of the world. Thus, when a peace was concluded upon principles which Urban had condemned, which dissolved the 'Catholic League' and the 'Evangelical Union,' by the concession of a full equality of political rights to the Roman Catholics, the Lutherans, and the Calvinists, secured the territorial rights of the German princes, and defined the powers of the Emperor², the Papacy found itself under the melancholy necessity of—protesting.

The articles relating to ecclesiastical affairs, in the Peace of Westphalia, 'were opened by a declaration that no regard should be paid to the opposition of any person, be he whom he might, and whether of temporal or spiritual condition³.' Thus was the death knell sounded of those dreams of universal conquest, in which the Papacy had for ages indulged. The causes which led to the check now imposed upon that august power which had planned, and even executed, enterprizes involving the most extravagant assumptions, are so plain that he who runs may read them. They may be summed up in this:—The practical abandonment by the Roman pastor of his spiritual functions, in the pursuit of the incompatible gewgaws of secular sovereignty.

[1] Ranke.
[2] 'Compendium of Universal History.'   [3] Ranke.

Urban VIII did not survive to witness the limitations imposed upon Papal claims by the Peace of Westphalia. But the very malady of which he died (A.D. 1644) was brought on by the distress of mind he experienced in signing the Peace of Castro. Strong in his misguided confidence that 'God and the world would be on his side,' Urban had put forth all his strength to wrest Parma from its duke. But in this attempt he found himself arrayed *against* God and the world ; for the Italians viewed with jealousy the repeated extensions of the ecclesiastical territory, and also the increasing power of France, of which country Urban was regarded as the determined ally. The growing resolution of the Italians to resist the encroachments of the Pontiff, at length compelled him to think of peace. The country was burdened with the most oppressive imposts. Bread, salt, wine, firewood, every article in fact of indispensable necessity, was heavily taxed; and the cost of the war had already reached 12,000,000 of scudi[1]. The treasury was exhausted.

In the failure of the expedition against the Duke of Parma, it was obvious that the Papacy, already humbled in its loss of influence in European affairs, had suffered a signal defeat at home. The proud Pontiff, without an ally, his resources exhausted, his enemies triumphant, the spiritual weapons of the Church contemned, had reached an extremity which moves the beholder to pity. But the gradations of anguish in which his life terminated were the natural and inevitable result of a career which, the more it is studied, the clearer grows the duty of moderating that 'harmful pity' which

[1] Ranke.

enervates the moral sentiments and blinds the judgment :—

> 'This too much lenity
> And harmful pity must be laid aside.
> To whom do lions cast their gentle looks?
> Not to the beast that would usurp their den.
> Whose hand is that the forest bear doth lick?
> Not his that spoils her young before her face.
> Who 'scapes the lurking serpent's mortal sting?
> Not he that sets his foot upon her back.
> The smallest worm will turn, being trodden on;
> And doves will peck, in safeguard of their brood[1].'

Few were the Italian hearts which throbbed with pity for the dying Pontiff, plunged though he was into a gulph of bottomless misery; an awakened conscience adding the tortures of remorse to his experience of bitterness. He died, praying that 'Heaven would avenge him on the godless princes who had forced him into war.' The life of this 'Vicar of Christ' had been in such strong contrast with that of our blessed Lord, that the contrast in the dying prayer seems consistent and natural.

The treaty of Westphalia, A.D. 1648, which closed one of the most terrible dramas of European history, extinguished the religious element which had coloured the policy and the wars of Europe for nearly a century. 'It closed,' says a modern writer, 'a very great and awful act in the history of the world. The battle of the Churches, as far as it was a matter of swords, as far as soldiers and statesmen had to do with it, was over; that is, it was over as a great European business, as a great scene in history[2].'

---

[1] Shakespeare.
[2] 'The Papal Drama,' by T. H. Gill. Longmans.

From the Peace of Westphalia to the close of the seventeenth century, the Papacy continued to sink into deeper ignominy and decrepitude, both as a spiritual and temporal power; nor were the personal characters of the Pontiffs such as to command the respect or the sympathy of Europe. The eldest son of the Church, the arch-persecutor of Protestants, insulted and humiliated the Power in whose name he persecuted heretics. In A.D. 1664, Louis XIV sent an army into Italy, and exacted a humiliating reparation from Pope Alexander VII, for an affront alleged to have been offered to his ambassadors at Rome. Twenty years later he humiliated his successor, Innocent XI, by curtailing the episcopal power in France, and claiming the right to appoint to vacant benefices. In vain Innocent launched bulls and briefs against bishops who had accepted benefices at the king's hands. 'In A.D. 1682 the clergy of France assembled, confirmed the right of presentation claimed by the king, and under the inspiration of Bossuet, drew up the four famous articles which denied the Popedom all temporal jurisdiction in foreign states, declared a General Council to be above a Pope, recognized in the canons and customs of the French Church, and other Churches, limitations of the Papal power, and pronounced the Papal decisions, even in matters of faith, liable to alteration, unless confirmed by the consent of the whole Church[1].'

The quickened intellectual life of France wielded its might against the Papal power and the Roman Church. The Papacy languished and dwindled, and the secular powers of Europe looked on with indifference.

[1] 'The Papal Drama,' by T. H. Gill.

The War of the Spanish Succession, the history of which is too familiar to require recapitulation, after disturbing Europe for thirteen years, was terminated by the Peace of Utrecht. The provisions of this treaty were favourable to Austria; but the peace which it promised did not last. Spain was excluded from Italy; but, by the advice of his bold and ambitious minister, Cardinal Alberoni, Philip V claimed the possessions in Italy, which, by the treaty of Cateau Cambresis, had been settled on the Spanish crown. He further claimed the Duchy of Parma, in right of his wife, Elizabeth Farnese, a descendant of the natural son of Paul III, for whom the duchy had been originally created. To resist these claims, the quadruple alliance was formed, between England, France, Holland, and the Emperor. The extinction of the reigning line of the Farnese family was imminent, and the parties to this alliance offered to the Spanish Bourbons the reversion of the Duchies of Parma and Tuscany. These terms were eventually accepted.

New causes of contention soon arose. As the Imperial power diminished, the independence of the sovereign princes was augmented, and it was not until A.D. 1749, that any permanent settlement of the territorial divisions of Italy was arranged. By successive treaties the power of Austria was crippled, until, by that of Aix-la-Chapelle, she had nothing left in Italy except the Duchies of Milan and Mantua. Parma was surrendered to the Emperor Francis I, Tuscany to the Duke of Lorraine, who, in exchange, assented to the surrender of his hereditary estates in France. The claims of Spain were allowed to the kingdoms of Naples and Sicily; the Duke of Savoy surrendering his claim to the latter in exchange for the island of Sardinia, with its kingly title. Hence the princes of his house have been since known in European history as Kings of Sardinia. These arrangements continued undisturbed up to the period of the French Revolution.

After the treaty of Aix-la-Chapelle, French influence was paramount in the States of the Church, and sycophancy to the dominant power became the recognized pathway to the occupancy of the chair of the Apostles. The Popes coquetted with Austria, but they feared France. It was an era of weakness and decline in Papal rule. Political and intellectual life there was none. Brigandage throve. The population of all the principal towns, Rome, Bologna, Ferrara, Imola, and others, dwindled to an extent that appears incredible. Education was neglected, and a priest-ridden people accepted the trammels of a priestly and oppressive, though not tyrannical, government[1].

Singularly this era was likewise distinguished by a line of Popes remarkable for their pureness of character, their learning, and personal greatness. Prominent amongst these stand forth Benedict XIV and Clement XIV, the former the wisest and best of the Popes. His wisdom displayed itself in a frank recognition of the insignificance of Papal power; and his goodness in disregarding pretensions which had become ridiculous, and in adapting his policy to the requirements of his time. 'He detested and discouraged persecution, not merely from his accurate discernment of the

---

[1] In A.D. 1740 the Counsellor de Bosses wrote:—'The Papal government, although the worst in Europe, is at the same time the mildest.'

time in which he lived, but by reason of a most gracious and benignant nature; he connived at the escape of some suspected heretics; he remonstrated with Maria Theresa against the oppressive acts of her troops in occupation of Genoa, oppression which provoked the heroic uprising of the Genoese and the ignominious expulsion of the Austrians on December 2, A.D. 1746, the noblest manifestation of Italian energy during the eighteenth century. He deprecated the persecuting practices of the vehement members of his own Church, and interceded for the oppressed Protestants in Languedoc[1].' He commanded the admiration and respect of Protestants as well as Catholics throughout Europe, and received the eulogy of the great assailant of Christianity—Voltaire.

The other conspicuous occupant of the Papal throne, towards the close of this century, to whom I have referred—Clement XIV—was a man too saintly, tolerant, and enlightened, for a Pope; conspicuous, not as a ruler, but for sanctity of life, and elevation of personal character. His Pontificate was distinguished by the suppression of the Order of the Jesuits; an act which they caused him to expiate by a lingering and torturing death from the effects of poison.

The Popes were pious, but feeble; the sovereigns of Europe—and particularly of France—were feeble too; they were also vicious, superstitious, and bigoted. But a mighty mind, which scorned all despotism, and, pre-eminently, the sovereigns who then so unworthily exercised it; which held in abomination not only vice and superstition, but religion also, swayed the intellect of Europe. Voltaire may be said to have prepared the

[1] 'The Papal Drama,' by Thomas H. Gill.

way, not in France only, but also in Germany and Italy, for that upheaving of the nations, symptoms of which were already apparent. Before he had tasted, in prison and in exile, the power of the existing governments to perpetuate the intellectual thraldom from which he aspired to awaken Europe, Voltaire rejoiced to leave all that he held dear in Paris, to enjoy for a season the invigorating freedom of the Hague. Monarchs contended to secure his presence to grace their courts. But, says his biographer [1], the baubles of vanity do not satiate souls impelled by the ambition of reigning over the minds of men—they do but supply new arms. The spectacle which Amsterdam presented of political freedom, honest commerce, and a hard-working population, had more attraction for the soul of Voltaire than the splendour of courts, and the flattery of sovereigns. At Amsterdam, he said, 'Nobody is seen who has to pay his court to anybody else; there people do not form a line to look at a prince passing. Industry and modesty alone are known at Amsterdam.' No doubt the suppression of the 'National Epic,' which he had designed to publish under the patronage of Louis Quinze, envenomed his hatred of that prince; and the fact that Louis was influenced by the Cardinal Dubois, on the ground of the fiery declamations against the Inquisition with which the Epic abounded, was at least not calculated to increase his love for the Church. His courage and his generosity were the dread of the oppressors who long had feared and hated him for his writings. Whatever the nation in which any striking injustice occurred—any act of bigotry, or insult to human nature—Voltaire carried it

[1] Condorelt.

before the tribunal of public opinion of Europe; and 'who knows,' exclaims Condorelt, 'how often the fear of this sure and terrible vengeance has withheld the oppressor's arm!'

We have to do with Voltaire as a politician and not as a controversialist. Whatever injury he was instrumental in inflicting upon true religion lies at the door of that Church, whose awful corruptions and implacable persecutions fired his soul with an inexorable hatred. The intensity of his indignation at the crimes of intolerance, and his fervid love for liberty of conscience, have secured for him the fame—to which it is impossible to concede his title—of having *invented* toleration. But for him, it has been said, the religious freedom of the nineteenth century would still have been but the dream of Utopian philosophers. All history gives the lie to such a notion. Rousseau himself was no less ardent an advocate of religious toleration, however inconsistent his theories of freedom, as propounded in his 'Contrat Social,' may appear with the whole tenour of his life, and with the mould that he impressed upon the French Revolution, which, it has been said, 'he had the fatal honour of forming in his own image [1].' Still more conspicuous was the ardent and enlightened love of liberty which breathes in the remarkable speeches of Mirabeau, and Rabaud-Saint-Etienne, in the National Assembly, who denounced the crimes and misfortunes caused by a State religion, and demolished the sophisms opposed to liberty of worship. These words of Mirabeau might serve as a motto for the Liberation Society, 'I do not come,' he cried, 'to preach toleration. The

[1] 'The Church and the French Revolution,' by E. De Pressensé, D.D.

most unlimited liberty of religion is, in my eyes, so sacred a right, that the word *toleration*, which tries to express it, appears to me, in some manner itself tyrannical, since the existence of the authority which has the power to tolerate, infringes on liberty of thought by the fact that it does tolerate, and that thus it might have the power not to tolerate.' Before we award to Voltaire the praise of having invented toleration, we must blot out the memory of Scottish Covenanters and English Puritans, and ignore the Holy Experiment of William Penn. In spite of the successful attempt of the Bishop of London to insert a clause, claiming security to the National Church, in the charter conferring those wild mountainous tracts which Charles Stuart christened with the Quaker's name, Penn inscribed RELIGIOUS LIBERTY at the head of his constitution. Every man, he said, in his provinces should enjoy *liberty of conscience*.

Surely it was the misfortune of France that her great apostle of toleration drew his inspiration from the evils inseparable from the fatal union of civil and religious despotism. The Church had already entered the arena wherein the great battle of progress—of humanity— was to be fought. To every aspiration which stirred the pulse of awakening Europe it opposed the obstacle of invincible intolerance. No wonder that the liberal cause was proclaimed to be antagonistic to religious faith. The greatest crimes of history had been perpetrated in the name of that holy religion against which, in terrible earnestness, an emancipated age was now in arms.

I will close this chapter with a quotation from a work to which frequent reference has been made. A man so rare among his species—in whom the enthusiasm of humanity was a real passion, is thus aptly portrayed:—'Voltaire was pre-eminently the assailant of Papal Christianity,—the distinctive doctrines of the Roman Church were those upon which the mighty mocker was most lavish of his scorn; the crimes and cruelties of the Roman Church were those upon which the great hater of oppression poured forth his intensest wrath. The supreme horror of history was his supreme horror; he shuddered at the Bartholomew business as though he had witnessed it; the butchery of Thorn, which in A.D. 1724 had stirred his youthful indignation, he remembered fifty years after in extreme old age with undiminished abhorrence. He fiercely denounced and most earnestly strove to arrest the horrible barbarities still now and then inflicted in France in the name of the Roman Church. . . . It was mainly the deeds of the Roman Church which made him mighty, which breathed into his imperial scorn its sovereign bitterness, and its awful power. . . . Foes of Christianity have sprung up in Protestant lands; but these men at the most gained a few followers and gave birth to a controversy; while the arch-mocker whom France bred and whom Rome provoked, became a great power and hastened on a great convulsion. The long reign of Voltaire was most disastrous to the Papacy; and his hand was felt in that terrible Revolution which so vengefully smote the French Church and the Roman See[1].'

[1] 'The Papal Drama,' by Thomas H. Gill.

CHAPTER IX.

WHEN the storm of the French Revolution burst over the Papal States, revolt was chronic, and received the powerful support of Napoleon, who readily connived at every act which was calculated to dismember the ecclesiastical territory, or to cripple the power of Austria, hitherto in full possession of the dignity and prestige of the Holy Roman Empire; occupying the most important fortresses in the States of the Church, and mistress of the destinies of Italy.

The news of Napoleon's approach to Rome threw the Council of the Vatican into great alarm. The First Consul appears to have revelled in his power of frightening these old gentlemen. He wrote in harsh terms threatening to crown his victories by the overthrow of the Papal power, which the Directory regarded as the irreconcilable enemy of the Republic. 'We find the martyr's crown more brilliant,' exclaimed the Pontiff, 'than that which we wear on our head;' and with something like dignity he refused the terms of peace offered by Napoleon, which included the withdrawing of the briefs by which Pius VI had condemned the civil constitution of the clergy of France. These clauses Napoleon, who was now anxious to terminate his Italian campaign, ultimately withdrew. A shameless peace was purchased by the surrender of the Legations, and the renunciation of the Pontiff's pretended rights over

Avignon; the forfeiture of large quantities of stores, and a war contribution of six million dollars. One hundred of the richest works of art, the contents of the galleries which Pius VI had beautified and enriched, were also surrendered, and to this day they constitute the greatest wealth of the Louvre; whilst a French army took possession of Rome.

The Directory were even more bent than was the First Consul upon the overthrow of the temporal power of the Papacy. Napoleon, as we shall presently see, had other aims in view. The treaty proved only a truce. Pius VI not only refused to ratify it, but, in conjunction with the forces of Austria, engaged in open hostilities with France. He committed himself to an unequal struggle. Napoleon, who had just vanquished the whole power of Austria, contemptuously crushed the feeble forces of the Pope, and forced him to accept, in the Peace of Tolentino, terms deeply humiliating to the Roman See. The city, the Patrimony, and Umbria, constituted all that was left to the Church of that fair domain secured to her by the Peace of Aix-la-Chapelle; and of this Napoleon appears to have thus early conceived the idea of despoiling her.

The Pope had passed the age of four-score years and, being afflicted with a dangerous illness, Napoleon generously awaited his demise before proceeding to establish a Republic in Rome, on the same model as that of France. His calculations were disturbed by the unexpected recovery of the Pontiff. Napoleon was then in Egypt, and the Directory, supreme in France during the First Consul's absence, dissatisfied with his Italian policy, and irritated by the intractable Pontiff who had recovered when they were impatiently awaiting his death, ordered General Berthier to march upon Rome. The Vatican was occupied by French troops, and Pius VI taken prisoner. The old man entreated his captors to let him die where he was. They scornfully replied that he could die anywhere, and proceeded to plunder the room in which he was seated, and his own person, taking even the ring from his finger. The Roman Republic was then proclaimed. Pius was at first allowed to find a shelter with the Grand Duke of Tuscany, but was afterwards carried captive into France, where he died, August 22, A.D. 1799; and the world believed that the Papacy had for ever fallen.

The Republican government at Rome was short-lived. Within one month after the death of the Pope, the King of Naples, supported by the English and the Austrians, compelled the French general to capitulate, and Rome was garrisoned by Neapolitan and Austrian troops.

After some delay, the cardinals, being unable to meet at Rome, assembled at Venice, and elected a new Pontiff, who took the title of Pius VII. The sovereigns who held Rome invited him to take up his abode at the Vatican, but he declined to reside there in any other capacity than as Rome's rightful and sole sovereign. Austria, anxious to recover her lost hold upon Italy, demurred; a compromise was at last effected, and, four months after his election, Pius VII entered Rome (July, A.D. 1800), and assumed the government; whilst the troops of Austria and Naples garrisoned the city. The election of Pius VII was due to the influence of Cardinal Consalvi, whom he immediately nominated Secretary of State. To his wise and temperate administration, in circumstances of unparalleled difficulty, the Papacy was indebted for internal quietude and stability and, after the downfall of Napoleon, for the consideration it received at the hands of the Protestant courts.

A policy of conciliation now served the purposes of Napoleon. The battle of Marengo had changed the position of Austria towards the Papacy, and had re-established the power of Napoleon in the Peninsula, and disposed him to acquiesce, for the present, in the continuance of the Pontifical government at Rome. Having resolved upon the restoration of a national religion in France, he made overtures to the Pope on the subject. Such a step, in the moment of his greatest triumph, captivated the heart of the Pontiff, who saw, in the restoration of the Catholic religion in France, the renewed subjection of that country to ecclesiastical authority. Never doubting that Napoleon was a sincere Catholic, and probably ignorant that, just a year before, the young hero had similarly cajoled the Ulemas of Egypt, by professing, with equal complacency, his conversion to Islamism, Pius VII and his cardinals rejoiced in the adhesion of the great conqueror who had made himself master of France, and France mistress of Italy.

By Napoleon religion was always regarded exclusively from a political point of view, and employed as a means of attaching its votaries to himself. Hence, whilst he was yet a Republican general, he praises the priests in Italy, who served his purpose by advocating the establishment of Republics in the Peninsula. 'Such priests,' he says, 'who have acknowledged that the political code of the Gospel is summed up in the liberty and sovereignty of the people, are the finest present that heaven can make a government.' After events proved that it was not their republicanism that Napoleon loved, so much as their docility. Only four months after he had employed these words he thus wrote to the Bishop of Malta:—'I do not conceive a more respectable character, nor one more worthy of the veneration of men, than a priest who, full of the true spirit of the Gospel, *is persuaded that his duties require him to render obedience to the temporal power*, and to maintain peace in his diocese.' The re-establishment of Catholicism in France was, in the eyes of Napoleon, a purely secular affair. Let him be judged by his own words. In familiar conversation, towards the close of A.D. 1800, the First Consul thus spoke:—'The people must have a religion; this religion must be in the hands of the government. Fifty emigrant bishops, paid by England, to-day lead the French clergy. We must destroy their influence; the authority of the Pope is necessary for that. He dismisses them, or makes them give in their resignation. It is declared that the Catholic religion being that of the majority of the French, the exercise of it ought to be organized. The First Consul nominates a hundred bishops, the Pope institutes them; they nominate the parish priests, the State pays them. They take the oath. The priests who do not submit are transported. It will be said I am a Papist. I am nothing. I was a Mahomedan in Egypt; I shall be a Catholic here, for the good of the people. I do not believe in religions, but in the idea of a God [1].'

The negotiations with Rome were now pressed forward. 'I have need of the Pope,' said the First Consul; 'he will do what I wish.' 'You wish,' answered Lafayette, to whom these words were addressed—'you wish to have the little phial broken over your head.'

[1] 'Mémoires sur le Consulat,' quoted by De Pressensé.

'We shall see—we shall see,' replied Napoleon. The sagacious courtier had gauged the true origin of the Concordat. The man who aimed at despotic power in a religious country could not afford to be indifferent to religion. Whether that religion were Islamism, or Roman Catholicism, was a matter of profound indifference to Napoleon. But he recognized the fact that France was Catholic at heart, and accordingly resolved, by a wise agreement with the Holy See, to consecrate his civil government by allying it with religion, and to attach to his person the whole body of the clergy. 'We have never seen,' he said, 'a State without religion, without worship, without priests. Is it not better to organize the worship and to discipline the priests, than to leave things as they are? Rather than exile the priests who preach against the government, is it not better to attach them to one's self? A Pope is necessary to me, but a Pope who brings together instead of dividing, who conciliates minds, reunites and gives them to the government that has issued from the Revolution. And for that there is necessary to me a true Pope—Catholic, Apostolic, and Roman.' Such were the views with which Napoleon entered upon the negotiations for the Concordat. It would be easy to multiply quotations from the recorded words of the First Consul[1], to show that the revival of religion was, in itself, a matter of perfect indifference to him. His central thought was to secure a functionary clergy, as an engine of support to his administration. 'What we are doing,' he said, whilst the negotiations with Rome were still pending, 'is inflicting a mortal blow on Popery.'

[1] See 'Mémoires sur le Conseil d'État,' c. xi.

Into the history of these negotiations I cannot enter. The Pope and his counsellors were animated by the desire of securing the great extension of the spiritual power which the Concordat promised, and the restoration of the temporal power of the Church in its ancient limits, for which they trusted to the gratitude of the First Consul. The capital of the Holy See, they reasoned, 'was no longer in proportion to the provinces which it still possessed.' By showing himself agreeable to the First Consul, the Pope might hope to obtain from his benevolence, either the principality of Sienna, or the restitution of the Legations, or an increase towards the Marches of Ancona; 'for it is the First Consul who to-day parcels out Italy.' 'Let us conclude the Concordat which he desires,' added other counsellors of the same party; 'they will know when it shall be ratified, all the immensity of its religious importance, and the power which it gives to Rome over the episcopacy in all the world[1].' The negotiations had not advanced many stages when these sanguine anticipations were discovered to be illusions. Napoleon valued the temporal power of the Pope only as the instrument of perpetuating his dependence upon France; and as the political interests of the Papacy were antagonistic to those of France, the French clergy must be separated from their head, subordinated to the ruling power in Paris,—'nominated, watched over, incessantly restrained by it.' Such was Napoleon's notion of the extension of the spiritual and temporal power of the Papacy, as regarded France.

The Concordat was signed on the 15th July, A.D. 1801. Whilst recognizing the sovereignty of the Roman

[1] De Pressensé, 'The Church and the French Revolution.'

Pontiff it subordinated his authority to the ruling power in Paris, and widened the breach between the French clergy and the head of Christendom. The political engagements of the new French bishops were reduced to a simple oath of fidelity to the government, to whose approval must be subjected all nominations to the cures of their dioceses.

The independence of Rome which the Gallican Church thus dearly purchased was destructive of its liberties. Its servility to the throne, in the seventeenth century, alone rendered possible that triumph of the League in France, which culminated in the revocation of the Edict of Nantes. The emasculated system retained nothing but the name in common with the Gallicanism which, in the fifteenth century, had dared to assert the independence of the French Church, and to set limits to, and exercise control over, the usurpations of the Papacy. Its vaunted liberties were now placed beneath the foot of the ruler who was supreme in spiritual as in temporal matters. The oppressive and vexatious intervention of the temporal power in spiritual interests naturally resulted in that preponderance of Ultramontanism which we now witness in France, so long distinguished as the home of a diametrically opposite principle. It became an object of solicitude with the French clergy to take precautions against the usurpations of the civil power. Their spirit of opposition to the Holy See, softened by the dangers which they recognized in the restriction of its rights, gradually disappeared; and Napoleon himself—prompted by his overbearing animosity to the bishops who had rejected the civil constitution of the French clergy, condemned by the court of Rome—compelled the Pope to sequesttrate their Sees. By a single stroke of his pen, Pius VII deprived of their dignity thirty-seven French bishops who had refused to resign, whilst at the same time he abolished all the episcopal churches for ever, and erected ten Metropolitan Sees and fifty Bishoprics [1]. A proceeding so arbitrary and unprecedented justifies the charge of the absolute and despotic power which the Roman Pontiff never fails to exercise when unrestrained by fear.

Napoleon had now unintentionally sacrificed to the interests of the Papacy the ancient constitution of the Church. He placed the French episcopate at the disposal of the Roman Pontiff, and thus furnished one of the most powerful incentives to the dissemination of those Ultramontane principles which he held in such intense abhorrence. 'A thing done,' say the Italians, 'has a head;' and it was in vain that Napoleon sought to neutralize this radical error in the stringent provisions of the Concordat which, in effect, confirmed and perpetuated it.

It was to the negotiator of this Concordat that Napoleon gave his celebrated instruction, 'Remember to treat the Pope as though he had 200,000 men at his command.' His usual penetration had preserved him from repeating the mistake of the Directory in their dealings with Pius VI, and convinced him that civility, and a semblance of deference, were better calculated to promote the object he had in view, than vainglorious threats of spoliation and schism.

The gentle and conciliatory Pontiff interposed few obstacles, glad to maintain even a nominal possession of his principality, and to win back again to the faith the infidel nation whose apostacy, during eight years,

[1] Dollinger.

had made her as formidable a foe to the Church as, in the days of her subserviency, she had proved to the Protestants of her own and other lands.

In the autumn of A.D. 1804, Napoleon commenced the preparations for the important solemnity of his coronation. The prescient jest of General Lafayette was to have its accomplishment, and the 'little phial' to be brought into requisition. He was well aware that 'with a large proportion at least of the rural population, the consecration of his authority by the ceremony of coronation was an essential particular, and that to all, of whatever latitude of opinion, it was of great political importance to prove that his influence was so unbounded, as to compel the head of the Church himself to officiate on the occasion. The Papal benediction appeared to be the link which would unite the revolutionary to the legitimate *régime*, and cause the faithful to forget in the sacred authority with which he was now invested the violence and bloodshed which had paved his way to the throne. Napoleon for these reasons had long resolved not only that he should be crowned according to the forms of the French monarchy, but that the ceremony should be performed by the head of Christendom [1].' The overtures which he presented to the court of the Vatican abounded with a profusion of simulated respect for the successor of the Apostles, and with vague promises of benefits which should accrue to the Papacy, from the compliance of the supreme Pontiff with the solicitations of the eldest son

---

[1] Alison's 'History of Europe,' vol. viii. I am disposed, however, to the opinion that Sir Archibald Alison errs in assuming that Napoleon ever contemplated receiving the crown at the hands of the Pontiff.

of the Church. To these solicitations Cardinal Consalvi had offered all the opposition in his power. As the representative of the Pope in negotiating the Concordat, he had already discovered the meanness and falsehood which, in the character of Napoleon, were blended with the highest genius. When, after endless debates, the terms of the Concordat had been settled, and Napoleon had consented to withdraw the Gallican doctrines which were so offensive to the Papal court, Consalvi had detected an attempted fraud, which was only too characteristic of the First Consul. At the moment when he was about to sign, the cardinal discovered that Napoleon had artfully substituted a document containing the obnoxious clauses, for the one to which he had agreed[1]. It is not, therefore, surprising that in the solicitations of Napoleon, Consalvi suspected a covered design of effecting the humiliation of the Pontiff. But the Emperor elect was now too powerful to be refused. He never intended to receive his crown at the hands of the Pope, nor was he allowed to officiate. With his own hands the Emperor placed the crown upon his head. *The presence of the Pontiff* only was desired, to adorn and consecrate the ceremony, and to render it more imposing. The relation which the Emperor had determined that *the Church* should sustain to *the Empire*, was thus shadowed forth—probably with design—that, namely, of an imposing and useful but always *subordinate* appendage.

The ceremony of coronation took place with every possible magnificence on the 2nd December, A.D. 1804. The Papal suite shortly afterwards returned to Rome,

[1] 'L'Église Romaine et le Premier Empire, 1800–14.' Par M. le Comte D'Haussonville. 3 vols. 8vo. Paris, Lévy, 1868.

charmed with their visit, and sanguine, with the confidence which a long-cherished desire too often inspires, as to the full realization of the important and durable benefits which the too credulous Pontiff expected to accrue to the Papacy from his condescension in crossing the Alps to sanction the coronation of the Emperor with the authority of the Church. Cardinal Caprera, the Papal legate at Paris, was largely responsible for these exaggerated anticipations. His appointment to this post had been insisted on by Napoleon, and M. D'Haussonville convincingly shows that he acted throughout these negotiations rather as the minister of the Emperor than of the Pope. Misguided by his representations, Pius VII was confident that, at the least, the three Legations ceded by the Peace of Tolentino would be restored. The flattering attentions which he had received from the Emperor, who used the same bait which had inveigled him into the Concordat—expressing the most liberal views, but abstaining from any definite pledge—encouraged these illusions.

Amongst the able statesmen who formed the Pope's cabinet, not a few were doubtful and anxious. Accordingly, and shortly after his return to Rome, Pius VII despatched a memorial to Napoleon, recounting the losses which the Holy See had sustained in the late war, and strongly urging him to imitate the example of Charlemagne, and restore these possessions. It is curious to note the fascination wrought upon the Pontiff, as upon all who personally approached Napoleon; and the affection, which subsequent events and his own cruel sufferings failed to obliterate, which Pius thenceforward entertained towards his unscrupulous oppressor. The evasive reply of Napoleon was followed, within a year from the date of his coronation, by the forcible seizure, and occupation by his troops, of the most important fortress in the ecclesiastical territory. To the Pope's expostulations the Emperor replied in disdainful terms, which, indicating the principle upon which he intended to act with regard to the temporal power of the Papacy, speedily destroyed all illusions. In this reply Napoleon asserted that all Italy must be subject to his law; that the Pope's situation required that he should pay the Emperor the same respect in temporal which he rendered to him in spiritual matters. 'You,' he said, 'are sovereign of Rome, but I am its Emperor.' To Cardinal Fesch, the French minister at Rome, he thus wrote:—'To the Pope I am Charlemagne, because, like Charlemagne, I unite the crown of France to that of the Lombards, and because my Empire extends to the boundaries of the East. I expect, therefore, that his conduct towards me should be regulated upon this principle. If good conduct is maintained, I shall not change the outward appearance of things; if not, I shall reduce the Pope to be only Bishop of Rome. In truth, nothing can be so unreasonable as the court of Rome [1].'

For two centuries, as we have seen, the struggle between the Popedom and the Empire had been less for supremacy than for existence. The Holy Roman Empire had fallen, and the Popedom seemed to be expiring, when by the new Emperor of the West the old struggle for supremacy was thus haughtily revived. The days were now past when, like Hildebrand, the Pontiff could imperiously claim the submission of the

[1] D'Haussonville, vol. ii. p. 78.

Emperor on the ground of his responsibility for the souls of all men; and the self-constituted heir of Charlemagne, aspiring to rule all Europe from Paris, was little likely to tolerate any independent exercise of the secular power by his puppet at Rome. The contest, indeed, was at an end; but about the resignation of the Pontiff there was a dignity which contrasted finely with the coarse threats, littlenesses, and treachery to which Napoleon was ever ready to stoop. In a despatch to his Nuncio at Paris, 31st of July, A.D. 1806, referring to the Emperor's threat that if Rome and the States of the Church were once in his hands, they would never come out of them, he says:—'His Majesty may easily believe this and persuade himself of it, but I reply frankly that if his Majesty has a right to be confident that power is on his side, I, for my part, know that above all monarchs there reigns a God, the avenger of justice and innocence, before whom every human power must bend.' His course, he declares, is irrevocable. 'Nothing can change it; neither threats nor the execution of those threats.' These sentiments, he declares, are his 'testament,' which he is willing to sign with his blood. 'But,' he adds, after instructing his Nuncio to convey them to Napoleon, 'tell the Emperor he still has my affection, and that I have every wish to give him every proof of it which is in my power, and to continue to show myself his best friend; but what is demanded is out of my power to do[1].'

Events now marched rapidly. On the 10th of January, A.D. 1808, Napoleon wrote thus to his brother Joseph:—'There is no end of the impertinences of the court of Rome; I am anxious to have done with it. I

[1] D'Haussonville.

have dismissed its negotiators. I wish you to assemble at Terracina a column of 2000 Neapolitan troops, infantry and cavalry, a French battalion of from 800 to 900 men, a cavalry regiment of 400 men, four Neapolitan and six French pieces of horse-artillery, which will make 3000 men and ten pieces of cannon. You will do all this quietly. You will put this column under the orders of a brigadier-general, who will wait at Terracina for orders from General Miollis, under whose command the column is to be. General Miollis is collecting 3000 men at Perugia, and General Lemarrois as many at Foligno. With these 6000 men Miollis will march towards Rome, as if he were going to rejoin the army of Naples. When he has reached Rome, he will take possession of the Castle of St. Angelo, and assume the title of Commander-in-Chief of the troops in the Papal States, and he will send orders to your division at Terracina to join him in Rome as soon as possible. You feel that this expedition must be kept very secret [1].'

Rome was thus beleaguered with a force of 9000 men, and its occupation, though delayed a whole year, might have been effected at any time without fear of opposition. But Napoleon, having thus made the Pope to feel his power, was willing to conciliate the Catholics of France by a show of forbearance. Concessions on the part of the Pontiff, which might be flaunted in the eyes of Christendom as the voluntary renunciation of untenable claims, would have been of far greater value to the Emperor than any which he could extort at the point of the bayonet. But the Pontiff was firm in his

[1] 'Napoleon's Correspondence with King Joseph,' vol. i. No. 350.

irrevocable decision to yield nothing but to force, which he was powerless to repel. His one answer to every overture involving the concession of one iota of his Pontifical claims being, 'What is demanded is out of my power to do.'

On the 2nd of February, A.D. 1809, the French troops took possession of Rome, and, within three months, a formal decree proclaimed that the territories of the Pope were united to the French Empire. The words of this decree, revoking 'the donations which my predecessors, the Emperors of the West, have made,' again curiously reveals the determination of Napoleon to be regarded as the successor of the Western Roman Emperors. Pius protested, but in vain; and though, either from generosity, or from motives of policy,—for the Emperor had declared that the Pope who should presume to denounce him to Christendom would cease to be a Pope in his eyes,—Pius VII shrunk from pronouncing the threatened personal excommunication of the Emperor, he issued a brief, which recounted the penalties to be pronounced upon those who presumed to invade the possessions of the Church. But the Papal interdict had lost its terrors; and Napoleon replied by sanctioning the arrest of the Pontiff.

Thus, just one thousand years after the establishment of the temporal power of the Popedom by Pepin and Charlemagne, France was the instrument of despoiling the Church of its own gifts. Originally the price of a base prostitution of religion, they had wrought incalculable mischief to the Church, which, for their possession, had abnegated her office as a teacher and pattern of morality. It had been well for the Church, for Italy, and for Christendom, had the allies, after

Napoleon's downfall, been less blindly determined to reverse his acts in every detail; and if, recognizing the wisdom at least of his Italian policy, they had suffered the Italians to enjoy that freedom from the oppressions of ecclesiastical rule which he had conferred upon them.

CHAPTER X.

It was from Vienna, in the spring of A.D. 1809, that Napoleon issued his decree annexing the territories of the Pope to the French Empire, 'by virtue of his right as the successor of Charlemagne.' He afterwards protested that he was not privy to the actual seizure of the Pope; which occurred, perhaps, sooner than he intended, but certainly had his entire approval. Preparations for the arrest of the Pontiff were made with sufficient secrecy to conceal the intention from the people of Rome. At three o'clock on the morning of the 16th of July, a body of soldiers, under General Radet, scaled the garden-wall of the Vatican, got into the palace by a window, broke through the locked doors opposing their advance, disarmed the Swiss guard, and so made a forcible entrance into the sleeping chamber of the Pontiff. Arousing the Pope from his slumbers, they demanded from him a categorical declaration that he would renounce all temporal pretensions, and withdraw the bull of anathema. Pius refused, protesting that he would rather accept the worst fate in store for him, than sign such an abdication; whilst he threatened General Radet with the anathema of the Church if he dared lay hands on the successor of the Apostles.

The General appears to have felt very little concern about these obsolete threats. He caused the Pope to be made fast in the arm-chair in which he was seated, and so lowered through the broken window into the street, where a close carriage was in waiting. The prisoner, with Cardinal Pacca, who was allowed to accompany him, was placed in this conveyance. The horses dashed off at full speed; and whilst the citizens were yet asleep in their beds, the *cortège* passed through the gates of Rome.

Napoleon offered the Pope the appurtenances of a court in any city he might choose in the south of France, with a revenue of two million francs; but Pius VII refused to hold intercourse with one under the ban. He was, accordingly, removed to Savona, on the shores of the Gulf of Genoa, and guarded as a prisoner. Here, through the medium of pamphlets clandestinely printed at Lyons, he continued to assail the Emperor's acts, and particularly his divorce from Josephine. To put an end to this factious opposition, and for greater security, Napoleon, after detaining his captive three years at Savona, caused him to be removed to Fontainebleau.

Meanwhile, the Emperor had issued a decree confirming that of Vienna of the 2nd April, A.D. 1809, and providing for the government of the States of the Church. By this decree Rome was declared to be the second city of the French Empire, and was to give the title of King to the Prince Imperial. It was also enacted that the future Emperors, after their coronation at Notre Dame, should be also crowned at St. Peter's at Rome[1].

According to his own acknowledgment, the object of Napoleon, in despoiling Pius VII of his dominions, was to effect the transfer of the Papal court to Paris—to make it a French and Imperial institution,—and by means of

---

[1] Dyer's 'Modern Europe.'

an ecclesiastical puppet and his Nuncios, to sway the conscience of Europe, as effectively as he already domineered over its politics through generals and diplomatists. He thus hoped to surmount the most formidable obstacles which impeded the accomplishment of his 'destined career[1].' But these acts of the Emperor redounded to the advantage of his victim, by producing a reaction of respectful devotion to the afflicted head of the Church. Thus, again, we see the despot who, determined to bend everything to his own iron will, had sought to supplant the Pope's supremacy in France, preparing public opinion for the revival of Ultramontanism.

Adversity had obliterated the amiable tractability which had characterized the Pope ten years earlier. He was aware of the sympathy which was extended towards him by millions who hated his captor; whilst such of them as were Catholics, lamented not only the indignities to which the Vicar of Christ was subjected, but the interference, thence arising, with the ministrations of religion in every land. His own sense of dignity and duty never entirely forsook him. The blandishments and threats of the Emperor were alike powerless to induce him to relinquish his Italian possessions. The rigorous treatment to which he had been subjected at Savona was relaxed at Fontainebleau; but it had produced lamentable effects, both mental and physical,

---

[1] 'What I have hitherto done is nothing,' he said one day at the camp at Boulogne. 'There will never be peace in Europe except under one chief—an Emperor, whose officers should be kings; who should distribute kingdoms to his lieutenants, making one King of Italy, another King of Bavaria,' &c.—' Mémoires de Comte Nicot de Melito.'

from which he never wholly recovered. Indications are not wanting that his sufferings had weakened the intellect, as, for instance, the frequent occupation of his time in *darning stockings*[1]; but pre-eminently in his falling into the snare of the Emperor in signing the fatal Concordat, by which he renounced his temporal power. 'The one error,' says Cardinal Wiseman, 'of his life and Pontificate. For there came to him men "of the seed of Aaron," who could not be expected to mislead him, themselves free and moving in the busiest of the world, who showed him, through the loopholes of his prison, that world from which he was shut out, as though agitated on its surface, and to its lowest depths, through his unbendingness; the Church torn to schism, and religion weakened to destruction, from what they termed his obstinacy. He who had but prayed and bent his neck to suffering, was made to appear in his own eyes a harsh and cruel master, who would rather see all perish than lose his grasp on unrelenting, but impotent, jurisdiction. He yielded for a moment of conscientious alarm, he consented, though conditionally, under false but virtuous impressions, to the terms proposed to him for a new Concordat [2].'

The Emperor was overjoyed at the complete success

---

[1] Perhaps *knitting* stockings,—an occupation for charitable purposes to which the aged of both sexes are much addicted in Italy. As recently as the 5th of May last the Roman correspondent of the *Morning Post* writes :—' Count Gaetano (a brother of Pope Pius IX) is an old bachelor, and very charitable to the poor of his native town, for whom he passes many peaceful hours in knitting stockings—an innocent amusement now getting rather out of fashion, but still practised in Italy.'

[2] 'The Last Four Popes,' by Cardinal Wiseman.

of this *coup-de-main*. 'Next morning,' says the historian of the French Revolution, 'decorations, presents, and orders were profusely scattered among the chief persons of the Pope's household; the joyful intelligence was communicated to the bishops. Te Deum was chanted in all the churches of France, all the restrictions upon the personal freedom of the Pope were removed; Mass was allowed to be freely celebrated in the palace of Fontainebleau; a numerous body of cardinals soon after joined his Holiness from their different places of exile. The Concordat was solemnly published as one of the fundamental laws of the State, the Emperor loaded the Pope and all the members of his court with that gracious and insinuating kindness which, when it suited his purposes, he could so well assume; and in the exuberance of his satisfaction, even gave orders for the liberation of his indomitable antagonist, Cardinal Pacca, from his long and painful confinement amidst the snows of Savoy [1].'

In permitting the Pope again to surround himself with his cardinals, Napoleon had not calculated the effect which the support of their presence and counsel would inevitably produce upon the Pontiff. Their remonstrances were earnest and importunate; and the weak-minded Pope perceived how completely he had been overreached by the specious arguments and clever artifices of the Emperor. With bitter remorse, and

'Tears from the depth of some divine despair,'

he acknowledged his mistake. But it was too late. Tears and imprecations were alike without effect upon the astute and exultant Emperor.

[1] Alison's 'Europe,' vol. xvi.

On the 24th of March, 1813, Pius VII solemnly retracted his signature to the Concordat, which he declared to be anulled, ascribing his compliance to the weakness of the flesh; and protesting that the concessions made were unjustifiable in the sight of God and man. The Emperor, not deigning to notice the recantation, forthwith published the Concordat as the law of the Empire, and obligatory upon all Archbishops, Bishops, and Chapters. Pius VII was soon avenged. His prolonged captivity, and his obstinate refusal to ratify the Concordat, had become a matter of serious embarrassment to Napoleon, who, after the fatal battle of Leipsic, in November, 1813, determined to assent to his liberation. Renewed but unsuccessful efforts were made to induce the Pontiff to purchase his freedom by concessions which might save appearances. He was removed from Fontainebleau to the south of France; but, under one pretext or another, his journey towards Rome was impeded, Napoleon apparently cherishing the hope that a return of fortune to his arms might enable him to detain so valuable and illustrious a prisoner. .

But the Emperor's downfall was now at hand. At that very Fontainebleau where he had cajoled the enfeebled Pontiff into signing the fatal Concordat, the allied powers compelled him to sign his own abdication. One of the earliest acts of the provisional government was to pass a decree expressing sympathy with the Pope, and charging the civil and military authorities to remove every obstruction to his journey, and to accord him all the honours due to his rank.

It is worthy of remark that, whilst three of the four allied powers to whom Pius VII owed his freedom were non-Catholic, it was to these three Protestant powers alone[1] that the head of that Church, which had so often strained every resource to effect the destruction of Protestantism, both in England and on the continent of Europe, now first expressed his desire of being reinstated not simply in those territories which Napoleon had, by his Vienna decree of April 2nd, A.D. 1809, annexed to the French Empire, but his hope of recovering the provinces ceded to France by the Peace of Tolentino.

As a steadfast sufferer, Pius VII received the sympathy and respect of the population in every town through which he passed. On approaching Reggio, the carriages that escorted him formed a long line of procession, followed by multitudes of horsemen and persons on foot. As the procession entered the town, the horses were removed from the Pontifical carriage, which was drawn through the streets amidst the enthusiastic shouts of the populace[2]. His return to Rome was, in fact, a grand triumphal progress in which, however, the demonstrations of joy probably sprang rather from a sentiment of commiseration on account of the persecutions which the Pontiff had endured, than from any respect for the tiara.

Wearied of the changes and tumults of the Revolution, there was a general disposition amongst the people of the Roman States to welcome a settled government, albeit not one of the people's choice. The conciliatory disposition of the Pope had been signally evinced at an embarrassing interview which he had held with Murat at Bologna. In the discussion

---

[1] Ranke.
[2] Butt's 'History of Italy,' vol. ii.

which then took place on the subject of the restoration of the Papal territory, the wily Murat had insisted that the desire of the Romans was to be delivered from the temporal sovereignty of the Pope, and to be incorporated with one of the secular Italian States; and he placed in the Pontiff's hands a petition, numerously signed by the inhabitants of Rome, of which this was the prayer. The Pope, perceiving that the original signatures were attached to the petition, calmly consigned the document to the flames, remarking that as he wished to know no enemies in Rome, he would not acquaint himself with the names of his rebellious subjects. The report of this generous conduct had reached Rome before his own arrival, and won the hearts of thousands, and of not a few even of those who had signed the petition. The return of Pius VII to his capital was celebrated by demonstrations of tumultuous rejoicing, the nobles fraternizing with the citizens and stimulating their mirth. The Duke Borghese, it is said, entertained the mob at a banquet which cost him £48,000!

By the treaty of Vienna, the whole of the Papal States, with the exception of a small district north of the Po, were restored to the Church. But Pius VII was far from satisfied with the simple restoration of his Italian crown. He demanded from the allied sovereigns the full and complete restoration of *the former power of the Church*; the reconstitution of the dissolved monasteries, with all their revenues; and the re-establishment of the bishops with their lands and prerogatives; 'Protestant rulers, especially, to yield up all the ecclesiastical lands which had accrued to them by the treaties of the last thirty years; above all, France to give back the principality of Avignon and the Comté of Veneissau to the apostolic throne, or incur the worst of all crimes, the crime of sacrilege.' The princes at Vienna were, however, unwilling, at the bidding of a Pope, to plunge Europe into the darkness of the middle ages; and Pius, with a solemn protest against all arrangements injurious to the interests of the Church, and the patrimony of St. Peter, eagerly clutched the prize of his restored sovereignty.

Pius VII was not behind the other minor sovereigns who recovered their paltry crowns, and were reinstated on their thrones by the treaty of Vienna, in his endeavours to obliterate all memory of French domination. In the pious but weak-minded Pontiff we are not surprised at any intensity of hatred towards the ruler who had been the spoliator of the Church, and his own unrelenting persecutor. But it is well-nigh incredible that the government of Rome should have descended to so ignoble a manifestation of their hatred of the French nation as to direct that the public clocks,—which had been bestowed on the city during the French occupation, and marked the division of the day on the system prevalent throughout the civilized world,—should have their dials either effaced or adapted to the effete practice of former days, the first hour commencing at nightfall, and so on until sunset. It is also said that the authorities proposed to abandon the practice of lighting the streets at night, because it had been inaugurated by the French. An edict was actually issued to suppress the public lamps, and although the endurance of the citizens was not tested by its being suffered to remain long in force, it did, for a while, leave them dependent for the illumination of their streets, upon torches which blazed at the doors of private houses, and the farthing candles burned at the images of saints. These freaks are illustrations of the petty and spiteful hatred which had their counterpart in Piedmont where Victor Emanuel I, determined to obliterate even the memory of his absence, issued a proclamation on the day after his return to Turin, by which all the laws of A.D. 1776 were restored. It is said that a court almanac of A.D. 1795 was handed to the king, who at once issued a warrant reappointing to their former offices all those whose names appeared in its lists. The grim monster, Death, had not forsaken Piedmont during the king's involuntary absence, and the result of course was that many persons, long since in their graves, were reappointed officers of State!

Throughout Italy the Code Napoleon was superseded by the intricate and semi-barbarous provisions of the German laws. The taxes imposed by the French were retained; but instead of being partly expended in making roads and other useful public works, in promoting education and encouraging manufactures, the whole found its way to Vienna. Such were the 'benefits' *the people* derived from the 'deliverance' which they celebrated with unreasoning enthusiasm. Nor was this blind hatred of Napoleon peculiar to the petty sovereigns who, after his downfall, recovered their thrones. It was shared equally by the restorers. Though by nature a despot, Napoleon had unwittingly conferred a priceless boon upon the Italians, by the abolition of the temporal sovereignty of the Pope; by the overthrow of the Bourbon despots of the South, and the hated Hapsburg dynasty in the North; thus demonstrating to Europe that the Italians were capable of self-government. It sufficed that *he* had done this. For no other reason was the political Papacy restored by the Protestant powers of Europe, and the Italians doomed to languish for another half-century under Papal, Hapsburg, and Bourbon misgovernment and oppression.

Europe was too intently occupied in the attempt to undo the work of the revolution, to take cognizance of a momentous act of the restored Pontiff destructive of the work for the accomplishment of which European statesmen had intrigued and toiled for half a century. Scarcely was Pius VII securely seated upon his Pontifical throne when, in defiance of the wishes of the lay sovereigns of Europe, he published a bull reviving the order of the Jesuits, that secret militia of Rome which, amid all the vicissitudes through which it had passed during the three centuries that had elapsed since its institution, had so marvellously fulfilled the design of its founder; insinuating its principles, and influencing courts and peoples by a hidden omnipresence. The order, as we have seen, had been repressed by Clement XIV in 1773. It is curious to note the name of D'Azeglio in the roll of the first reception of novices which took place at Rome. This was the brother of Massimo D'Azeglio, the man who perhaps, more than any contemporary statesman, contributed by his writings and his extensive influence to create in Italy that mental independence and civil liberty which Jesuitism abhors,—that atmosphere of free thought which is fatal to its existence. But it must be said that the Jesuit Marquis was as imperfect a Jesuit as he was upright, liberal, and patriotic as a man. Insisting upon the absolute obedience due from believers to the head of the Church, he nevertheless boldly affirmed that when, as sovereign of Rome, the Pope addressed his subjects, his decrees must be discussed at the tribunal of public opinion; and be examined and judged by the law, which is the same for those who govern and those who are governed, and the observance of which constitutes the common justice of civilized nations[1].

The re-establishment of all the monastic orders followed, in quick succession, the revival of the order of the Jesuits; and the Holy Office of the Inquisition was resuscitated. The system of government by ecclesiastics was completely restored, and the spirit of freedom and nationality in the Papal States, as throughout Italy, was crushed.

The territories which constituted the States of the Church were distributed into five great divisions;—the District of Rome, and the Four Legations. These five divisions were subdivided into provinces; the provinces again into governments; and the governments into communes. In the District of Rome were included, besides Rome and the country immediately adjacent, three provinces:—Viterbo, Civita Vecchia, and Orvieto. The four Legations were:—

I. Romagna, comprising four provinces:—Bologna, Ferrara, Forli, and Ravenna.

II. The Marches, comprising six provinces:—Urbino and Pesaro, Macerata with Loreto, Ancona, Fermo, Ascoli, and Camerino.

III. Umbria, comprising three provinces:—Perugia, Spoleto, and Rieti.

---

[1] See 'The Court of Rome and the Gospel,' by the Marquis Roberto D'Azeglio.

IV. Marittima and Campagna, comprising three provinces:—Valletri, Frosinone, and Benevento[1].

At the restoration of Pius VII the whole of these districts were subject to his despotic sway, and were declared to be the inalienable possessions of the Papal See. The collapse of the Holy Roman Empire, and the overthrow of Napoleon, relieved the Papacy of that rivalry of the secular with the spiritual government which, during a period of eight hundred years, had occasioned so many vicissitudes to both. There remained, however, the power of Austria, the most abominable despotism in Europe, which, by the arrangements of the treaty of Vienna, had acquired increased influence in Italy. With the extension of the fatal grasp of Austrian power the last vestige of Italian policy disappeared from the States of the Church. Upon Austria the Papacy now leaned for support. Her troops were indispensable for the preservation of order. Her intervention was sought in every province in which the flame of liberty still flickered. The clerical party came back to power, her avowed instruments, pledged to maintain the maxims and the institutions of the Middle Ages, and thus to plunge Italy into a state of thraldom.

I have said that Italian policy had disappeared. So also had the policy of the Popedom. The great contests for Papal prerogatives of which Christendom, with bated breath, had been through long ages the interested spectator, are forgotten. The imperious voice of Rome in the council-chambers of foreign Courts is silent. Bullied by Austria, the feeble Pontiff, who clutched more convulsively at the shadow of power as the

[1] 'The Church and the Churches,' by Dr. Dollinger.

substance eluded his grasp, avouches his subserviency. How are the mighty fallen! Had Pius VII possessed the daring to embrace the liberal opinions which he was powerless to smother, he might now have assumed the leadership of Italy under circumstances more favourable than ever Roman Pontiff enjoyed. We can only speculate upon the later glory with which he might have surrounded the tiara. But he failed to appreciate the destinies of Italy; and this failure precipitated the inglorious and rapid decline of that effete system, which, though galvanized into new life by the will of the Allied Sovereigns, was antagonistic to the interests of Italy and of the world. 'Praise,' said Lord Byron, 'is the reflection of virtue.' 'Gratitude,' said Seneca, ' is so easy a virtue, that the sluggard may be grateful without labour.' But the Papacy had established no claim to the praise or the gratitude of Italy; and it languished, dishonoured and unlamented.

Pius VII quailed before that cry for liberty in which, favoured by the prevailing public opinion, he might have firmly rooted the power and enhanced the glory of the Roman See. The opportunity came, and went; and returned no more. Sycophancy to Austria was his only policy. Doing her bidding, he sanctioned political inquisitions and condemnations which deprived him of his most worthy subjects. And, most fatal error of all, he sanctioned the formation of a political sect in support of his tottering power. Lending the name of religion to an association, unnatural, irreligious, and antinational, this act proclaimed the utter incompatibility of Papal rule with the true happiness and prosperity of Italy.

Here we pause. The politico-religious sects which

divided Italy, and especially the States of the Church, at the commencement of this century, were the natural outgrowth of the system of terrorism wherewith the head of the Roman Church vainly sought to arrest the rapid decay of his temporal power. For a short account of some of these 'sects,' and their influence upon the social and political life of Italy, the reader is referred to the Appendix.

CHAPTER XI.

WITH the settlement of the treaty of Vienna and the restoration to the Roman See, under Pius VII, of those territories of which Napoleon had despoiled the Church, my allotted task is completed. It is my purpose to narrate the vicissitudes of the Papacy under the eventful Pontificate of Pius IX in a separate work, which, if the exigencies of a busy life allow, I hope to offer to the public at no very distant day. I shall here confine myself to a brief narration of those events of the present Pontificate, issuing in that large restriction of the temporal power which seems to herald its speedy abolition.

The Pontificates immediately preceding that of Pius IX were amongst the most unpopular on record. The power of ecclesiastics in temporal matters was infinitely greater than it had ever been before; the spy system was increased; the press was completely gagged; feuds between the rival sects of the Sanfedists and the Carbonari disturbed the peace of every town; political assassination was not accounted a crime, and the hands of the adherents of both parties had been freely imbued in blood: but the former sect, instituted in aid of the government, and now openly allied with it, was triumphant. Every man who was suspected of Carbonarism was dogged day and night by the police; evidence against such was collected with secrecy, and, on the testimony of irresponsible and unknown informers, hundreds of peaceable and inoffensive citizens were arrested and placed in irons. The prisons afforded insufficient accommodation; convents, and even private dwelling-houses, were rented by the government to receive the accused. Abortive conspiracies contributed to embitter and intensify the alienation between the Popes and their unwilling subjects.

Gregory XIV and his notorious minister, Bernetti, turned a deaf ear to the expostulations and advice of the Great Powers who, after the suppression of the insurrection by which his Pontificate was inaugurated, and again after the ill-fated rising at Rimini, urged upon the Pontifical government the necessity of conceding the reforms which it had been the object of these insurrections to secure. A chronic condition of revolution was only held in check by the threatening attitude of Austria and a large increase in the Swiss mercenaries in the pay of Rome. But the disaffection of the people was complete. Political assassinations were of frequent occurrence, and, by a necessary consequence, the governments became more persecuting, espionage more prevalent, and the political sects more bitter in their mutual antagonism. By means of military commissions which imprisoned and shot offenders at pleasure, and of the dreaded tribunal of the Inquisition, the government contrived to suppress revolt, whilst it imbued the whole population with the hatred engendered by despair.

Such was the condition of things when, on the 16th of June, 1846, Pius IX was raised to the Papal throne. His election was a good omen for Italy. The great act of grace by which he inaugurated his reign sent a thrill of joy throughout and beyond his dominions, for the amnesty restored liberty to one-tenth part of the active population of the Papal States, who were either exiles or languishing in the Papal dungeons.

The apparent earnestness and sincerity with which Pius IX set about the reform of abuses won the hearts of the most inveterate haters of the Papacy. He became the idol of the populace, whose adulations were so extravagant that wise men trembled for the result, and the Pontiff himself counselled moderation. If noble qualities of heart, alone, constituted a good sovereign, undoubtedly the subjects of the newly-elected Pontiff were singularly blessed in their ruler. But it soon became apparent that Pius IX was bent upon converting the infatuated devotion of his people into an instrument for securing and extending the prerogatives of a priestly government. For a while the Romans, disappointed at the inactivity of the government, and the weary postponement of the promised reforms, vented their indignation upon the ministers of the Pope, and refused to believe in the unwillingness of the popular idol to confer that full freedom which they deemed consistent with the Papal prerogatives.

The projected Council of State, in which the Romans saw the germ of an elective and representative assembly, was a reform of the Pontiff's own conception, and commanded the enthusiastic commendation of the people. But when, at the first meeting of the *Consulta*, Pius IX declared that his purpose in convening the members in a permanent Council was to hear their opinions 'when necessary,' and that in relation to these he 'should consult his conscience and confer on them with his ministers of the Sacred College;' when he denounced as Utopian the views of those who saw in the Council 'the germ of an institution incompatible with the Pontifical sovereignty,' the confidence of the multitude, and of those especially who were adverse to constitutional government, was rudely shaken. It was impossible that what the Pope offered could content the great body of the people. It was from Rome that the oft-repeated lesson of history was again proclaimed to the purblind despots who then, as now, refused to perceive that the gift of a sham liberty to a people aroused by long privation to demand FREEDOM, is a more dangerous expedient than undisguised and unmitigated despotism.

The line of policy pursued by the Pope in the war with Austria alienated the great body of the liberals, who now saw in Pius IX only the Priest-King, jealous of his prerogatives, and willing, for their retention, to barter the freedom of Italy.

From this period the faith of the people in Pius IX, as the renovator of Italy and the reconciler of estranged factions and antagonistic institutions, declined, and has never revived. A large section of the liberals, distinguished by the appellation of Moderates, did indeed still profess their respect for the Pontiff, their faith in the successful working of the constitution which he had reluctantly conceded, and their preference for the established order of things to the Republican institutions advocated by the *Giovine Italia*. This party was of great numerical strength, and embraced many adherents of whose names Italy is still justly proud. They adhered to the Pontiff with a tenacity which their more ardent compatriots could neither comprehend nor respect. But when, at last, the Pope stood revealed, a traitor to Italian freedom, declaring that he would do nothing for Italy which would injure the priesthood or weaken the Popedom, when it became apparent that the realization of the national aspirations had but one obstacle, the Papacy, Pius found himself deserted by the men who alone possessed sufficient influence with the people to support a form of government which was utterly detested. It is noteworthy that this severance between the Pope and his subjects was coincident with the advent to power of that remarkable man who, for a period of twenty years, has been the true Pope of Rome, Cardinal Antonelli, designated by his countrymen '*il Cardinale Diavolo.*'

On the 16th of September, 1848, Pius summoned the distinguished, but unfortunate, Count Rossi to form an administration. To a Supreme Pontiff, as to ordinary mortals, wisdom often comes too late. Rossi had great claims upon the respect, the gratitude, and the confidence of the Italians; but it was now inevitable that the man chosen by Pius IX for such an office should immediately fall under popular suspicion. Rossi, moreover, had been the representative of monarchical France at the Papal Court, and the intimate friend of M. Guizot. Such credentials rendered his name odious to the Republicans. Political assassinations were now of frequent occurrence at Rome, as elsewhere, and were hardly accounted a crime. To the eternal disgrace of the party of action, as they were termed,—composed of the dregs of the volunteer regiments, whose insubordination in war had proved Austria's best ally, and who had now returned to their dishonoured homes to cause fresh misery in Rome, which became a hotbed of sedition and tumult,—Rossi fell before the stiletto of an assassin. This foul murder was honoured with festivities and illuminations throughout and beyond the limits of the Papal States.

Ten days later, the Pontiff, terrified by the threatening attitude of the multitude, quitted Rome in disguise in the dead of night; Antonelli and the Bavarian Ambassador alone being privy to his purpose. Pius IX found a safe and a hospitable asylum at Gaeta. In this pleasant retreat, free from the anxieties and cares of government, he acquired, it is said, that obesity of person which has since characterized him, and was at leisure to fulminate the anathemas of the Church against the authors of 'the sacrilegious and miserable attempt' to establish a Republican government at Rome.

It was impossible that the Catholic powers of Europe could acquiesce in the permanent establishment of a Republican government in the capital of Roman Catholic Christendom. Its duration was only a question of time, dependent upon the settlement of the rivalry amongst these powers for the honour of reinstating the Pope upon his throne. Austria, anxious to re-establish the relations broken up by the Italian war, was jealous of the claims of France, as the eldest son of the Church, to prop up by her bayonets the tottering power hated by every Italian. Antonelli, consistent through life in his hostility to France, inclined to accept the assistance of Austria, and steadfastly opposed the overtures of the Moderate Liberals in Rome for a reconciliation with the Pope. In vain they urged the possibility of his return to Rome with dignity, and with proper securities against the risk of having again to quit his capital. In vain they pleaded that if the Pope believed it essential to his dignity to return to Rome with a show of force that should strike terror into the hearts of the anarchists, he should seek that assistance from Italy rather than from any foreign power, and that Piedmont was ready, and even forward, to render such service to the Holy See. The Holy Father, the Servant of Servants, the Vicar of the Prince of Peace, replied that 'nothing but *force* would serve to restore effectually his authority, spurned as it had been by a most audacious faction.' And Antonelli was resolved that that force should be, if not Austrian, at least not Italian.

On the 7th of February, 1849, a consistory of cardinals was held at Gaeta, when it was resolved that Piedmont should be struck out of the list of Catholic powers whose aid would prove acceptable to the Pope, and that the armed assistance of Austria, France, Spain, and Naples should be immediately solicited.

The Republicans of France were not entirely devoid of sympathy with their brethren in Rome. They desired that the Pope's restoration should at least be preceded by a manifesto, promising moderation, if not the restoration of a liberal government. Hence arose prolonged and embarrassing negotiations at Gaeta. But the great aim of Louis Napoleon in sanctioning an interference in the affairs of Rome, was to secure the instrumentality of France in the restoration of the Pope, and thus to prevent the recovery by Austria of her former prestige in Italy; and the latter power, however reluctant to yield her hold upon Italy, was fully occupied with Venice and Hungary.

Whilst the Court at Gaeta was wearied with protracted negotiations and diplomatic wranglings, the selfish and unpatriotic squabblings of the vainglorious sectarians who polluted the very air of the

Tuscan cities unexpectedly solved the difficulty, and brought upon Italy the double bane of riveting the hold of Austria upon Tuscany, and opening the way for the French occupation of the Papal States. Leghorn had become the refuge of all the Tuscan adherents of the Republic whose love of tumult inspired them to resist the restoration of the constitutional ruler upon which the state was determined. The wild excesses of these demagogues were more serviceable to the despotic governments than a powerful army. Louis Napoleon, anxious to get into Italy without the danger of lighting up a European war, was now enabled to accomplish his purpose. Tuscany was surrendered to Austria, whilst that power in return allowed France the boast of that share in the Catholic crusade upon which Louis Napoleon had set his heart. The consent of Antonelli was reluctantly accorded; and the ground of his objection is indicated in an anecdote which appears worthy of credence. When intelligence of the sail of the French expedition reached Gaeta, Pius IX, who was at dinner with his royal hosts and some cardinals, filled his glass 'to the safe arrival of our friends.' 'Say rather,' interposed Antonelli, '*of our masters!*'

On the 24th of April information arrived in Rome that the French government had despatched an armament to the Roman States. On the following day General Oudinot disembarked his troops at Civita Vecchia. French intervention, long threatened, had now become an accomplished fact, and the Italians soon learned the true objects of that expedition which M. Drouyn de Lhuys had affirmed, and Oudinot had reiterated, was projected in the interests of Italy, to facilitate a reconciliation with the Pontiff, the only hope to the Romans of avoiding an unconditional restoration.

I cannot enter here into the story of the two months' siege of Rome, which I hope to narrate in detail hereafter. On the night of the 29th of June, 1849, the French troops entered Rome, and ten months later, April the 12th, 1850, Pius IX re-entered his capital, escorted by a body of French troops under Baraguay d'Hilliers and a squadron of Neapolitan cavalry. Flowers were strewn in the pathway of the Pontiff; banners waved over his head; but the accents of triumph were uttered in a foreign tongue. The city wore a look of sullen discontent, but the military at least performed their allotted part with an enthusiasm which was well calculated to inspire dismay in the breasts of Republican plotters. An attempt to fire the Quirinal on the very night of the Pope's entry would suggest to any mind, but that of Mr. Cochrane, that the ecclesiastical government which was thrust upon the Romans at the point of French bayonets was as hateful to the people as when, eighteen months earlier, they had celebrated with wild enthusiasm the flight of the Pontiff whose rule was abhorred, and whose possession of a temporal principality they believed to be hurtful to the interests of religion, and fatal to the freedom and prosperity of Italy.

With the process by which the restoration of the Pontifical government was established we are not here concerned. France had recovered her lost hold upon Italy, her supremacy at Rome. The Popedom had become that which the first Napoleon had designed to make it—an institution, not indeed French and Imperial, but dependent for its existence upon the support of French bayonets; the least intimation or rumour of the withdrawal of which sends at once dismay into the inmost recesses of the Vatican, and a thrill of exultant hope through Italy.

The history of the transformation of the little State of Piedmont into the Kingdom of Italy is too familiar to require even a passing notice. It is well known that the people of Central and Southern Italy had no special love for Piedmont, but the aspiration after Italian unity was universal, and overbore every obstacle which local jealousies interposed. The Emperor Napoleon's scheme for a kingdom of Central Italy, though appealing to the municipal jealousies which have so long proved the source of weakness and division to Italy, could not withstand the universal passion. However bitter the disappointment throughout Italy at the supposed treachery of Napoleon in concluding the inglorious peace of Villa Franca, Italians did not forget the appeal made to their patriotism in the Emperor's proclamation when the glorious victory of Magenta had rescued Milan from the Croats. That proclamation concluded with these words: 'Animated by the sacred fire of patriotism, be soldiers to-day, that to-morrow you may become *the free citizens of a great country!*' The appeal was made to the Italian troops, but it awakened a responsive echo in every Italian heart. The transfer of the crown of Lombardy from Francis Joseph to Victor Emanuel; the union of Tuscany with Piedmont, after the second flight of her Grand Duke; the brilliant campaign of Garibaldi in Sicily; the complete success of the revolution, undertaken and accomplished against the will of the King and of Cavour; the yet more brilliant success of the quondam-Republican general's attack upon Naples in the teeth of the remonstrances of Louis Napoleon and of his sovereign, whom he desired to make the unfettered monarch of a free and united Italy, only intensified the longing of the populations of the States of the Church to become participants in the common joy of Italy.

Louis Napoleon was strongly opposed to the advance of the Piedmontese army beyond the Papal frontiers. His opposition, however, gave way when it became apparent that the invincible Garibaldi, with his volunteers, would respect no Royal, much less Imperial decrees; that the question of the invasion of the Papal States was already decided, and that which alone admitted of solution was, whether the invasion should be that of Napoleon's ally or of the army of the revolution. 'The invasion of the Papal States by a Sardinian army,' says Mr. Dicey[1], 'was the master-stroke of Cavour's political genius. It had become imperatively necessary to stop Garibaldi's progress to restore Sardinia to the position of leader of the Italian revolution.' The advance of Garibaldi to Rome would have added greatly to the embarrassments of Napoleon's position, and not less so to that of Victor Emanuel. 'We are forced to act,' Cavour wrote to Baron Talleyrand on the 10th of September, 1860. 'If we are not at Cattolica before Garibaldi we are lost; the revolution will invade Central Italy.' On the 29th of September Ancona was captured; and, the heart of Italy united to the new Italian kingdom, Garibaldi, addressing the population of Naples from the balcony of the palace, could say, 'All the provinces enslaved by the Pope are free!'

[1] 'Life of Cavour.'

There is something touching in the noble patriotism which—unhurt by the opprobrium cast upon him by diplomatists, and without a trace of jealousy that the honour of effecting this liberation had been snatched from his hands—cordially rejoiced in the issue, careless as to who were the instruments of its accomplishment, and had only words of congratulation and eulogy for his 'brethren of the Italian army.' 'The valiant soldiers of the North,' he said, 'have passed the frontier and are on Neapolitan soil. Soon we shall have the good fortune to clasp their victorious hands.'

The stereotyped '*non possumus*' of Pius IX could not avert that catastrophe of the Papacy which made Italy radiant with joy—the formal annexation of the States of the Church to the Italian kingdom. Italy was one, and the heart of the nation sent up a triumphant shout of gratitude to heaven for the deliverance it had granted them. It was impossible but that the fond dreams of an exultant and impulsive people should lead them to expect, and even demand, the withdrawal of the French troops from Rome, as the last and necessary act in the drama of liberation. The calamity of Aspromonte was necessary to dissipate these illusions.

Pius IX has never recognized the alienation of those States which now constitute a part of the kingdom of Italy, and still pleases himself with an annual anathema of the 'Sub-Alpine king.' But the obsolete and perfunctory *non possumus* of an Italian priest is powerless to arrest the progress of events—the march of Italian unity. The September Convention must prove equally futile. Without Rome, unity is for ever menaced, liberty jeopardized, and constitutional government proclaimed incapable for the task of working out Italy's

o

regeneration. 'To the common Italian mind,' said Cavour, 'the idea of Italy was inseparable from that of Rome. An Italy of which Rome was not the capital would be no Italy for the Italian people. *For the existence, then, of a national Italian people,* the possession of Rome as a capital was *an essential condition.*'

But are the people of Rome hostile to the government of the Pope? Are they for Italy, or for Pius IX? It is the question of questions for Italy. That to a certain extent the benign and good-natured Pontiff has recovered the popularity which he enjoyed before his great act of treason to Italy, is no doubt true. But what does this imply? Most assuredly not the acquiescence of the Romans in the perpetuation of Italy's humiliation, or in the priestly government to which they are subject. The bourgeoisie are benefited by the maintenance of the Papal court at Rome[1], and the appearance of the Pope in public is attended with acclamation; but his government is entirely wanting in all the attributes of popularity. A feeling of insecurity pervades all classes. Full well does a Roman know that a careless word may jeopardize his liberty, and that the overcrowded state of the prisons affords him no hope of an unwillingly accorded immunity. The characteristic reply of Antonelli to the official who

---

[1] Such, at least, is the prevailing opinion. But it is impossible to ignore the fact that immense relief would be afforded to the citizens by such a diminution of the number of the priesthood as would inevitably result from the acquisition of Rome as the capital of Italy. In a population of 170,000, no less than 10,000 human drones are to-day supported out of the common funds. 'Every sixteen lay citizens—men, women, and children—support out of their labour a priest between them.'—Dicey's 'Rome in 1860.'

represented to him this difficulty,—'Well, we have the catacombs left,'—has dissipated any hope based upon such a foundation. It is essential to the liberty and even to the life of a Roman to be on good terms with his *curé*, who is imbued with the spirit of priestly pretension to hold absolute sway over the intellect and life of every individual. The rigours of an ecclesiastical government are reserved for the intelligent—for the man who reads and thinks, and deports himself as a man; especially for such as presume to allow their speculations to touch the sacred domain of politics. But politics is the absorbing passion of the Roman. He thus finds himself at war with a government between which and himself there can be no sympathy.

A temporal government in the hands of ecclesiastics cannot be liberal, while its despotism is so petty as to expose it to contempt, so exacting as to constitute it an object of hatred and fear. The Pontifical sovereignty is an antiquarian relic of no mean interest, and in the ages that are gone, and with which have perished systems as effete as itself, it has played a conspicuous and important part in the drama of the world's history. Its vitality has survived its use. Its continued existence is only pernicious and, its chief advocates being witness, is incompatible with liberty and with Italian unity. At the accession of Pius IX the Pontifical sovereignty was tolerated by a people who had not then been aroused by the stirring events of his Pontificate, and who, in their degradation, preferred the profits accruing to the guardians of a museum to the noble but grave responsibilities of a free nation. Now all Italy re-echoes the words which Napoleon haughtily addressed to Pius VII, 'The ancient Romans conquered the world by their arms; the Popes have taken advantage of the ignorance of nations, and Rome still holds the sceptre and the censer. But formerly there was, at any rate, political talent and intelligence, but now there is nothing but ignorance, inactivity, and folly.'

The twenty years' struggle which the Papacy, as a temporal power, has waged with revolution, has proclaimed its defeat, and its inability under a mild and benevolent ruler to produce those fruits of love and obedience, of contentedness and prosperity, which it is the incumbent duty of a government to secure to the governed. It has created only mistrust and bitterness, and has proved that 'neither can cannon destroy ideas, nor police and spies eradicate opinions[1].' Every tittle of historical evidence bearing on the subject proves the temporal dominion of the Papacy destructive of its spiritual interests. Those who affirm that the maintenance of the temporal sovereignty is essential to the dignity of the Holy See, and to the interests of Catholic Europe, would do well to recall the words of Italy's greatest bard—

> 'Say thou henceforward that the Church of Rome,
> Confounding in itself two governments,
> Falls in the mire and soils itself and burden[2].'

To affirm the essential union of the two powers it is necessary to ignore the fact that for seven centuries of the Papacy the temporal power, however coveted, eluded the grasp of the Pontiffs, and that until the close of the twelfth century, when Innocent III obtained from the Emperor a formal recognition of his

---

[1] Hemans' 'Catholic Italy.'
[2] Dante, 'Purgatorio,' xvi. 127–9.

claims to territorial sovereignty, the Popes could not be said to reign. They were the nominees of the German Emperors, who levied tribute to the Imperial exchequer, and whose effigy was stamped upon the Roman coinage. Nor when the Popes seized upon the Imperial jurisdiction was it from any alleged concern for the interests of Christendom, but simply the gratification of a long-cherished political ambition, which the disorders of the age and the weakness of the Imperial power placed within their reach. The interests of Catholic Europe are now much what they were in the twelfth century, and the attempt to justify the union of the two powers on any such theory is one of those curiosities of ignorance which provoke a smile.

CHAPTER XII.

The French occupation of Rome has but confirmed the evils of a government which was, and will ever remain, powerless to prolong its own existence. It has at the same time thrown vexatious hindrances in the way of the consolidation of that union after which Italy aspires, and has robbed France of the gratitude of a powerful and impassioned nation—her natural ally—numbering 24,000,000 souls. Italy is charged with ingratitude towards the man who made her a nation; but granting that French arms won Lombardy from the Croats, Italians may well disavow all pretence of gratitude for the attempted subversion of their country's destiny, in order to the fulfilment of the Napoleonic dream of an Italian federation, so arranged as to convert the Holy See into a French bishopric. In spite of Papal denunciations and French rebuffs, the cry, Italia una! still rises above the din of diplomatic wrangling; and hatred of the French ruler who, unthanked by the Pope and execrated by the nation, persists in propping up the tottering power of Rome, is the universal sentiment of Italy.

France still defends against all comers the temporal power of the Roman Pontiff, which she re-established; but the day that her protection is withdrawn the Pontifical sovereignty will expire. That this will favour the spiritual interests of the Papacy, it is impossible to question. It was when the Roman Church had her spiritual interests alone to look after, that she placed those interests always in the ascendant, and established her supremacy throughout Europe. As the things of earth yield their present precedence over the things of heaven, the spiritual power of the Papacy, now shaken to its foundations, will doubtless acquire new vitality. The religion of Rome, now tolerated in the land of its birth, and of its most fanatical ascendency, will recover the hold which it is losing upon the hearts and consciences of men; and the Papacy may again enjoy that dignified calm which centuries of vain ambition, and of undignified effort to maintain a false position by the basest subserviency to France or Austria, have forfeited. Rome must learn the lesson, that if the temporal prerogatives to which she so tenaciously clings cannot make, they most assuredly can destroy a Church; whilst that which alone can truly establish or render it durable against all the attacks of time, or of earthly foes, is the Truth which that Church contains, its fidelity to that truth, and its zeal in propagating it in all its native purity.

All history testifies to the fact that the temporal sovereignty of the Pope makes him in reality the most dependent man in Europe. Out of limited resources he is compelled to maintain the dignity of a sovereignty which the world is expected to recognize as the most august in the universe! He is thus constrained to fall back upon foreign armaments for the police of his territory, and at once to insult the national sentiment, and to place the spiritual no less than the temporal power which he wields, in the hands of a foreign potentate. Meanwhile, the increase of the Papal troops, the cannon which are being accumulated in Rome, and the fortifications that are constructed out of all proportion to financial means and to political necessities, and in direct contravention of the September Convention, indicate an intention on the part of the Pontifical government of making due preparation for contingencies that are foreseen, but with which the power which we instinctively feel to be the most glaring political solecism of the nineteenth century, will assuredly be powerless to cope. Coincident with this we have recently witnessed the assembling of a so-called Œcumenical Council, convened to define the dogma of the personal infallibility of the Roman Pontiff; in other words, to declare him the privileged representative of the Divine will, of a nature superior to our common humanity, possessed of truth absolute and complete.

The revival of these inordinate pretensions of the Papacy will but bring new conviction to the minds of Italians of the incompatibility of the temporal and spiritual powers, and of the tremendous peril to Italy involved in the recognition of their union in the person of a priest enthroned in the Vatican,—the puppet of a foreign and, of necessity, hostile power.

Sooner or later this fanatical and tenacious grasp of the temporal power must condemn the Papacy to the humiliations and calamities which it suffered at the hands of the first Napoleon. It renders it at once indispensable and impossible that the supreme head of the Church should observe strict neutrality in those political complications, into which he cannot throw himself without imperilling his spiritual authority, and abandoning the claim to a universal charity, covering with its wings the whole of Christendom. But as a temporal prince the Roman Pontiff cannot, even with his present shred of territory, escape the contingencies and responsibilities of his position. As in A.D. 1806, it will again prove the vulnerable point which will endanger the very existence of the Papacy in its ancient seat. Napoleon, always ready to adapt his arguments to the exigencies of his political ambition, thus aptly expressed the radical defect of the Papal pretensions:— 'Jesus Christ, born of the blood of David, never would be king. For centuries the founders of our religion were never kings. There is not a single doctor or faithful historian who has not admitted that temporal power has been fatal to religion. The Pope, as head of Christianity, ought to have an equal influence all over the world; nevertheless this influence ought to vary according to the political circumstances of States. No personal interest ought to impede spiritual affairs; and yet how could it be otherwise when the interests of the Pope as sovereign and those of the Pope as pontiff are contrary? *"My kingdom is not of this world,"* said Jesus Christ, and by this doctrine he for ever condemned the mixture of religious interests with worldly affections.' The Emperor's reasoning was admirable! But it was the possession of a temporal sovereignty which presently placed Pius VII in the power of Napoleon, who was not slow to discover new arguments, sufficiently convincing for his purpose, showing the necessity for its being respected.

That Pius IX and his ministers will not read the plain lessons of history furnishes only a new illustration of the familiar proverb, '*Quem Deus vult perdere prius dementat.*' The famous and emphatic 'never' of M. Rouher may but veil the intentions of his Imperial master. 'Italy shall *never* go to Rome;' the Garibaldians 'never' insult the throne of the holy Father. So said the now discredited minister of Napoleon III. The Pope, then, *is* deposed, and France rules in Rome as Austria ruled in '48. It is not the Italians who depose him of the authority which rests exclusively upon French chassepots. The Italians wish but to regulate, in conformity with the interests of a great nation and of advancing civilization, a deposition already accomplished; and maintain with reason that the Pope can never be more subject to foreign pressure than he is at this moment[1]. Public indignation is excited in France at the clerical policy of Rome, and however determined the Emperor or his quondam minister may be that the Revolution shall not triumph, the former at least, whilst yielding to popular pressure at home, is not likely permanently to place himself in conflict with all that is intelligent and living in Europe, all that is earnest and true in France, by constituting her the guard and bailiff of a Pope who answers his advice with haughty surprise, and maintains towards him an attitude of studied neglect.

It may be that the Emperor is willing to let the court of Rome so compromise itself towards Italy, and discredit itself before Europe, as to hasten the termination of an intervention which has been the cause of much embarrassment, and that the pretentious assumptions and fanatical decrees of the so-called Œcumenical Council may herald the fulfilment, in regard to the Papacy itself, of the prediction of Holy Writ, 'A stone was cut out *without hands,* which smote the image upon

---

[1] See Taine's 'Italy—Naples and Rome.'

his feet that were of iron and clay, and brake them to pieces.'

But it must be acknowledged that the signs of the times point in quite another direction. Every attempt which has been made to reconcile Rome with modern progress, whether in religion, in politics, or in science, has encountered the uncompromising hostility of the pretentious theocracy which recognizes no note of harmony, no point of agreement, between modern civilization and historic Christianity. The following travesty of Liberalism appeared in a recent issue of the *Civiltà Cattolica*, which the Pope, by special decree, has appointed official journal to the Church:—'As the Church teaches that God created man, the Liberals will not believe it, and maintain they descend from apes. They have chosen that animal for their progenitor because Satan, the first conspirator, the first revolutionary, and the first Liberal that ever lived, was the ape of the Deity. Further, they have observed that, as the ape is notoriously impudent, malicious, and above all prone to theft, he possesses the same qualities as themselves. The Liberals are the apes of the Church and of God, and follow in that the example of the devil, their lord and master. From this come their hatred and animosity to the Church. Does the Pope summon an Œcumenical Council at Rome? The Liberals propose at Naples an assembly of free-thinkers. In short, Liberalism is only a grand piece of aping.' Whilst Liberalism is thus traduced, science is proscribed as the insurrection of godless intellect against the Bible, and constitutional government as the last lure of Satan whereby nations are tempted to their ruin. And so great, even in its senility, is the influence of the Papal See in the Roman Catholic world, that it appears strengthened rather than jeopardized by its intolerant presumption, never more dangerous than when the central power is weak, nor more aggressive than when it has lost all strength but in the credulity and infatuation of zealots. To a dreamy imagination, whether that of a marquis, a curate, or a sentimental belle, the mysticism of Rome offers a natural aliment; her intolerance and presumption are but evidences of her Divine authority. It is hardly surprising that, even in Protestant communities, dreamy and restless spirits occasionally 'take refuge from their own scepticism in the bosom of a Church which pretends to infallibility, and, after questioning the existence of a Deity, bring themselves to worship a wafer [1].' This principle of authority once admitted, the power of the Church can be jeopardized by no presumptions, however intolerant and absurd. Hence we see the finest intellects, the learned and most truly honest divines of the Roman Church, however lively and often painful the interest with which they receive every novelty coming from Rome, take meekly the rebuke which their liberal tendencies draw down, and with humble submission to Mother Church, continue to throw their energies into the Papal cause. A signal illustration of this phenomenon is furnished in the painful position of an English divine—one of the brightest ornaments of the Roman Catholic Church in these or any other realms. Dr. Newman, a theologian as conspicuous for refinement of taste as for genius and learning, reluctantly avows that he deprecates the affirmation of Papal Infallibility and the measures by which some persons

[1] Lord Macaulay.

are advocating its definition. But, however bitter the struggle, Dr. Newman will humble himself, and prostrate his reason before the one authority which cannot err. The *Tablet* comes to his rescue with the casuistry, in which it is so great an adept, but which his refined taste and honest mind will assuredly spurn, and suggests that the learned Doctor's disapproval of *some* persons, and *some* measures, does not include *any* mode of soliciting the definition! Simultaneously we have the following avowal of the Editor of the *Literarische Handweiser* of Munster, an influential literary organ of Germany. A formal profession of belief in the dogma of Infallibility is followed by a distinct enunciation of *the inopportuneness of the definition*. 'But,' he adds, 'if the Council should proclaim the dogma, I shall renounce immediately, *and regret as an error*, my opinion of its inopportuneness.'

The Church of Rome, never more haughty than when in the lowest depths of humiliation, grows stronger and wins heartier homage, as its head is most bent on crossing the currents of thought and of life which flow most strongly. The only alternative of the malcontents is to start a schism, with the moral certainty that they would not be followed or supported by their flocks who, whether in France, Italy, Germany, or Spain, know little, and care less, as to what may or must be believed, and, trained in the school of Romanism, regard religion in the light of an undertaking to accept whatever may be prescribed by the head of the Church. 'Catholicism,' it has been said, 'is less a doctrine than a resolution, or, if you like the term better, an attempt to believe; the Catholics of the present age are much less followers of a fixed creed than believers in a general sense, and you find many of them rather candidly inclined to think that the more they succeed in believing, the more Catholic they are.'

The fact is incontrovertible that the Papacy, under Pius IX, has recovered the hold upon Catholic Christendom which, at his accession, was purely theoretical; and that no Pope has for three centuries been regarded with an affection and interest so great as the present Pontiff commands. It is foreign to my purpose to attempt, in this place, any exhaustive enquiry into the reasons which may be held to explain this phenomena. I can but glance at some of those which lie upon the surface. It has been said that we are witnessing the last leap of the flickering flame before it dies. It may be so; at least it is not wise for the impartial observer to discard an opinion so strongly corroborated by facts; and pre-eminently by the sensational expedient by which the holy Father now seeks to galvanize an effete system into spasmodic and artificial life—simply because it has been propounded in former crises which the Papacy has survived. Passing by the fact that modern Romanism presents a charming quietism, the fit asylum for the morbid, and the natural refuge of a shallow sentimentalism, we readily detect, in more transient causes, one element at least of the present power of the Papacy. As the sufferings of Pius VII aroused the sympathy of entire Christendom, and caused Napoleon to tremble for its effects, so the sufferings of Pius IX, and the loss of his temporal dominions, have awakened an almost universal sympathy and respect, which his personal character has enhanced; thus consolidating the influence of the Papacy in a far larger degree than can be effected by the semi-comic spectacle of an Œcumenical Council.

In the sympathy thus extended to the Pontiff,
> 'The tears most sacred, shed for others' pain,'

it is forgotten that the cry for freedom, so long vainly uttered by three million oppressed Italians—raised to the pitch of frenzy as they witnessed the noble effects upon their compatriots in Piedmont of that freedom which they coveted for themselves, and at length changed into a shout of triumph—was essentially *a cry of justice*. Pius IX may hurl his annual anathemas at the head of the 'King of Sardinia,' but in no sense can Victor Emanuel be called the spoliator of the Church. His part has been but to assist these down-trodden and unwilling subjects of the Pope to *reclaim* the rights of which the Church had despoiled them, and which, with purblind fanaticism, it still seeks to reassume.

Of the many illustrations which crowd upon us of the growing popularity of the Pontiff, perhaps the most singular is the proposal, of which we have recently heard, to confer upon him the title of 'Great;' a distinction shared by two only of his 256 predecessors. The past year, with a jubilee at its commencement, and an Œcumenical Council at its close—the most memorable in his long Pontificate—has witnessed the growth of Papal assumptions in a degree which severely tests the toleration of Christendom. Excited by the homage offered to him, the condition of mind into which the Pope has worked himself differs only from the mental state of visionaries like St. Francis, in that the language which expresses it is that of a later era; and although the title 'Pius the Great' can hardly be regarded as due to his acts, his courage, or even his virtues, the present occasion will probably be seized for surrounding his name and his Pontificate with a lustre which may dazzle the vulgar, but to which the nineteenth century will assuredly not recognize his claim.

The pretensions of the Papacy have ever been the source of its decadence; and so, in the interests of religion and of freedom, we must hope that it will be again. Pius IX has already successfully accomplished the unprecedented attempt to enunciate a new dogma on his own unaided responsibility, after having simply consulted the dispersed members of the Episcopacy. It is not then surprising that he has proceeded to convene a General Council, charged, if semi-official reports speak truly, to define dogmas the acceptance of which would plunge Europe into the darkness of the fourteenth century, and cause the Papacy itself to be execrated by every Catholic power.

Pius IX believes that he has a mission to replace the obnoxious principles of the Revolution of A.D. 1789 by those of the Syllabus which simply proclaim a pure theocracy antagonistic to, and destructive of, the civil and municipal law, and would bind Europe once more to accept the absolute rule of the priest. The Council is expected to pronounce the Syllabus canon law. 'The guidance of the Holy See,' Pius IX tells us, 'is the brief and compendious rule whereby we may persevere in the profession of Catholic truth.' In his Encyclical addressed, on the occasion of his exaltation to the Pontifical throne, to the bishops of the universal Church (November 9, A.D. 1846), we read, 'Hence it clearly appears how great is the error of those who, abusing reason, and dealing with the oracles of God as if they were a human work, rashly presume to explain and interpret them according to their own judgment, although God himself has established *a living authority* to declare the true and legitimate sense of His Divine revelation, to confirm it securely, and to terminate *by an infallible judgment* all controversies of faith and morals; lest the faithful, being circumvented by error, should be carried away by every wind of doctrine through the wickedness of men. Which living and INFALLIBLE authority exists only in that Church which was built by Christ our Lord upon Peter, the Head of the whole Church, the Prince and Pastor whose faith he promised should never fail, having always, without interruption, its Pontiffs deriving their origin from the same Peter, placed in his chair, and both heirs and defenders of the same doctrine, dignity, honour, and power. And since where Peter is, there is the Church, and Peter speaks by the Roman Pontiff. . . . it is evident that the Divine oracles are to be received in that sense which this Roman Chair of the Blessed Peter held and holds. . . . We, therefore, who, by the inscrutable judgment of God, are placed *in this chair of truth* earnestly exhort, &c.'

In the Encyclical to the Bishops of Italy, on the 8th December, A.D. 1849, Pius IX thus expresses himself:— 'Let your faithful people remember that here, in this See,' lives and presides in his successor, Peter the Prince of the Apostles, whose dignity is not removed even from one who is unworthy to be his heir. Let them call to mind that Christ our Lord established the foundation of his Church *in this invincible chair of Peter.* . . . Hence it follows that it is by communion with, and obedience to the Roman Pontiff, that the nations *have a brief and compendious rule by which they may persevere in the profession of Catholic truth.'*

Nothing can be clearer than the teaching conveyed

in these words. The only feeling of surprise which they awaken is, that the Pope, who thus claimed by anticipation all the prerogatives which the Council in its wildest flights could confer upon him, should have thought it worth while to encounter the risks inseparable from its convocation.

'It might have been supposed,' says Dean Milman, ' that nowhere would Christianity appear in such commanding majesty as in a Council, which should gather from all quarters of the world the most eminent prelates and the most distinguished clergy; that a lofty and serene piety would govern all their proceedings; profound and dispassionate investigation exhaust every subject; human passions and interests would stand rebuked before that awful assembly; the sense of their own dignity as well as the desire of impressing their brethren with the solemnity and earnestness of their belief, would at least exclude all intemperance of manner and language. Mutual awe and mutual emulation in Christian excellence would repress, even in the most violent, all un-Christian violence; their conclusions would be grave, mature, harmonious, for, if not harmonious, the confuted party would hardly acquiesce in the wisdom of their decrees; even their condemnations would be so tempered with charity as gradually to win back the wanderer to the still open fold, rather than drive him, prescribed and branded, into inflexible and irreconcilable schism. History shows the melancholy reverse. Nowhere is Christianity less attractive, and, if we look to the ordinary tone and character of the proceedings, less authoritative, than in the Councils of the Church. It is in general a fierce collision of two rival factions, neither of which will yield, each of which is solemnly pledged against conviction. Intrigue, injustice, violence, decisions on authority of a turbulent majority, decisions by wild acclamations rather than after sober inquiry, detract from the reverence and impugn the judgments, at least of the later Councils. The close is almost invariably a terrible anathema, in which it is impossible not to discern the tones of human hatred, of arrogant triumph, of rejoicing at the damnation imprecated against the humiliated adversary[1].'

[1] ' History of Latin Christianity.'

CHAPTER XIII.

None but the man who, twenty-four years ago, flattered himself that he could organize St. Peter's Patrimony into a Constitutional State, could now have persuaded himself that it was for the Pope's interest to summon an Œcumenical Council. This bold act of the Pontiff suggests a train of reflections upon some of which a few remarks may be appropriate. I select the following:—The constitution of the so-called Œcumenical Council. The position, in relation to it, assumed by the lay governments of Europe. The probable nature and bearings of some of its decisions.

I dismiss, as improbable, the vague rumours with which the special correspondents of certain newspapers have made us familiar, to the effect that the perplexing questions which are pressing for solution will necessitate an early and indefinite prorogation, and that the last actual session of the Council will be held before Easter. History furnishes no precedent for a course so completely at variance with the traditions of the Roman See, which never forgoes a claim she has once put forward; whilst the ambition of the Pontiff, the unyielding obstinacy of 'that insolent and aggressive faction,' who have elicited the protest of Dr. Newman against the definition of the Dogma of Infallibility, and the actual majority of the Fathers, certain now, but at the least doubtful in the future, who may be relied upon for obsequious obedience, are guarantees that whilst so many good things are upon the anvil, Pius IX will strike hard and long.

The question of the constitution of the Council is one of considerable interest and importance. By an Œcumenical Council we understand a Council representing the whole of Christendom, and preserving, in harmony with the law of progress, the evidences of organic continuity with the great Councils of antiquity to which by common consent the title of 'Œcumenical' has been accorded. The first thing which strikes us is the revolutionary character of a Council representing neither the governments of Roman Catholic countries, nor the various branches of the Christian Church separated from the communion of Rome,—devoid, therefore, of all organic continuity with those which have preceded it. With that utter disregard of historical facts which has marked every encroachment of the Church of Rome, it is now contended by high dignitaries of the Church that 'the Pope alone enjoys the right of convening an Œcumenical Council.' None know better than the legislators of the Roman Church the value of a bold assertion in entangling the understanding and perverting the judgment. Presuming then to discard Archbishop Manning's dictum, that 'to appeal to history is both a heresy and a treason,' let us bring this unblushing assertion of the Bishop of Orleans to the test of historical fact,—remembering that it is the pivot upon which hangs the fulfilment of those conditions which constitute the validity of the Council now assembled at Rome.

The first Councils of which we have any authentic record were brought together for the settlement of the paschal question, at the close of the second century.

But neither these, nor the more systematic Provincial Synods of the third century, have any claim to Œcumenicity. No one has claimed for them any inherent authority binding upon the conscience of Christendom. Their convocation was regarded in the light of expediency rather than as a matter of right and duty [1].

The fourth century witnessed the rise of General Councils and the firm establishment of the principle that their decisions were infallible. These Councils *were convened and presided over by the Emperor* (without any consultation with the Bishop of Rome); or, in his absence, by a Commissioner or Patriarch chosen by himself irrespective of rank; nor was any Bishop of Rome selected for this distinction prior to the Council of Chalcedon, A.D. 451. From this period one hundred and thirty-six years elapsed before any Roman Bishop presumed to claim the privilege in right of his See. It is evident that no such priority amongst the Apostles was claimed by St. Peter, inasmuch as not he, but St. James, presided at the Council in Jerusalem. The Councils were attended by Imperial Commissioners whose duty it was to maintain discipline, and regulate the whole business *according to the will of the Emperor*. The Œcumenicity, and consequently the dogmatic authority, of these Councils depended on the co-equal concurrence of the Pope and the Episcopate.

Glancing briefly at the Seven General Councils which preceded the disintegration of the Roman Empire, we find that the first—that of Nicea, A.D. 325 [2]—*was summoned by the Imperial mandate*, whilst the

---

[1] Riddle's 'History of the Papacy,' vol. i. p. 101.

[2] I have been furnished with the following mnemonic doggrel,

presence of the Emperor gave its chief weight and dignity to the assembly. It was the first time that an Œcumenical Council had been possible, for never until now had the East and West been united under a sovereign professing the Christian faith. The mandate for the convocation of the Council necessarily emanated from the Emperor, who alone possessed the requisite authority; and the principle of placing these assemblies under the control of the State was firmly established.

The appearance of Constantine in the Hall of Council was welcomed by the bishops as an unprecedented condescension, the whole assembly rising to do him honour as he advanced to the golden seat prepared for him. In the traditional pictures in the convent of Mount Athos, the Sacred Dove hovers over the head, not of the bishops but of the Emperor[1]. The Emperor was assiduous in his attendance at the meetings of the Council which were prolonged over a period of two months. Whilst abstaining from direct partici-

---

with which Continental Catholics recall the previous Councils of the Church.

Ni—Co—E—
Chal—Co—Co—
Ni—Co—La—
La—La—La—
Lu—Lu—Vi—
Pi—Con—Ba—
Flo—La—Tri.

These syllables stand for Nice, Constantinople, Ephesus, Chalcedon; then Constantinople twice; Nice again, Constantinople again, Lateran four times; Lyons—that is, Lugdunum—twice; Vienne, Pisa, Constance, Bâle, Florence, Lateran, and Trente (Tridentinum).

[1] See Article on the Œcumenical Council. 'Edinburgh Review,' October, 1869.

pation in the acrimonious metaphysical discussions, he listened with patience, softening asperities by a judicious exercise of his authority, countenancing those whose language tended to peace and union, and conversing familiarly, in the best Greek he could command, with the different prelates [1]. He thus contrived to exercise a most important control over the theological conclusions at which the Council ultimately arrived, and was regarded as the highest judge in all causes. The Bishops of Rome 'considered it a distinction to be allowed to plead for themselves before his Council, after the example of St. Paul [2].'

The second Œcumenical Council (the first of Constantinople), A.D. 381, *was summoned, controlled, and eventually dismissed by the Emperor* Theodosius. This Council, as is well known, was convened for the re-establishment of Trinitarianism as the doctrine of the East; and although the bishops, in the following year, sent an account of their proceedings to the Western bishops assembled at Rome, it was to solicit their co-operation in carrying their decrees into effect, not at all as recognizing any necessity for their ratification by the Bishop of Rome [3].

The third Œcumenical Council assembled at Ephesus, after the lapse of half-a-century, A.D. 431; and twenty years thereafter, A.D. 451, its successor met at Chalcedon, In the former, *summoned by the Imperial mandate*, the Count of the Imperial Domestics was present throughout, and exercised his rightful prerogatives; whilst it is clear that the Bishop of Rome claimed no right of precedence, as he sent his legates to the Council,

---

[1] Milman's 'Latin Christianity,' vol. i.
[2] Robertson's 'History of the Christian Church,' vol. i.
[3] Riddle's 'History of the Papacy.'

knowing well that the Emperor had delegated the Bishop of Alexandria to preside. In the latter, although the Bishop of Rome was represented by two legates, *the Emperor Marcian presided*, and reserved to himself the right of ratifying its decrees. It is worthy of notice that the formulary of faith finally adopted by this Council *was brought forward by the Imperial Commissioners* [1].

After the lapse of 240 years *Justinian II summoned at Constantinople* the Council which has been denominated the Quinisext—its object being to complete the acts of the fifth and sixth Councils previously held. The theological opinions promulgated in the Canons of this Council at the instigation of the Emperor and of Theodora were highly offensive to the Church of Rome; the timid Pontiff welcoming the sudden death which relieved him from the imperious commands to receive the Decrees of the Quinisextine Council [2].

The lapse of another century brings us to the seventh and last truly Œcumenical Council of the Church—the second of Nice, A.D. 787; if indeed this Council, whose decrees were not received in the West [3], can be rightly considered Œcumenical. *Summoned by the Empress* Irene to decide the great question of image worship, the decrees of this Council bear the impress of the ambitious mind, deeply tinged with superstition, of the crafty but omnipotent woman who, by the restoration of image worship, thought to secure the blessing of the Virgin and the saints, whom she thus honoured, upon her schemes of power.

Up to this period, then, the right of assembling General Councils was recognized AS BELONGING TO THE

---

[1] Milman's 'Latin Christianity,' vol. i.   [2] Ibid.
[3] Riddle's 'History of the Papacy,' vol. i. p. 326.

EMPERORS ALONE, and to them, or to their envoys, were assigned the first places of dignity in the Council chamber. The right of the Popes came in gradually, and, like most of the Papal usurpations, was supported by supposititious credentials; but from first to last every Council claiming to be Œcumenical, has at least contained within itself the representatives of the secular governments. At the third Council of Constantinople, and the four Lateran Councils, *the sovereigns of Europe were represented by their ambassadors*, whilst at the former the Emperor took a prominent part in the discussions.

The Council of Lyons, A.D. 1245, witnessed the discomfiture of the great Innocent at the hands of the intrepid Thaddeus of Suessa, the principal Proctor of the Emperor who, with calm dauntlessness, unmasked the insincerity of the Pope, and forced upon him that fourteen days' adjournment of the Council which, but for the pusillanimity of his master, might have averted the bitter struggle between Pope and Emperor—that dire fatality which thereafter hung over the house of Hohenstaufen, and the implacable hatred of the Papal See, extinguished only in the blood of its last representative on the scaffold at Naples.

The Council of Constance, A.D. 1414, was once more *summoned by Imperial edict*, and presided over in person by the Emperor Sigismund; whilst at those of Pisa, Basle, and Trent, the *presence and active influence of the Emperor and the ambassadors* is likewise a matter of history.

In the face of these historical facts it is now gravely asserted that the Roman Pontiff alone has the ancient and indefeasible right to summon a General Council! Not only without concert with a single European sovereign, but in spite of such warnings as the attitude of hostility assumed by the lay governments; the defection of the intellect of Roman Catholic Christendom, as indicated by the cautious but significant protest of the German prelates assembled at Fulda, who declared that 'a General Council never can and never will proclaim new doctrines;' the strong remonstrance, echoed back almost from the grave, by that fervent Catholic and distinguished patriot and statesman, the late Count Montalembert, expressing his adhesion 'to the manly and Christian' manifestations of the liberal Catholics of Germany, as 'a ray of light shining in the night;' the hardly less significant letter of Father Hyacinthe to the General of his Order, announcing his retirement from it in consequence of the censures of the Vatican,—Pius IX has presumed to convoke, in his own palace, an assembly in which no lay representative has place or voice, and to insult the intelligence of Christendom by denominating it an ŒCUMENICAL COUNCIL!

An essential condition of the Œcumenicity of a Council is that *it shall embrace all sections of the Christian Church*. The Œcumenicity of the important Council of Sardica, A.D. 433, is disallowed on the express ground of the secession of the Eastern bishops. The Œcumenicity of the first Council of the Lateran has similarly been challenged on the ground of the imperfect representation of the Oriental thrones. The Greeks, contending that the representatives of their communion at the Council of A.D. 869 were impostors, with forged credentials [1], to this day reckon the Synod of Constantinople, A.D. 879, as the eighth General Council. At the first Council of the Lateran, the precedent set by

[1] Robertson's 'History of the Church,' vol. ii. p. 353.

the earlier Councils of inviting the representatives of each of the two great sections of the Christian Church had been adhered to. The tinge of heresy was accounted no ground of exclusion. But if this adherence to precedent was needful to maintain the semblance of unity in the Church in the ninth century, how much more so has it become in the nineteenth, when all the intellect of Christendom is Protestant, and the Greek Church, after a thousand years of schism, maintains its ancient antagonism! The rupture of the Reformation, however much it may have increased, did not create the difficulty of a combination of all Christendom in a cosmopolitan Synod. If it be said that the possibility of intercommunion between the different sections of the Christian Church no longer exists, this is but to echo the opinion of one of the ablest modern apologists of the Papal theory[1], that 'in these days an Œcumenical Council has become a chimera.' A better illustration of the correctness of this judgment could not be afforded than is presented by the assembly now sitting in Rome. Summoned by a Pope, confined to ecclesiastics, and restricted to one of the three great divisions of Christendom, it proclaims itself a merely Provincial Synod, or at best a General Council of the Latin Church, strictly forbidden to decide controverted points of belief, and devoid of all constitutional identity with the Councils of the early Church.

'All such a Latin Council can do is to condemn what it considers to be error, and to recognize or enounce "pious opinions," in matters *de fide*; but it cannot legitimately impose acceptance of its decrees even on the communion it represents, and much less on the Œcumenical world, as articles of faith necessary to

[1] Joseph de Maistre.

salvation. All its decisions are subject to revision, either in confirmation or rejection, by a genuine Œcumenical Council, when such may meet. And if it oversteps its powers, the responsibility of any scandal or schism that may ensue, arising from the violence done to the consciences of men, will lie exclusively at its own door, and that of those who promote and carry it through[1].'

There is a widely prevailing popular belief that an invitation was addressed by the Pontiff to the Protestant Churches of Christendom, if not to take part in its deliberations, at least to grace the Council with the presence of their representatives. It is wholly devoid of foundation. Without distinction of Church or sect, they have been excluded as outside the pale of salvation, and insulted by a warning to repent of their errors and to seek admission to the true fold.

The case of the Eastern Churches is somewhat different. An invitation to the Council—not general, but addressed to some of the Churches—was given with much unctuosity. But the invitation was conveyed in terms which rendered its acceptance impossible, and drew from those *whose authority it thus recognized* an unanswerable condemnation of the Pope's presumption. Whilst the Patriarch of Alexandria laments that 'whatever views we share in common stop short at the desire to effect the union of all the Churches of Christ,' he emphatically adds, 'all beyond is delusion and discord.' Eschewing controversy he states in plain and convincing terms three principal objections to the Papal programme. 'In the first place, it overthrows and abolishes the equality which exists among the Holy Churches of God, and their

[1] Lord Lindsay's 'Œcumenicity and the Church of England.'

individual independence proclaiming withal that Rome holds uncontrolled sway and sovereign dominion over the other thrones equally self-governing and independent—a pretension evidenced by the mode adopted for convoking this General Council; whilst, as is universally known, the honour of precedence is all that was conceded to the Pope of Rome by the Holy and Œcumenical Synods, and not the dominion over other Churches; so that he, of his own authority, has no right to convoke General Councils without the previous consent of the other most holy Patriarchs. In the second place, his Holiness the Pope also gives us to understand that salvation is to be found exclusively in Rome, that there alone Divine grace operates effectually, that there alone is the centre of ecclesiastical verity—in virtue, as he affirms, of the privilege conferred on the blessed Apostle St. Peter by our Saviour; whereas the grace of God, through the divine energy of the Church of Christ, is not restricted to Rome, or to any definite place, but has operated, and continues to operate, throughout the habitable globe, and has expanded itself and shed abroad its radiance to the ends of the earth. In the third place, he intimates that he convokes the General Council to assemble on the Festival of the Immaculate Conception of the Mother of the Lord, a dogma, be it said, wholly unknown to the Church—a recent invention, therefore, and by no means a solitary one.'

The Patriarch of Constantinople observes that 'the Œcumenical Councils were convened in other fashion than as his Holiness has convened this,' and proposes the adoption of an expedient which has at least the merit of simplicity;—

'Since it is manifest that there was a Church in existence ten centuries back, which held the same doctrines in the East as in the West, in the old as in the new Rome, let us each recur to that and see which of us has added aught, which has diminished aught therefrom; and let all that may have been added be struck off, if any there be, and wherever it be; and let all that has been diminished therefrom be re-added, if any there be and whatever it be; and then we shall all unawares find ourselves united in the same symbol of Catholic orthodoxy from which Rome, in the latter centuries having strayed, takes pleasure in widening the breach by ever new doctrines and institutions at variance with holy tradition.'

Those of the Eastern bishops who treated the Papal briefs with less of contumacy than was bestowed upon them by the Patriarchs of Constantinople, Jerusalem, and Alexandria, took care to affirm that it was because they viewed them in the light of private communications; and that they equally rejected the appeal of the Pope who, 'with the two arms of crucified love' had opened to non-Catholics 'the bosom of living unity,' by inviting them to his Œcumenical Council[1].

The *Times* of the 15th September, 1869, has the following remarks upon the attitude assumed by the Eastern bishops:—

'On the 29th of June, 1868, the bull of the indiction of the Council was duly promulgated. This was followed on the 8th of September of the same year by an apostolic letter addressed to all the bishops of the Oriental rite not in communication with Rome, inviting them to be present at the Synod, "even as

[1] See Father Felix's 'Conferences' in *Notre Dame*.

their ancestors had been present at the second Council of Lyons and that of Florence," where they were not allowed to vote, and had to sit apart. Abbate Testa was delegated to deliver these missives personally to the schismatic bishops or patriarchs. Finally, on the 13th of September, that apostolic letter to all Protestants and other non-Catholics was indited, which exhorts them to "embrace the opportunity of this Council" (*occasionem amplectantur hujus concilii*). We remarked at the time that the effect upon the schismatic mind of the East was scarcely to be called encouraging. The Greek Patriarch would not look at the letter, though it was handsomely bound in red morocco and emblazoned with gold letters bearing his own name. He had read all about it in the newspapers, and did not see how the Council could do aught but lead to further strife. The peace once arrived at by the two Churches had long fallen to the ground. His mind was perfectly easy on the subject. And so the gorgeous volume was taken from the divan and handed back to the delegate, who was bowed out, and departed in peace. The Metropolitan of Chalcedon returned the Encyclical, with the simple but graphic "Epistrephete," which might be freely rendered "Avaunt." The Bishop of Varna did not see how he could accept what his master had refused, and so he sent back the Encyclical. The Bishop of Salonica had no less than five reasons for his declining, to wit—1. What would his Patriarch say? 2. Why at Rome, why not in the East? 3. Because the Pope wants to get us into his grasp. 4. The Pope wears a sword, which is against Scripture; let him put it down and disband his army. 5. Let him give up the

"Filioque" and there will be no more disunion between Greeks and Latins—which last proposition, all things considered, is very delicious. Yet there were some exceptions, which the official Roman press calls "consoling." One schismatic bishop returned the letter, yet with the promise that he would think about it for himself; and another, the venerable Bishop of Trebizond, well stricken in years, seems to have been quite overcome, and received the Œcumenial with the most profound tokens of reverence and admiration, pressed it to his forehead, then to his bosom, looked at it from all sides, for, alas! he knew not the mystery of Latin characters, and exclaimed from time to time, "Oh, Rome! oh, Rome! oh, Holy Peter! oh, Holy Peter!" But, adds the official account quaintly enough, it was utterly impossible to get anything else out of him—notably, whether he meant to come to the Council or not.'

It is difficult to arrive at any other conclusion than that the venerable Churches of the East were excluded from participation in the Council of Pius IX as deliberately, in spite of these specious negotiations, as were the whole body of the Protestant Churches who were not invited at all. But the recognition of their right to participation *condemns by anticipation the Œcumenicity of a Council from which they are absent.* The Council may not be without importance. Everything indicates that it will prove pregnant of the most important results to the Roman Catholic Church; and we rejoice both in the Council and in the claims on which it is based, inasmuch as both combine to show priestcraft in its true colours. It is, however, only in pure ignorance or perversion of the historical significance of the name that the Council can be called Œcumenical.

However impressive the splendours of its ceremonial, or however pompous its claims to speak with authority upon the various questions by which the Christian society of the age is convulsed; however imperious the restraints it may impose upon the free utterance of opinion; however malicious and all-embracing its anathemas; or however momentous the decrees it may embody in formularies binding upon its adherents, the disdainful apathy with which it is universally regarded to-day reflects the verdict of posterity, who will treat its pretensions with scorn,—softened perhaps with a touch of sympathy for the aged Pontiff whose baffled ambition has exposed him to the contempt of the scoffer, and to the hatred of those who, with himself, he has made the laughing-stock of Europe.

The attitude assumed towards the Council by the lay-Catholic powers is significant rather for what is implied, than for what is said, in the recondite utterances from which alone it can be gathered. If, abandoning its pretensions to Œcumenicity, the Council had busied itself only upon matters of ecclesiastical discipline and matters of doctrine, such as were indicated in the series of propositions originally submitted by the Roman curia to the Roman Catholic Bishops, the secular courts of Europe would have disdained interference in such controversies. But as the pretensions of the Roman See became more apparent, and the rumour—first vague and improbable, but soon surrounded with such a pomp of circumstance as to remove all doubt—was circulated of the avowed intention to elevate the syllabus of A.D. 1864 into a dogma, a challenge was thrown down which it was impossible for any Catholic power to ignore; and here and there an appeal on behalf of more moderate counsels was addressed to Rome. That of Prince Hohenlohe, the Prime Minister of Bavaria, and himself the brother of a Cardinal, will be remembered. When Rome, overstepping the limits of ecclesiastical jurisdiction, threatened to impose ordinances upon her clergy which conflicted with the civil laws of other lands, the governments of such countries were at once placed on the defensive, and from all quarters we hear the echo of the same word—Hold!

True it is that three centuries have elapsed since Europe has been agitated by the question of the Pontifical right to absolve subjects from allegiance to their rulers; but the bull *Cœna Domini*, to which reference has been made, and which claims this power as properly belonging to the Holy See, is still in force, and though obsolete, so long as it is not formally repealed, remains a source of danger to the peace of the world, and justifies the jealous scrutiny of every new Papal pretension by the lay governments of Europe.

But if the promulgation of the doctrines of the Syllabus is thus fraught with danger, much more is there cause for alarm in the projects, no longer concealed or apologised for, of dealing similarly with such matters as the Temporal Power and the Personal Infallibility of the Pontiff. Pius IX boldly declares himself the enemy of modern civilization, detesting from his heart all that the broad stream of modern thought assumes to be good and true, whilst his pleasure will certainly be law to an immense majority of the assembled prelates. Hence the justifiable alarm of the French and

German bishops, and the attitude of hostility assumed by their respective governments. Whilst the two leading Catholic powers, Austria and France, hold the same views, German and American prelates, with many distinguished Italians, are united in their approval of a policy of common-sense, as opposed to the projects of the Ultramontanes. The Berlin correspondent of the *Times* makes the following statement in reference to the position assumed by Germany towards the pretensions of Pius IX:—

'On the subject of infallibility it is becoming more and more evident that all German sovereigns and many German bishops are arrayed against the Pope. Not to speak of conscientious scruples, the bishops are obviously afraid that to declare the Pope a god will outrage the feelings of every civilized being among their flocks, and cause many hitherto accommodating, though perhaps somewhat indifferent, members of the Church to desert, renounce, and attack it. As to the sovereigns, they have no wish to assist the Pope in arousing a religious movement which might go any length, and which, should it attain serious proportions, would be sure to extend to Protestantism also. In Germany, religious apathy—the prevailing feature of the age—is accompanied with so much downright opposition to all that has been hitherto considered orthodox, that for the Pope to treat this country on a footing of intellectual equality with Italy, Spain, and France, and desire the Germans to adore and idolize him in the same way he asks others, is to let off squibs over a barrel of gunpowder. They need not necessarily ignite the inflammable material over which they fly and crack, but they may do so. Already Protestant

Liberalism is preparing for such an event. . . . . In the meantime, two more Catholic professors of theology have publicly declared against infallibility, viz. Professor Michelis, of the Clerical Seminary of Braunsberg, in East Prussia, and Dr. Schulte, one of the most renowned professors of canon law at the University of Prague. In addition to these literary announcements of opinion we have to record an address sent by the leading ecclesiastics of the diocese of Paderborn to their Bishop, the notorious partisan of the Pope in the Council. The address declares against infallibility, and entreats the Bishop to conform his attitude to the wishes of his chapter and flock.'

The publication of the Twenty-one Canons, to which I shall refer more particularly hereafter, afforded the Governments of France and Austria the opportunity, of which they were not slow to avail themselves, of energetically protesting against the definition of the threatened dogmas. In a despatch remarkable alike for its candour, dignity, and conciliatory tone, the Foreign Minister of Austria pointed out to the Court of Rome the complications and dangers likely to arise from a struggle between Church and State. In a communication addressed by Count Beust to the Austrian Ambassador at Paris, of which the following is an abstract, he lucidly states the reasons for the firm attitude of remonstrance assumed by the government of Francis Joseph:—

'The Catholic Powers, and more especially Austria and France, being anxious to leave the Church at liberty to conduct its own concerns, have not interfered with the arrangements for the Council and resigned the right properly belonging to them of sending representatives to that assembly. In thus abstaining from all interference they had been actuated by a wish to show their respect to the Church, and likewise by a recognition of that principle of modern civilization which accorded full and unrestrained liberty to Church and State within their respective spheres. For France it had been more easy to adopt such a course than for Austria, the former, by her treaties with the Pope, being entitled to stop the promulgation on her territory of any objectionable ecclesiastical decrees, a right which the latter, by her own Concordat, did not possess. In view, therefore, of what was preparing at the Council, and remembering the protests a short time ago couched by the Austrian bishops against the new school and marriage laws, and the agitation to which their resistance had given rise, Austria could not but feel uneasy concerning the future. It was not, indeed, the intention of the Council to enact Papal Infallibility that disquieted her, for he trusted that this doctrine, if proclaimed at all, would be expressed in a mild and merely theoretical form, similar to the one adopted by the Florentine Council, and, therefore, without much practical influence on the course of events. Nor had the State a right to object to the proclamation of other purely religious dogmas, such as the immaculate conception and glorification of the Virgin Mary. But it was different when the Church was about to claim a permanent and comprehensive supremacy over the State, and to arrogate to herself the right of deciding which of the laws laid down by the secular powers were binding on the subject and which not. Unfortunately, this was the standpoint assumed in the Twenty-one Canons submitted to the Council, and warmly advocated by certain parties. But, not content with establishing so unacceptable a principle, the canons proceeded at once to make use of the prerogative claimed, and declared many of the fundamental laws of all modern and civilized states to be unsound, invalid, and, in short, accursed. The canons, for instance, anathematized liberty of religion, liberty of the press, liberty of instruction, civil marriage, the amenability of the clergy to the criminal code, and a variety of other statutes asserted in them to be contrary to the laws of God and Holy Church. Now, supposing these *Schemata* to be really passed by the Council the danger to France would be very small, as the principles denounced had been the law of the land for nearly a century, and were likely to be upheld by the common consent of society. But in Austria legislation had only recently begun to recognize the necessity of enacting the laws long introduced in France, and the consequences resulting from clerical opposition to the new statutes would, therefore, be much more unpleasant. For this reason the Austrian Government had applied to Rome, and pointed out the disastrous results likely to arise from a struggle between Church and State. Whatever might be enjoined by the Church, the Austrian courts of law would not be induced to look leniently on those that broke the laws or incited others to break them. Add to this that the majority of the Austrian Bishops were opposed to the canons, and in the event of their being passed would be subjected to the cruel alternative of either not publishing them or of doing so against their better judgment, and it could not be denied that there were many reasons for apprehending an undesirable issue. Rome should beware of throwing down the gauntlet to the civilized world.'

The protest of Count Daru, conveyed in his now famous note of the 20th February, is yet more emphatic than that of the Austrian minister. Nothing can be more explicit than the language in which he commends the firm attitude of the minority of the bishops who oppose the adoption of the Syllabus and the promulgation of the dogma of Infallibility; and significantly hints that an imprudent persistence in this course would imperil not only the Concordat, but the protection which alone has rendered the meeting of the Council possible. 'People cannot be so blind as to suppose that the maintenance of our troops would be possible the day after the dogma of the Infallibility should be pronounced. We might be willing to leave them in Rome, but we should not be able.' It is true that His Excellency has recently been represented as so uncompromisingly hostile to the project for the withdrawal of the army of occupation, that he has threatened to resign his portfolio sooner than accede to it. However plausible the reasons assigned for the reversal of the policy sketched out in Count Daru's note of the 20th of February, it is difficult to believe that the cabinet of the Tuileries can have so misjudged the temper of the French nation, or miscalculated the endurance of Italy, as to commit the egregious folly of adopting a policy distasteful to 'that generous French nation,'—recently eulogized by Pius IX to the disparagement of their ruler,—hostile to Italy, and subversive of the September convention. However this may be, it is unquestionable that the issues raised by the publication of the Twenty-one Canons, appeared to the French government so to modify the position of neutrality which it had originally taken up, as to warrant the claim to representation in the Council by a special envoy.

It is stated that an attack of gout, especially affecting the hands[1], accounts for the dilatoriness of Cardinal Antonelli in replying to the French note. That reply however, has now reached the Tuileries; and the conflicting rumours concerning its import suggest that, consistently with all the diplomacy of Rome, it is ambiguous and indecisive. The *Patrie* of March 26 says:—'The reply of Cardinal Antonelli is lengthy, and very skilfully framed. The most remarkable facts to be noted are—first, that it does not dispute the authenticity of the text of the canons as published by the *Gazette d'Augsburg*; and, secondly, it opposes to the demand of direct intervention on the part of the French Government in the Council a series of obstructive reasons which do not go so far as to offer a definitive and categorical refusal. The cardinal takes pains to show that a signification and consequences have been attributed to these canons such as the court of Rome has never understood to be ascribed to them; that in such matters it is essential to distinguish between the absolute and theoretical and the relative and practical sides; that, the Church being a spiritual and divinely constituted society, it is its duty to offer to men's consciences solutions of all the problems which human life encounters; but the note adds that the exercise of this spiritual right in no way implies an intention on the part of the Church to meddle with political questions; and that in all cases, with regard to nations with which she has concluded Concordats,

[1] It is a well-known fact that Cardinal Antonelli is in the habit of writing his own despatches.

the Church will always remain faithful to the clauses of the treaties to which she is a party. In conclusion, Cardinal Antonelli expresses a hope that the explanations contained in his despatch may appear sufficient to the Cabinet of the Tuileries, and that they will induce it not to insist upon the demand conveyed in the note of Count Daru. We know not what resolution will be adopted by the Cabinet of the Tuileries in consequence of this Roman despatch, the effect of which, however, must previously have been made known by M. De Banneville. We have reason to believe, however, that at the moment we write no determination has been arrived at.'

The question of the representation of France in the Council remains, therefore, in abeyance. But it appears probable that this reasonable claim of the Emperor will, eventually, be conceded. Meanwhile, the Papal court—which has everything to gain by delay—secures a plausible pretext for adjourning the discussion of the *schema* relative to infallibility, from the considerate disposition to give France time to consider her ways.

The Council, whose duration it was boldly prognosticated would not be longer than that of Chalcedon—that is, that its labours would be completed within three weeks, and the promulgation of its decrees form a fitting close to the most eventful year of the Pontificate of Pius IX—has now been in session upwards of four months. The Pontiff, whose inflexibility of purpose sufficed to bring the Council together, has probably abandoned all hope of witnessing its termination.

The motives for the convocation of the Council, from which Pius IX anticipates the regeneration of the world, however transparent, were certainly not specified with any distinctness in the Bull of Convocation, in which they were nowhere more clearly expressed than in the following passage:—'In this General Council, then, there must be examined with the greatest care, and established, whatever, above all, especially regards, in these most difficult times, the greater glory of God, the integrity of the faith, the dignity of divine worship, the eternal salvation of souls, the discipline of the secular and regular clergy, the salutary and solid instruction of the clergy, the observation of ecclesiastical laws, the correction of morals, the Christian education of youth, and universal peace and concord betwixt all. It must also be endeavoured with the most active zeal that, with God's help, all evils may be kept away from the Church and civil society, and that unhappy wanderers may be called back to the right path of truth, justice, and salvation; and that, vices and errors being once for all extirpated, our august religion and its salutary doctrine may revive in the whole world, spreading and governing more and more: so that piety, honour, probity, justice, charity, and all Christian virtues may acquire vigour and flourish to the greatest advantage of human society.'

It is self-evident that this programme of the deliberations of the Council is incomplete, as it affords no justification for bringing together 700 ecclesiastics—most of them advanced in years—from every corner of the habitable world, at the cost of personal sacrifices which it is deplorable to contemplate, and at an expense of £1000 per diem to the already exhausted Pontifical treasury. The solution must be sought in the extreme elasticity of the phrases employed. Nor can it be denied that they afford scope for the widest possible range of interpretation.

In opposition to the materialism of the age, to the advancing power of science and of unfettered thought, Pius IX desires to exhibit the moral power of the Church, of which he claims to be the infallible head; to assert for it alone the right and power of leading the progress of mankind; and to receive the plaudits of his contemporaries, as well as of posterity, for this closing act of a Pontificate which, commencing in the throes of revolution, has presented to Europe the unique spectacle of a Pope governing upon Constitutional principles; the spectacle, more familiar, of a fugitive Pontiff, with a Republic proclaimed at Rome in his absence; the spectacle of a Pope restored, to the disgust of his subjects, coerced into submission by foreign bayonets; and, finally, of a Pope, despoiled of four-fifths of his territory, claiming authority, and gravely asserting spiritual pretensions worthy of a Boniface, and the first announcement of which Christendom, Catholic and Protestant alike, received with incredulous amazement.

The court of Rome is bent upon surrounding the proceedings of the Council with such profound secrecy that, not content with imposing the penalty of excommunication upon any violation of confidence, it has actually prohibited the publication of the names of the speakers. It is thus in a position to answer those upon whom we are dependent for information with the charge of misrepresentation—that frequent resource, with a certain class of mind, when suffering under the process of exposure. I shall not attempt to probe unrevealed mysteries, but rest content with a cursory glance at the present position of the two great parties in the Council, and an inquiry into the probable effects of the decisions which may be expected on some of the leading questions upon which the Council will have to deliberate.

It is now reported that in the event of the ultimate disallowance by the Vatican of the French Emperor's proposal to send a special envoy to the Council, or of its disregard of the legitimate influence of the lay governments, the liberal prelates will withdraw from Rome in a body. It may be anticipated that this course will either be immediately adopted, or definitively abandoned, as a secession now, it is affirmed, would imply nothing more than a protest; whereas, at a later stage, and after an important division—say, on the subject of Infallibility—it would amount to a schism. Would Pius IX congratulate himself on being thus rid of his opposition? If the French, the Austro-Hungarian, and the American prelates, to the number of two hundred, withdrew from the Council, even Pius IX must allow, in deference to the precedent established by the disavowal of the Œcumenicity of the Council of Sardica, A.D. 433, that the Œcumenicity of the Council of the Vatican is wholly destroyed. It is a matter of certainty that this plan for nullifying the decisions of the Council is under the consideration of those whom it concerns. These prelates inveigh bitterly against the disadvantageous position in which they are placed by that peculiar organization of the Roman and Italian Episcopate, which secures to the Italian prelates a most unfair and absurd majority of numbers. But this is the very reason why the Council is necessary to the Pope. His court, a senate of cardinals, *is too exclusively Italian.* This source of weakness is appreciated in Rome. It is a scandal which irritates against her every national sentiment in the world. 'It is the majority of her own subjects that she is now in difficulties with. The boasted majority she has not the courage to use represents mythical sees, decayed orders, a multitude of petty bishoprics near home, and purely official creations of her own temporal power. The minority represents the people—that is, the majority of the Roman Catholic communion throughout the world[1].'

The merest glance at the representative composition of the Council suffices to establish the reasonableness of the grievance alleged by the recalcitrant prelates. Italy with her population of 27,000,000 is represented by 230 cardinals, bishops, abbots, and fathers-general of monastic orders; whilst France, with her population of 34,000,000 has to content herself with sending eighty-four reverend fathers to the Eternal City. Nineteen million German Catholics are represented by nineteen deputies. Spain sends forty, South America thirty, the Orientals forty-two, China fifteen, Australia thirteen. We must cap this list by observing that 3,000,000 of semi-civilized Sclavonians are represented by no less than twelve docile deputies, all pledged to support the utmost pretensions of the Holy See. Allowing, in consideration of their more advanced civilization, and their proportionately-enhanced moral responsibility and rightful influence, *double this proportion* of numerical representation to Italy, France, and Germany, Italy should have 216, France 264, and Germany 152 delegates. The actual numbers are, Italy 230, France 84, and Germany 19[2].

[1] The *Times*.

[2] See letter of the Berlin correspondent of the *Times*, February 19th, 1870. In *Times* of February 24th.

Notwithstanding the statement of so great an authority as Archbishop Manning, that 'the ranks of the opposition are daily melting like snow in the glance of Pio Nono;' or the assurances of the *Tablet* that an opposition has hardly an existence; we prefer the testimony of facts to the word of an Archbishop, or to the asseverations of an ultramontane journal pledged to the demonstration of a foregone conclusion. The courtiers of the Vatican predicted, with real or simulated confidence, that so soon as the Council met the personal infallibility of the Pontiff would be voted by acclamation. The programme was imposing, and, while the Pontiff lent a willing ear, its success was not so utterly improbable but that Europe listened, with bated breath, for the firing of cannon and the ringing of bells which should announce the intelligence to the world. We were told, and we received the information with befitting credulity, that every bishop attending the Council would, by his presence alone, have signified his adherence to the programme laid down by the Jesuits. The great dogma was to be proclaimed 'by the inspiration of the Holy Ghost;' and a distinguished English clergyman, who was in Rome at the opening of the Council, was told by a high dignitary of the Church that the non-acoustic properties of the Council Hall constituted its special recommendation; 'for,' he naively added, 'we don't want any debating!'

The Jesuits had laid their plans with that precision and adroit organization of which they have ever proved themselves the most consummate masters. The time was come, they held, when those who were not with the Pontiff must understand that they were against him. The opportunity of the great influx of Catholics into Rome during the festivities of the centenary of St. Peter, in 1867, was seized to administer the following oath to thousands of both clergy and laity.

'Holy Prince of the Apostles, St. Peter, I, N. N., moved by a desire to offer to thee, and in thee to thy successors in the apostolic chair, a tribute of especial devotion, which may be, on the one hand, for thee and for the Church a compensation for the outrages done to the see of Rome; and, on the other, may bind me more to honour her, do swear to hold and to profess, if necessary at the price of my blood, the doctrine already common among Catholics, which teaches that the Pope is infallible when he defines in his character of Universal Master, or as it is called, *ex cathedrá*, what must be believed in questions of faith and morals, and that consequently his dogmatic decrees are irreformable and binding in conscience, even before they have received the assent of the Church.'

Six hundred and fifteen bishops, we were told, had committed themselves to teach, support, and defend, *usque ad effusionem sanguinis*, if necessary, the dogma of Papal Infallibility. No debate would be permitted. The business of the Council was simply to define and enforce the dogma.

Such were the confident vaticinations of the Jesuits in Rome. But they did not avail to drown the notes of discord which heralded the crowning act of the Pontificate of Pius IX. The astute cardinal who, for twenty years, has been the most influential of the Pontiff's advisers, foreseeing how the projected Council would be received by the cismontane Catholics, after vainly exerting himself to save the Church from a gratuitous peril accepted a qualified disgrace rather than give in his adhesion, all at once, to a forlorn project for framing new bonds of union out of ignorance and fanaticism. The press of France teemed with urgent appeals for protective measures against the black designs of the Council. And although thousands of Catholics in France, as in Italy or Spain, would probably accept any dogmatical creed propounded by the Council with that indifference which the comprehensive faith of Roman Catholic Christendom engenders, it soon became apparent that no encroachments upon the civil law or political independence of the State would be for a moment tolerated. But the less comprehensive faith of the Germans rebelled against all dogmatic absurdities. Austria, exulting in the new life quickened by the adoption of constitutional institutions which had their birth in the abrogation of the Concordat, was little likely to tolerate any despotic encroachments of the court of Rome: whilst in Bavaria the Roman Catholic Premier—the brother of a cardinal—conferred with other German cabinets, and solicited the opinion of the most eminent Roman Catholic theological faculties in Germany, upon the course to be adopted in the event of the Pope's infallibility being dogmatically promulgated, or the Ultramontane faction, i. e. the Holy Father, deriving additional authority in the State, from any decrees that might be voted by the Council[1]. All doubt was re-

---

[1] The following are the questions which were submitted, and to which the faculty of Munich replied emphatically in the sense of the government:—

1. If the theses of the Syllabus and the Papal infallibility are raised into dogmas at the forthcoming Council, what changes would arise therefrom in the doctrine of the relation between

moved that the Liberal Catholic party in North Germany, though disapproving equally with Bavaria of the assembling of the Council, would make a combined effort with the prelates of Austria, France, and Italy, who were hostile to the pretensions of the Ultramontane party, not only to secure free discussion, but also to

Church and State as hitherto held, both theoretically and practically, in Germany?

2. Would in that case the public teachers of dogmatics and ecclesiastical law feel bound to make the doctrine of the divinely set rule of the Pope over the monarchs, either as *Potestas directa* or *indirecta*, as binding to the conscience of every Christian, the basis of their teaching?

3. Would the teachers of dogmatics and ecclesiastical law consider themselves bound forthwith to receive into their lectures and writings the doctrine that the personal and real immunities of the clergy are *juris divini*, and belong to the province of religious doctrine?

4. Are there any generally acknowledged criteria whereby it can with certainty be decided whether a Papal utterance, *ex cathedrâ*—according to the doctrine of the Council eventually to be fixed—is absolutely binding to every Christian's conscience? And if there be such criteria, which be they?

5. How far might the prospective new dogmas, and their necessary consequences, exercise an altering influence also upon popular education in school and church, and further upon the school-books, the catechisms, &c., now in use?

'On this last point they give the very decided answer, that there would, indeed, ensue very considerable changes in the catechisms, changes which they point out as clearly as may be. The juridical faculty to whom the same questions have been submitted has not answered yet, nor has the theological faculty at Wurzburg sent in their reply. But there is no question about its purport. Europe in general passes the Council by silently. Catholic Germany speaks through its highest authorities, and unconditionally condemns its aims and purports.'—*Pall Mall Gazette.*

wring from the Council an authoritative sanction of their proposals for the complete separation of Church and State, the suppression of the Index, and other reforms for which they had petitioned and agitated [1].

[1] In a lengthy abstract of a paper which, according to the *Wanderer*, the Bohemian clergy proposed to submit to the Council, we find the following bold suggestions. The paper begins by saying that in a time like ours, when the fundamental doctrines of Christianity are being called in question, when doubts are expressed as to the existence of a God and the nature and immortality of the soul, the Council would be guilty of an error in tactics if it were to employ its forces against the light troops of a doubtful ally instead of directing its whole attention to the attack that threatens the very centre of the fortress. 'The task of the Council is therefore solemnly to define and proclaim those doctrines which are calculated to support religion in general, revelation, and the authority of the Church.' It is advised to follow the example of the Council of Trent, in avoiding, as far as possible, a philosophic terminology, as it is liable to be misunderstood, and thus open up a way for objections. Certain boundaries, too, must be observed, and even those doctrines to which true believers are sincerely attached should not be inserted in the dogmatic code without weighty reasons. 'Thus the Council should not proclaim the infallibility of the Pope. This is the sincere wish of the most learned, intelligent, and earnest of the adherents of the holy chair.' Such a step would only give rise to ridicule among unbelievers, while for believers it is quite unnecessary, as their attachment to the Roman See was never greater than at present. It seems equally unadvisable to make any further authoritative statements as to the corporal assumption of the Virgin Mary, the state of nature, the cause and means of supporting grace, the manner in which the body is governed by the soul, and similar matters. These have already engaged the attention of former Councils, particularly that of Trent, and may now safely be left to theology. With respect to the Index of forbidden books, it is urged that before a work is condemned the opinion of the bishop in whose diocese it appeared should be asked.

In Rome rumours were rife of revolutionary plots, formed for the purpose of preventing the meeting of the Council, or of cutting short its deliberations by assassination and incendiarism. The Council was not only distasteful to the Mazzinians; it was opposed by many of the Italian episcopacy. The Archbishop of Genoa resigned his see, and retired to Savoy, rather than consent to attend, and the government deemed it prudent to employ large bodies of firemen to watch the erection of the structures in St. Peter's for the accommodation of the members of the Council. Provision was also made for a large number of fire-engines in different parts of the cathedral, and for the permanent accommodation of the requisite number of firemen.

It was said that the Jesuits were alarmed, as well they might be, by such indications of the apprehension entertained, in official quarters, of an outbreak of popular disaffection. Certain it is that many of them would fain have persuaded the Pope to abandon the Council of which they had been the chief projectors. But the Pope stood firm. In the course of nature his Pontificate must soon come to an end; and there was nothing he was unwilling to risk for the sake of the grand spectacle which should close his eventful career. To every suggestion of expediency or of danger he turned a deaf ear. The quicksands before which an Antonelli stood appalled, affrighted him not. As to a schism upon matters of faith, he cheerily dispersed, with the ready joke ever upon his lips, the mists of apprehension and doubt which obscured the intellects, and paralyzed the hands, of less resolute cardinals.

There is much reason to believe that the infatuated Pontiff was less prepared than were many members of the *curia* for the determined attitude which was early assumed by the compact phalanx of a powerful opposition. The violent and arbitrary measures which have been adopted for their suppression—as, in addition to others already mentioned, the prohibition of unofficial meetings of the bishops even in private houses—have immeasurably strengthened their position. The most nervously apprehensive mind amongst the members of the *curia* probably little anticipated that, by the proceedings to which they lent themselves, a machinery was being called into existence utterly beyond their power to manipulate.

The information which reaches us of the character of this opposition is so cumulative and circumstantial, that it is impossible to ignore its general authenticity, however it may be challenged in some of its details. The bold assault of Strossmayer, Archbishop of Bosnia and Syrmia, on the eighteen propositions brought before the Council in January, and the censure of Cardinal de Luca for not stopping the debate; the threat of the Archbishop of Paris, supported by many of his brethren, that in the event of any attempt being made to carry the new dogma by acclamation, he would leave Rome and protest against the validity of the Council, are matters of fact. So also is the following Anti-Infallibility address drawn up by Cardinal Rauscher, Archbishop of Vienna, and signed by a large number of bishops:—

'Most Holy Father,—We have received the draught of a petition circulating among the Fathers of the Œcumenical Council, and calling upon them to declare supreme and infallible authority to be vested in the Roman Pontifex when imparting Apostolical teaching to all the faithful upon subjects connected with religion and morals. It is certainly strange that the judges of matters religious should be asked to decide a question before it has been discussed, but as thou, most Holy Father, divinely appointed to attend the flock of Christ, so piously takest care of the souls redeemed by His blood, and with paternal compassion lookest upon the dangers threatening them, we have thought it right to address ourselves to thee in this matter. The times are past when the Catholics used to contest the rights of the Holy See. We all are aware that as the human body, without the head, is but a mutilated trunk, so can no Council of the entire Church be held without the successor of St. Peter; and we all obey the mandates of the Holy See with ready willingness. As regards the authority which the faithful are obliged to concede to the Roman Pontiff, this has been settled by the Council of Trent, and also by the Council of Florence. The decrees of the latter, particularly, ought to be the more faithfully observed, inasmuch as, having been enacted with the common consent of Latins and Greeks, they are destined some day, when the Lord will take pity on the Orient now oppressed by so many evils, to become the basis of the reunion of the Church. Nor must we leave it unmentioned that at a time when the Church is compelled more earnestly than ever to wage war against those who denounce religion as a mere fiction, vain and idle indeed, yet pernicious to the human race, it cannot be opportune to exact of the Catholic nations, already exposed to so much seduction and temptation, heavier duties (*majora*) than were enjoined on them by the Council of Trent. It is true that, although Bellarminus, and with him the whole

Catholic Church, affirms that matters of faith are to be chiefly decided by Apostolical tradition and the common consent of the Church, and although the best way to ascertain the decision of the Church is to convene a Universal Synod, yet from the Council of the Apostles and Elders of Jerusalem down to the Council of Nice have the innumerable errors of the local Churches been checked and extinguished by the decisions of the successors of St. Peter, approved by the entire Church. Nor do we deny that while all faithful believers are bound to obey the behests of the Holy See, there are pious and erudite men teaching over and above this that any utterances of the supreme Pontiff on matters of religion and morality, when formally (*ex cathedrá*) made and announced, must be held irrefragable, albeit lacking the express consent of the Church. Yet we must not omit stating that grave objections to this teaching may be based on the acts and utterances of the Fathers of the Church,—objections supported by the evidence of genuine historical documents and the Catholic doctrine itself. Unless the difficulties arising from this circumstance are entirely solved and done away with, it is possible that the doctrine advocated in the above-mentioned petition will some day be inculcated on the Christian people as one revealed by the Almighty. We have no wish to dwell upon this prospect (*verum ab hisce discutiendis refugit animus*), and confidently entreat thee to obviate the necessity of such a discussion. We think we may say that performing episcopal functions among the more eminent nations of the Catholic world, and being by daily experience well conversant with the state of things in our respective countries, the enactment of the doctrine proposed will only supply fresh arms of attack to the enemies of religion, and enable them to rouse invidious feelings even in better and more virtuous men (*melioris notæ viros*) than themselves. We are certain, moreover, that such an event in one part of Europe, at any rate, would be taken advantage of by the Governments to infringe the remnant of rights still possessed by the Church. Having laid this before thy Holiness with the sincerity due to the common father of all true believers, we beseech thee to prohibit the discussion in the Œcumenical Council of the doctrine recommended in the above-mentioned petition. Prostrating ourselves at thy feet, both in our own name and on behalf of the nations which we have undertaken to guide to the knowledge of God (*ad Deum perducendos*), we ask for thy apostolical blessing. We remain the most humble, most obedient, and devoted servants of thy Holiness.'

Hardly less important is the following protest of the German and Hungarian bishops against the regulations of the Council:—

'Most Holy Father,—All the Bishops of the entire world, and among them we the undersigned, most ardently desire that the Œcumenical Council, so happily inaugurated under the auspices of your Holiness, may be successfully continued, so that it may supply the various nations with remedies against the many new evils oppressing them, and impart to the Holy Church of God fresh means and strength to fulfil the mission divinely imposed upon it. In order that this object may be the more surely attained, we take the liberty of acquainting your Holiness with the anxiety we feel concerning a matter connected with the debates of this ecclesiastical assembly. In taking this step we are animated by that devotion to the Holy Apostolical See always felt by the Bishops of the entire world, and never more so than at this present time.

'In the rules and regulations of the Council prescribed by your Holiness, the most important clause, perhaps, is the second, referring to the privilege of the members to direct the attention of the assembly to such matters as they may think fit to introduce. There are those who think that by the clause in question the right of the assembled Fathers to start any discussion they may deem conducive to the public weal has been taken away, its exercise having been made dependent on a favour to be only exceptionally accorded. Most Holy Father, we are all firmly convinced that the body of the Church cannot be strong and healthy unless possessed of a lofty and powerful head, and that the proceedings of the Synod cannot be correct and orderly unless the Divine rights of the Primacy are properly protected and observed. But if this is undoubtedly true, it is not less so that the other members of the mystical body of Christ likewise require to be protected in their special functions, and that the College of Bishops, more particularly, must be in a position to exercise the rights inherent to them by virtue of their office and character, if the head is to retain its proper strength, and to act safely and undisturbedly. By God's ordinance the head and the body are intimately connected and inseparably united with each other. Equally as, therefore, in the exercise of your Holiness's undoubted privilege, your Holiness has condescended to lay down the manner of procedure in the Holy Synod, and prescribe the wisest and most effective rules concerning the manner and order of treatment of the subjects introduced, so the Fathers of the Council, if feeling prompted to prefer aught connected with the welfare of the Church, or to make a proposition aiming at the furtherance of the same, have always justly enjoyed the right to do so by virtue of their position and office, the only condition exacted being that they should speak with the devotion and veneration due to the Head of the Church. We state this the more confidently, inasmuch as your Holiness has yourself condescended to exhort us to express freely whatever we may consider to be calculated to promote the public weal; and inasmuch as, in taking this step, we are only following in the footsteps of the most celebrated Council of Trent (Sess. XXIV., cap. 21).

'In our opinion, therefore, there can have been no intention to infringe our rights by the abovementioned clause; and we should be greatly strengthened in this our conviction if your Holiness would kindly permit that the committee appointed for the preliminary examination of propositions introduced by members be reinforced by some Fathers elected by the Council out of their own midst, and also that members introducing propositions be allowed access to the said committee, to enable them to take part in the examination thereof.

'In submitting this, with filial devotion, to your wise consideration and judgment, we hope, Most Holy Father, that what, animated by the purest intentions, we have been prompted to prefer will be well received.

'Prostrating ourselves at the feet of your Holiness, we are the most obedient servants of your Holiness,—

'Cardinal Schwarzenberg.

'Fürstenberg, Archbishop of Olmütz.

'Gregor Scherr, Archbishop of Munich.
'Michael von Deinlein, Archbishop of Bamberg.
'Ludwig Haynald, Archbishop of Kolosa.
'Heinreich Förster, Archbishop of Breslau.
'Pancratius Dinkel, Bishop of Augsburg.
'Valentin Viery, Bishop of Görz.
'Gregor Simonovicz, Archbishop of Lemberg (of the Armenian Rite).
'Bartholomaeus, Bishop of Trieste.
'Joannes Zirzik, Bishop of Budweis.
'Georg Dobrila, Episcop. Parent.
'Jacobus Stepnisnigg, Episcop. Lavantin.
'Alexander Bonnaz, Bishop of Csanad.
'Matthaeus Eberhard, Bishop of Trier.
'Eduard Jacob, Bishop of Hildesheim.
'Michael Fogarassy, Bishop of Transylvania.
'Joseph Strossmayer, Bishop of Bosnia and Syrmia.
'Stephan Lipovniczky, Bishop of Crosswardein.
'Sigismund Kovacs, Bishop of Fünfkirchen.
'Ludwig Ferwerk, Bishop of Lemberg.
'Joannes Beckmann, Bishop of Osnabrück.
'Georg Smiciklas, Episcop. Crisiens.
'Hieronymus Zeidler, Abbas Strahoviensis.
'Wilhelm Ketteler, Bishop of Mayence.
'Petrus Kenrick, Archbishop of St. Louis, United States.'

In the face of these events it is impossible to doubt that the opposition, whilst growing in numbers and in moral weight, is organizing a consistent policy of resistance, and threatening a crisis for which Rome is unprepared. Already it has inspired in the Jesuits a misgiving which is likely to deter them from bringing forward some of their most monstrous propositions. In addition to several cardinals, more than two hundred bishops are enrolled in its ranks. It is instructive to note that whilst *the members of the Council* who are in opposition to the Pontiff and his Jesuit advisers are a minority, they *represent* no less than 80,000,000 members of the Roman Catholic Church, whose adherents throughout the entire world cannot be computed at more than 170,000,000; a circumstance which invests the remote chance of schism with a terrible significance. The really representative men are in the ranks of the opposition. The Archbishop of Paris, it has been said, 'represents more Catholics than *all the Roman bishops together.*'

This formidable opposition has awakened the keenest irritation in the minds of the Papalist party, and of the Pontiff himself, who denounces them in language as remarkable for its boldness as for its energy, considering the recent exposures of 'the historical frauds' upon which Papal pretensions are based. In a recent letter to an Ultramontane Benedictine his Holiness denounces the 'madness,' 'obstinacy,' 'corrupt practices,' 'audacity,' 'folly,' and 'spirit of hatred, violence, and artifice,' which distinguish the party represented by Doupanloup, Strossmayer, and Dollinger. 'They undertake,' he says, 'to reform even the divine constitution of the Church, and to adapt it to the modern forms of civil governments, in order more readily to lower the authority of the supreme chief whom Christ has appointed, and whose prerogatives they dread,' employing in their nefarious work 'historical frauds ... and sophisms of all kinds.'

A significant illustration has been recently afforded of the lengths to which these Infalliblists are ready to go in despotically silencing their opponents. The *Augsburg Allgemeine Zeitung* informs us that when, at a recent sitting of the Council, Dr. Strossmayer declared that a new dogma of faith could not be established without a moral unanimity of the Fathers, he was ordered by the President to leave the Council[1]! The desperate attempts of 'this insolent and aggressive faction' to recover lost ground, and by any means to carry the dogma upon which their hearts are set, have proved the occasion of the claim now put forward by France to send a representative to the Council. At the same time Baron Beust, on behalf of Austria, asserts the right, 'properly belonging to the Catholic powers,' to direct representation in the Council, which however he abstains from claiming out of respect to the Church, 'and a recognition of that principle of modern civilization which accords full and unrestrained liberty to Church and State within their respective spheres.' All the Catholic powers in fact concur in the views of France, and, although advancing no similar claim, have resolved mutually to concert measures to insure, by existing laws, each in its own territory, respect for those civil rights menaced by the *schemata* submitted to the Council.

[1] The Roman correspondent of the *Cologne Gazette* informs us that when the Bishop began to touch on the question whether the dogmas should be passed by a majority of votes, or only, as in former councils, when all the members are unanimous, the Council lost all patience. Cries of 'Hæreticus! hæreticus!' and 'Damnamus eum!' were heard on all sides. One bishop exclaimed, 'At ego non damno eum,' upon which the others repeated 'Damnamus,' and shouted to the speaker, 'Tu es protestans! taceas! ab ambone descendas!'

CHAPTER XIV.

I SHALL limit my observations upon the probable decisions of the Council, and the consequences which may be expected to flow from them, to the following. The proposal to elevate the Temporal Power into a dogma. The definition of the corporeal assumption of the Virgin—and, as is now added, of St. Joseph. The Syllabus. And, lastly, the main business of the Council, the enunciation of the dogma of the Personal Infallibility of the Pontiff, in direct contradiction to the decision of the Council of Constance, which subordinated the Papal authority to that of a General Council.

The pretensions of the ecclesiastical politicians by whom Pius IX has surrounded himself are as unlimited, and far more utterly in conflict with the spirit of the age, than were the wildest dreams of the Gregories and the Innocents of the Middle Ages. Nor is there any attempt to veil the fact. The Council, says the *Civiltà Cattolica*, 'may enact dogmatic decrees or disciplinary regulations contrary to the spirit of modern times.' The probability is only too apparent; and the *Civiltà*

Cattolica answers by anticipation the enquiry—What, then, will the civil governments have to say to the Decrees of the Vatican Council? Will they venture upon maintaining the majesty of law in their respective countries at the risk of doing violence to the consciences of their Roman Catholic subjects? 'If they do,' says this organ of the Vatican, 'they will stand guilty of criminal tyranny, and their opposition must be treated by the bishops with contempt.' And again, 'All laws contrary to the Decrees of the Council will be radically null and void, and will in no way compel the consciences of their subjects.' Here we have the very spirit of the Bull *Cœna Domini*, the theory of which survives and flourishes more vigorous than ever.

The erection of a dogma for the belief of the necessity for the Pope's temporal power is assuredly one that may be embraced in the elastic formulary of 'decrees contrary to the spirit of modern times.' Further, it is declared in the Syllabus that all Catholics are bound to hold most firmly that doctrine concerning the Pontiff's civil princedom which is therein clearly laid down. The necessity is there affirmed for the temporal power to secure the Pope that liberty which is required for his spiritual office; that it is ordered by Divine Providence; that all Catholics are bound to unite against every effort to overthrow it; that the aggressive acts of its assailants are *de jure* null and void; and that the spoliation of the Roman territory by Victor Emanuel was nefarious and sacrilegious. The definition of this dogma is, however, improbable to the last degree. However anxious the Roman *curia* may be to secure the preservation of the temporal authority of the

Pontiff, it can hardly be affirmed to furnish the elements of a dogma. Civil society, moreover, tolerant of the discussion of doctrinal and disciplinarian questions, could not afford to overlook a decision pregnant with danger, and arrogantly disregarding accomplished facts. At the same time it is apparent that a grave discussion of the question might afford the Jesuits an opportunity, of which they would gladly avail themselves, to divert and perhaps disintegrate the opposition by the introduction of a topic upon which they may be beguiled into fierce controversy, prolific of rancour and dissension. In this sense the Roman correspondent of the *Times* has recently remarked: 'Upon this matter of the temporal estate there are few bishops, even among the foremost in the present opposition, who have not committed themselves in a manner some, no doubt, would now gladly know undone, but from which others (and they are the more numerous) will hardly dare to recede. Many a hasty and unfounded word has fallen at times from episcopal lips on this matter of temporal power which at this moment threatens to hang like a millstone around the speaker's neck; for now that things are being pushed to their logical end, and men on being driven into a corner have at last to make a stand, it will be found that between the tenets of Papal Infallibility and the Pope's indefeasible right to a Temporal Power there is internal affinity and correlation. If, therefore, at this moment, when a truly formidable opposition has formed itself against the dogma of Infallibility, the coherence of this opposing phalanx could be loosened by the introduction on the scene of that other tenet, the Temporal Power, with the creation of a divergence of opinions and the production of dissensions, the move would be strategically a very good one in the interests of those who have the chief voice in directing the business of the Council.' It is indeed broadly asserted in the *Schema de Ecclesia Christi*, to which I shall presently have occasion to refer, that the connection between the Temporal and the Spiritual Estate of the Holy See, is one 'prescribed by the law of God,' from which *none can deviate without risk of salvation*, and that it is not lawful for any one to assert that the lay authority is called upon to restrict coercive measures against the violators of the Catholic faith to that which may be only requisite for the maintenance of the public peace [1]. But it is probable that the Council will content itself with an imposing protest, after the model of those of 1862 and 1867, against the spoliations endured by the Pope *contra sacrilegos ausus et conatus guberni subalpinii*, &c.

The theological bearings of the Council are beyond our sphere. Their exposition in the daily papers may be read *ad nauseam*, and those who desire to see them arraigned with the bitterness proper to polemical strife, may be abundantly edified from the same source, from platform, pulpit, the hustings, or wherever men do congregate. True to our motto, then, we will review 'lightly and on tiptoe' these topics with which the subject of this treatise has but slender affinity, although such as cannot be wholly ignored.

The dogmatic definition of the doctrine of the Corporeal Assumption of the Virgin—to which the *Tablet* has added the Assumption of St. Joseph, the third Person of the earthly Trinity, as it profanely calls him—is the

---

[1] See letter of *Times* correspondent already quoted.

natural sequence of the 'honours' already rendered by Pius IX to the mother of our Lord. The Commission of Dogmatic Theology has by a large and decisive majority pronounced in favour of the definition, and effective opposition is not anticipated from any quarter.

The great question of the Syllabus, 'the banner of retrogression' as it was termed the other day in the Italian Chamber, is one upon which the docility of the assembled Fathers will be severely tried. It is well known that the errors which the Pope lays down as worthy of condemnation, are enunciated in the decrees of Councils held by all Christendom to have been Œcumenical, which, on the Roman theory, involves their infallibility. The Syllabus was not composed all at once in 1864, but consists of condemnations of modern principles, emanating as well from other Infallibles as from the present Pontiff. Pre-eminently it raises the question of the infallible authority of the Church, in whom it resides, and with what limits. It is a code which regulates the relations of the court of Rome with civil society. It raises amongst other questions, too numerous to specify, that of the validity of civil marriages; of the connection of Church and State; of the right of the ecclesiastical power to exercise its authority without the permission and assent of the civil governments. Hence the lively apprehension evinced by the civil powers, and by prelates such as the Archbishop of Paris, habituated to the liberty enjoyed under a Concordat wrung from Rome when she was anxious, *upon any terms*, to gain a footing in a country where religion had ceased to exist —a liberty not shared by any other Catholic country.

It is now well known that, exasperated by the

threatened promulgation of the doctrines of the Syllabus, the Government of Louis Napoleon intimated to the Roman *curia*, before the close of last year, that however great the reverence which his Imperial Majesty might feel for the spiritual authority of the Holy See, the Papal pretensions and the narrow system of absolutism upon which the temporal power was conducted, could not command the sympathy of a constitutional country. Studiously avoiding any threat of coercion, but at the same time significantly reminding Pius IX that the recall of the French troops 'is with his Government a settled purpose,' the Emperor besought the 'benevolent' Pontiff to have recurrence to the liberal ideas proclaimed by him in 1846—in other words, to emulate the reforms now inaugurated by his Imperial monitor [1].

---

[1] The Roman correspondent of the *Pall Mall Gazette*, writing on March 10, says:—'Count Daru has charged the Marquis de Banneville to press again on Cardinal Antonelli the necessity of an entire reform of the Pontifical Government and the granting of a constitution to the Roman people. The French ambassador declares that both England and Prussia urge the Emperor to make these demands, and that the Imperial Government will be unable to continue the occupation if they are not promptly complied with. Several French bishops, in obedience to commands from the Tuileries, have supported the ambassador's counsels, and among these prelates is the Bishop of Bayeux, to whom Count Daru addressed his two famous letters. But the Pope, guided entirely by the Jesuits and the Ultramontane *camarilla*, has resolved to meet the propositions of the French minister with a peremptory refusal. Many of the cardinals and prelates are in favour of concession, and express a belief that the Holy Father must ultimately yield. I must not omit to add that the Marquis de Banneville also asks for a general amnesty for political offenders. The French Government is believed to have

'The Catholic religion,' Pius IX recently said at the inauguration of the Exposition, 'loves and cherishes all the arts of true progress instead of opposing them.' Such a declaration was calculated to lead the unreflecting to anticipate a favourable reply to the missive of the Protector of the Papacy. That reply was in two kinds, the one addressed by Antonelli to the Tuileries, the other, through the columns of the *Civiltà Cattolica*, to the Catholic world; and it is instructive to note the customary duplicity of all that emanates from Rome, providing for a specious show of consistency in the ultimate adoption of that course which may appear the more expedient. The diplomatist replies that the abolition of the reforms of 1847 was justified on the ground that concessions had been shown to weaken the hands of authority and open the way to revolution and anarchy; that to grant reforms would be to give weapons to an enemy; and that his Holiness has profited by the warnings conveyed in the agitation that has followed the change of government in Austria, Spain, and France. But that if the Holy See could put an end to the dream of Italian unity by recovering its

fixed on Duke Albert De Broglie as its lay representative at the Council. It would be difficult to choose an ambassador more distasteful to the court of Rome; and the views held at the Vatican about the duke are embodied in a most abusive article by Monsignor Nardi, in a late number of the *Osservatore Cattolico* of Milan. I am assured that the Pope was pointing at the Duke De Broglie, when, in his speech at the Exhibition, he said that the Church would never have its '89. The Pope has intimated that he will receive no more addresses on the subject of Infallibility, whether they favour or oppose the dogma, as this question is now virtually before the Council, and his reception of addresses might interfere with the deliberations of the Fathers.'

lost possessions, then political reforms might be possible. Widely different is the reply addressed to Catholics through the Pope's own organ. Here it is contended that the principles denounced in the Syllabus *are* the principles which inspired the reforms with which the Pontificate of Pius IX was inaugurated, and which won for him the name of the 'Benevolent Pontiff.' He never changed from what he began, and when Napoleon exhorts him to return to the counsels of 1847, he commits himself to an approval of the Syllabus. The following remarks of the *Times* correspondent (20th February) place in a clear light the argument for consistency put forward by Rome:—

'In the very infancy of his Pontificate, it seems, Pius IX exposed the great league of unbelief called Rationalists, who repudiate the light of supernatural faith, and give the supremacy to proud reason and the dictates of nature. It was then he raised his voice against all private interpretation of the Word of God in contempt of the only legitimate, infallible authority of the Church of Christ and His Vicar, the Pontiff. Nor was it to religion and Scripture and the Dogma that the Pope confined himself. He denounced the impiety which disregarded the laws of the Church, but, not less, all contempt of rights and lawful civil authority. His predecessors had already laid their anathema on the secret societies vomited forth from the regions of darkness for the ruin of Church and State. Pius IX, it seems, singled out for his own special anathemas the Bible Societies instituted by heretics for the spread of their secret poison. Under the same ban he laid religious indifference, the opposition to religious celibacy, and the establishment of a soul-destroying philosophy under the pretence of education. It was then he warned. the faithful against the pernicious tracts sown broadcast by wicked hands, and, in a word, all free thoughts, free speech, and, above all, the free Press. Certainly it is not amiss the world should be reminded that it was Pope Pius IX who did all this; that he did it when he was, so to speak, a child of the people, and that it passed with scarcely animadversion—nay more, that the bare fact may be almost said to be forgotten.

'But the Pope's apologists are not content with the natural inference that he was always the same man that he is now; they must also establish a splendid and elaborate unity of design. It is a policy that is to be defended, and the world is triumphantly asked why it interferes too late with the completion of the edifice it has had the opportunity of watching from the very foundations, and seen slowly rising story after story in a Pontificate providentially prolonged for this very work. As it is a question that concerns France a good deal more than ourselves, I need not hesitate to assist the Pope and his privileged champions in putting it well before the world. It appears that as early as November, 1846, the Pope condemned the Proposition numbered the fourth in the Syllabus, and then, or shortly after, expressed himself in like manner as to the Propositions numbered sixth, seventh, sixteenth, fortieth, and sixty-third in the Syllabus. But the fourth paragraph is simply a quotation *in extenso* from the earlier document, and various letters and allocutions from January to December, 1847, are referred to, the titles given, in order to prove that the Syllabus and, consequently, the Propositions now before the Œcumenical Council were all anticipated, more or less literally, on or before the very year 1847 now brought into question. When, therefore, Napoleon III asks the Pope to return to the counsels of 1847, it is nothing more nor less than advising him to return to the Syllabus — a most needless piece of advice, inasmuch as the Vicar of Jesus Christ has never departed from those counsels, and is not likely to depart from them. If, too, it be said that all this refers only to religious principles, not to those relating to temporal matters, and that Pius IX has certainly somewhat departed from his first temporal policy, and has shown a want of fixed principles, an answer is at hand, these writers inform us. In the first month of 1847 M. Guizot wrote a series of despatches to the French Minister at the court of Rome, bringing before the newly-elected Pope certain articles agreed upon by the five European Powers in 1831, with a view to the improvement of the Papal Government. Pius IX entered heartily into the programme, and immediately upon his coronation had the entire series of papers collected, with all the appended documents, and these he kept in his own room in the Quirinal, with his private papers, intending to make the fullest use of them. When, however, he was driven into exile, these papers, with many others, were stolen and dispersed or destroyed. The Pope had made no secret of his reason for collecting the papers, said to have been very bulky, and lumbering his private room with them. His intention was to study them diligently, and by their light to give to the Pontifical Government that completion which he felt it still needed. Of course, it is a great pity that the loss of these papers should have entirely stopped for twenty years all reform at the Holy See; but, for the present, I will return to the Syllabus, and its growth from the sapling of 1847 to the Œcumenical Council of 1870. The present argument worked out elaborately before us that if the world stood by quietly and watched with approving smiles the first inception, the scattered anticipation, and the slow progress of this enormous design, it has no reason to interfere with the final execution. The argument is addressed, of course, to those who are directly concerned in the result, and who also had the power always in their hands. Why did they let the work go on towards its evil and bitter end? But the argument is still liable to the rejoinder—If all that comes of allowing Pius IX to begin as he did, and go on as he did, what in the world will not come of letting him work it out to the very end of all?'

The famous despatch of Count Daru of the 18th of February, and the subsequent claim of the Emperor's Government to send an envoy to the Council are the consistent steps of a policy the ultimate object of which must soon be placed beyond the realm of conjecture. It is said that Count Daru is the only member of the Imperial Government who desires to assert the claim of direct representation at the Council, and that the result of the further deliberations of the Cabinet will be the withdrawal of the demand [1]. By this means the

---

[1] The *Journal of Geneva* recently published an analysis of the note addressed by Count Daru to the Vatican, and of Antonelli's reply. According to this journal, Count Daru's despatch does not touch upon the question of the Pope's infallibility so lightly as was supposed. He claims for the French Government the right of being heard in the discussion of matters of a mixed

threatening rupture with Rome may be averted; but it is instructive to note the grounds upon which the Ultramontane press disallows the claims of France. 'At the Council of Trent,' says the *Tablet*, 'the ambassadors represented Catholic sovereigns and stable governments, whereas now there is not a Catholic government in Europe—since Jews, Protestants, and Atheists may be members of any of them.' Quoting with approval similar remarks from the *Pays*, the *Tablet* cannot believe that the French Government can persist in offering counsels to the Head of the Church, or authorize any kind of ambassadorial agent to present himself in its name, 'in order to talk Latin to the Council.' The Cabinet, the *Tablet* thinks, will content itself with having made a blunder, and will not persist in converting it into a fault. But if France remains obdurate, let her know that a French envoy, talking against the Syllabus, 'would be disarmed by the smiles of his audience, and feel himself crushed with ridicule under a sense of his own presumption!'

character, but does not insist upon it to the extent allowed at the Council of Trent. The French Minister for Foreign Affairs says that the Government would be satisfied to have a French bishop explaining in the Council the condition and the rights of the country; and he concludes by proposing a modification of the programme of the Council in the above sense, even if it should be found necessary to prorogue the Council. Count Daru's despatch does not make any threat in the event of a refusal being received from the Vatican. Cardinal Antonelli, in his reply, represents that a bishop could not reconcile the double duties of an ambassador and a Father of the Council. Nevertheless he does not decline to receive observations from France before the discussion on any particular question, but neither can he undertake that the recommendations which may be given will be adopted.

But the Syllabus, as interpreted by the articles *De Romano Pontifice*, contains in its eighty propositions the germ of almost every dogma to be submitted to the Council, not excepting the Pope's secular right to the temporal estate. It would identify the constitution of the Church with a particular domestic establishment, 'notoriously the stone of permanent offence to the unity of Italy, and thereby to the secular peace of a most important part of Catholic Europe.' The elaborate tissue of dogmatic propositions, composing this document, upon which it is sought to set the final seal of authority, are framed to secure to the powerful party now dominant in Rome the retention of their power, and to stifle the uprising of a contrary influence. Very suggestive upon this point is the following proposition bearing upon *the* question of the day:—'The government of the public schools in a Christian State cannot belong, and ought not to belong, to the civil authority.' These—and not simply questions bearing upon the minute points of ecclesiastical discipline cunningly brought into prominence in the Syllabus—are matters upon which the Council cannot avoid the responsibility of discussion. 'It is more probable,' says a writer in the *Pall Mall Gazette*, 'that the bishops will be requested to sanction it in the complex by an open and unanimous adhesion, and to explain in detail such of the condemnations as are obscurely worded or erroneously interpreted by the public. Such is said to have been the advice of the majority of the consultors of the Commission for politico-ecclesiastical affairs.'

Whilst these pages are passing through the press, intelligence reaches us of the 'unanimous' voting of the first *Schema de Fide*, on the 11th of April. According to the official journal of Rome, 515 bishops voted for the *schema* unreservedly, and 83 conditionally. The Ultramontane press is triumphant, and wisely reticent concerning the 100 bishops now in Rome who were conspicuous by their absence from the division.

The Jesuits have undoubtedly achieved a triumph greater than they could have anticipated, and at which they have some right to be jubilant. But, amid the vociferous applause with which it is communicated to the world, it is well that we should realize what, stripped of the trappings of polemical bedizenment, this success really means. It is simply this, that nearly five months of debate in the Council, which the *Civiltà Cattolica* prognosticated would be of as short duration as that of Chalcedon, has produced the nett result of carrying one of the fifty-three *schemata* on the Council programme, and that only in the extremely modified form imparted to it by Cardinal Bilio's committee, in deference to the strictures of the opposition in the preliminary discussions.

That the entire Constitution *de Fide* will now be carried no longer admits of doubt. But the tones of Pius IX, while gladdening the hearts of the Ultramontane bishops, as he pronounces these deplorable articles of the Syllabus to be the law of the Church, will pronounce the final severance of Rome, with her intolerable pretensions, from the current of modern thought—the divorce, final and complete, between reason and faith.

The Consitution *de Fide* consists of eighteen canons, distributed under four articles:—Of God, the Creator of all things; Of Revelation; Of Faith; and Of Faith and Reason. The first pronounces the curse of the Church upon all those who encounter metaphysical difficulties in their conception of the Creator. 'If any one shall say finite things as well corporeal as spiritual, or at least the spiritual, have emanated from the Divine substance, let him be anathema.' How many simple God-fearing souls will be consigned to perdition for their 'damnable error' of failing rightly to comprehend the mystery of creation,—'the Lord breathed into his nostrils the breath of life, and man became a living soul?'

The second article anathematizes all those who reject as uncanonical 'the whole books of Holy Scripture, with all their parts, as set forth by the Council of Trent, or deny that they are divinely inspired,'—the legend of Bel and the Dragon, introducing us to 'the company of the priests *with their wives and children,*' and the licentious story of Susanna and the Elders included.

The third article reiterates the curses of the Church upon all such as receive the doctrine of justification by faith. And

The fourth pronounces anathema upon those who accept the teachings of science when in seeming opposition to revelation, or 'to the sense which the Church has always attributed to dogmas.'

The period for the discussion of the great question draws on apace. The papers referring to the *Schema Deuxmano Pontifice*, embracing the question of Papal Infallibility, will, it is said, be distributed to the Fathers immediately after the promulgation of the Constitution *de Fide*. Then we shall learn the real strength of the opposition,—whether their courage has evaporated in words, or, being heaven-born, will brave the consequences of earnest and conscientious protest.

But it is easy to perceive that, with the present organization of the hierarchy, it is a hopeless undertaking for a few, or even for many bishops, to resist the programme of the Jesuits, supported by the supreme head of the Church with all the authority with which his Apostolic chair is now surrounded.

The Church of Rome ascribes many of her misfortunes to the want of accurate definitions. Such is the justification put forward for the present Council, and for the great dogma which, in some form or other, will doubtless be promulgated. The success with which, in former ages, the Church has addressed itself to the settlement of complicated theological and speculative questions, encourages the Jesuits to make light of the quicksands amongst which they are now moving. They are as buoyant with hope as are those 'perfidious enemies' of the Pope that hail the infatuation of the men who will 'cause the Papacy to stultify itself beyond all cure.'

Speculation upon the vicissitudes of this great question would be profitless and tedious, and it is unnecessary to review the history of a controversy which has been brought to the foreground of all discussion upon the proceedings of the Council.

The Fathers of the Council demand freedom of speech, and the Pope has recently declared that he did not wish any bishop to return to his diocese 'without having said all that he thought it his duty to say.' The spirit of independence which is developing itself in the very bosom of the assembled episcopate is reflected by, or is perhaps itself the reflection of, the same spirit in their flocks out of doors. In rapid succession, the most important towns of Germany have declared themselves against the dogma of Infallibility. Bonn, Breslau, and Cologne have united with ultramontane Wurzburg, and the not less ultra-Roman laity of the city of Munich, in doing honour to the courageous and orthodox theologian, Dr. Döllinger, for his fearless advocacy of Catholic freedom, whilst the King of Prussia has addressed to him an autograph letter thanking him for those manly theses in which he demolished Rome's pretensions to infallibility.

Will that freedom of debate upon this crucial question, claimed by the bishops, and in words conceded by the Pope, be allowed? There are unmistakable indications that anything like free discussion will be suppressed; and the so-called deliberations of the Council, however protracted, will issue in the formal registering of the dogma, enunciated, like that of 1854, on the sole responsibility of Pius IX. Few will be found to emulate the temerity of those who have presumed to avail themselves of the promised liberty of debate.

The following warning which has recently appeared in the *Civiltà Cattolica*, the infallible echo of Vatican law, might well disturb the equanimity of the most resolute of prelates. 'What,' it asks, 'is the Pope in relation to the episcopate in council assembled? As the successor of Peter, he is, according to Scripture, the corner-stone of the Church, the possessor of the keys of heaven, the shepherd of the flock of Christ. According to the Council of Lyons he is the guide of the Universal Church; according to that of Florence, he is the head, the master, the father of all Christianity. . . . . These are the relations between the Pope and the Church, whether the latter be considered in its isolated and special groups, or as a whole, *in corpore*, or in council. What, then, tell us these relations between Pope and Church in their special groups or in council? SUPREME AUTHORITY AND SUBJECTION:—*the former vested in the Pope, the latter the part of the assembly of the bishops!'* 'No doubt,' observes a writer in the *Pall Mall Gazette*, 'liberty of speech is an indispensable prerogative of any council not a sham; but to those who reckon on the warrant of sacred right to secure them against despotic encroachments by a holy Father, we would recount a little fact that happened in 1854. There was then also a question of promulgating a dogma, very dear to the heart of its promoters, and the bishops had been worked assiduously as now, until they were all as soft as butter. There was then also a so-called deliberative assembly, professing gravely and conscientiously to discuss pros and cons, the conclusion being all the while foregone. And, moreover, there was then in Rome one, Abbé Laborde, who was innocent enough to believe words were meant to be taken at their sense, and accordingly begged to be allowed to state, not at all his dissent from, but merely the grounds on which he desired further argument in behalf of, the proposed dogma. Abbé Laborde received the following reply. He was then and there taken neck and crop and forcibly expelled from Rome [1].'

[1] The *Pall Mall Gazette* gives the following account of a 'scene' enacted at the latest sitting of the Council:—'The amenities of debate were, perhaps, not too closely observed; at any rate, two right rev. Fathers, Cardinal Schwarzenberg and Monsignor Strossmayer, were "called to order." Until we have had an authoritative denial of the incident, there can be no harm in saying that, according to our correspondent, the cardinal attacked the revised scheme *De Fide*, especially denouncing the canons which anathematized Protestants as contrary to the spirit

Already the original regulations of the Council, which afforded too much scope for the dangerous eloquence and excessive earnestness of the opposition, have been modified by a decree requiring the Fathers to present in writing to the Commissions any objections which they wish to urge. *The substance of these objections* will then be laid before the Council by the Commissions, and the debate strictly limited to their defence or refutation. Further, when the Council shall decide that any point of doctrine or discipline has been *sufficiently discussed*, the vote upon it will be taken at once, the Fathers being allowed to express their opinion simply by votes of *placet* and *non placet*. The Pope has been much annoyed at the protracted debates upon *schemata* which are preliminary to the grand issue, and, if the Roman correspondent of the *Pall Mall Gazette* is to be credited, he has hit upon a novel experiment for expediting the debates. He declares that the Fathers

of the Gospel. He eulogized the sanctity and genius which ennoble many Protestants, and declared that such men " could not be precipitated by words into hell." The cardinal is even said to have characterized the threats of eternal torment so held out as " profane and impudent." He then thanked God that the time for these cursings between Catholics and Protestants was now passed, never to return. The cardinal is reported to have closed a remarkably vigorous speech with the declaration that he longed to begin the great work of religious conciliation, and he frankly tendered his hand to those Protestants whose benevolence and piety he had so eloquently extolled. The storm which immediately arose in the Council was not allayed when Monsignor Strossmayer " ascended the tribune, and, amid a profound silence, delivered the most eloquent panegyric on Protestants that ever fell from a Catholic bishop." A scene of great confusion ensued, and, as the tumult could not be repressed, the legates broke up the assembly.'

can only be taught despatch by their stomachs. The other day he said to his household, 'If they are kept without dinner till they do something, you will see how quick the affairs of the Council will proceed.' Accordingly, the supplement to the regulations is to be further supplemented by a decree that the Fathers are not to leave the Council Hall till they have agreed upon the question in debate.

Such are the tactics to which it is found necessary to resort, in order that the doctrines of the Syllabus shall not be set aside by an assembly in which the Pope commands a large and faithful majority, made up of Italian, Spanish, and Missionary bishops, and of the Vicars-Apostolic, the creatures of the Pontiff. 'Bishops,' said Bossuet, ' are pastors in relation to their people, *but sheep in relation to Peter.*'

In illustration of the grim fanaticism, as pretentious in the nineteenth as in the eleventh century, which inspires the Roman *curia*, no apology is necessary for the introduction of the following series of dogmatic formulas from the *Schema Constitutionis Dogmaticæ de Ecclesia Christi*, submitted to the Council at its first session after Christmas, and which it is believed were the occasion of the intimation given by the French Government of its inability to consider with indifference any extreme resolutions adopted by the Council. In this document, which forms a volume of 200 pages, we have presented the full civil code, as conceived in the nineteenth century, of a corporation claiming, under the direct inspiration of the Holy Ghost, to proclaim the mind of Christ, whose Church is founded in love and peace and good-will to all mankind. The second section of the *Schema* contains the following twenty-one

T

canons, expressing dogmatically a series of propositions previously developed.

The Church of Christ.

Canon I.—Whosoever says that the religion of Christ is not existing and expressed in any community established by Christ Himself, but that it can be rightly held and exercised by each individual for himself, and without regard to any community which constitutes the Church of Christ, let him be anathema.

Canon II.—Whosoever says the Church has not received from Christ any positive and unchangeable organization, but that it is, just like any other human community, mutable and transformable according to the changes of the times, let him be anathema.

Canon III.—Whosoever says the Church of Divine Promises is not an external and visible community, but a purely internal and invisible one, let him be anathema.

Canon IV.—Whosoever says that the true Church is not a body in itself, but consists of different and dispersed denominations, and is diffused throughout them all; or that the different communities opposed to each other in their professions of faith, and divided in their spirit, equally form members or parts of the one common Church of Christ, let him be anathema.

Canon V.—Whosoever says that the Church of Christ is not an institution absolutely necessary for reaching eternal happiness, or that men can arrive at this blessing through the exercise of any other kind of religion, let him be anathema.

Canon VI.—Whosoever says that the authority with which the Catholic Church proscribes and condemns all religious sects separated from its communion is not prescribed by Divine right; or that about religious truths only opinions, not certainties, can exist, and that therefore all religious sects are to be tolerated, let him be anathema.

Canon VII.—Whosoever says that this very Church of Christ can fall into darkness or error, and so deviate from the Holy Truth in faith and morals, and fall away from its original institution into depravity and corruption, let him be anathema.

Canon VIII.—Whosoever says that the present Church of Christ in not the last and highest institution for reaching eternal happiness, but that there is another to be expected through a new and more complete effusion of the Holy Spirit, let him be anathema.

Canon IX.—Whosoever says that the infallibility of the Church is restricted only to things contained in the Divine Revelation, but is not extended to other truths which are necessary to the integral maintenance of the Revelation, let him be anathema.

Canon X.—Whosoever says that the Church is not a perfect institution, but merely a corporation, or that it is of such a nature, with regard to civil society or the State, as to be subject to temporal power, let him be anathema.

Canon XI.—Whosoever says that the Church, divinely instituted, is like a society of equals, and that the Bishops, having offices and duties, possess no governmental power bestowed upon them by Divine right and which they can freely exercise, let him be anathema.

Canon XII. — Whosoever says that Christ, our Saviour and Sovereign, has conferred upon the Church the power to direct only by advice and persuasion those who turn aside, not to compel them by orders, by coercion, and by external verdicts and statutory punishments, let him be anathema.

Canon XIII.—Whosoever says that the true Church of Christ, out of which there is no salvation, is any other than the holy Catholic and Roman Apostolic Church, let him be anathema.

Canon XIV.—Whosoever says that the Holy Apostle Peter was not appointed by Christ as the first of the apostles, and as the visible head of the whole Church Militant, or that he had only the honorary supremacy, but not the true and real jurisdiction, let him be anathema.

Canon XV.—Whosoever says that it is not according to Christ's own will that St. Peter has permanent successors in his supremacy over the whole Church, or that the Roman Pope is not the successor of Peter in this primacy by Divine right, let him be anathema.

Canon XVI.—Whosoever says that the Roman Pope has only the office of superintendence and direction, not the highest and fullest power of jurisdiction over the whole Church, or that this power is not direct and legitimate over the whole of the various Churches, let him be anathema.

Canon XVII.—Whosoever says that the independent Church authority, as established by the Catholic Church and bestowed upon her by Christ, and the supreme civil power cannot exist together, so as to preserve the due rights of both, let him be anathema.

Canon XVIII.—Whosoever says that the power necessary for the government of a civil State does not emanate from God, or that one is not bound by Divine law to submit himself to such power, or that such power is repugnant to the natural liberty of men, let him be anathema.

Canon XIX.—Whosoever says that all rights existing between men arise from the political State, and that there is no other authority besides that so constituted, let him be anathema.

Canon XX.—Whosoever says that the supreme rule for public and social conduct is in the law of the political State, or in the public opinion of men, or that the judgments of the Church concerning what is lawful and unlawful do not extend to such actions, or that there may be something allowed by civil rights that is not allowed by Church rights, let him be anathema.

Canon XXI.—Whosoever says that the laws of the Church have no binding power, excepting so far as they are confirmed by the sanction of the civil power, or that this civil power has the right, consequent on its high authority, to pronounce judgment or decisions in matters of religion, let him be anathema.

There is nothing new in the cursing propensities of a Church whose power, from the days of Gregory the Great, when her insatiable thirst for wealth and power obscured the image of her Founder, has been built upon interdicts and anathemas. But the question presents itself, Is this indeed 'the Rock of unshaken Truth?' is this 'a photograph of the Bride of Christ?' Let us see who it is upon whom heaven's wrath is here denounced. It is well that we are not left to deduce this from the fevered diatribes of polemical and heretical controversialists. We have before us the deliberate production of the legislators of the Roman Church, unfettered save in their devotion to him whom they regard as its infallible head.

He, then, who receives the Saviour's words 'Other sheep I have which are not of this fold,' is accursed.

He who does not believe that our Saviour erred in giving his commission to '*other seventy*' besides the Apostles, confirming it with those suggestive words '*he that despiseth you* despiseth ME,' is accursed.

He who holds with Peter, that God is no respecter of persons, but in every nation he that feareth Him, and worketh righteousness, is accepted with Him, is accursed.

He who, with Paul, recognizing that there is not in every man the same knowledge, scorns to become a stumbling-block to a weak brother, is accursed.

He who listens to the admonition of the Apostle James, 'So speak ye, and so do, as they that shall be judged by the law of liberty,' is accursed.

He who does not believe that the Master erred when He said 'My kingdom is not of this world,' is accursed.

He who hesitates to ignore, and when necessary to deny, historical facts which militate against the Papal pretensions, is accursed.

Finally, he who accepts that most accursed heresy, that 'Love is the fulfilling of the law,' or believes that the infallibility of St. Peter himself must not be assigned to a date posterior to his exhortation to the elect, '*Above all things* have *fervent* charity among yourselves,' and again, to his antecedent reprobation of the perverse rendering of the charge 'Feed my sheep,' by himself commenting upon it thus, 'Not as lords over God's heritage,' is accursed.

The curses of the Church extend not only to every

man who doubts her most overweening pretensions, they embrace him also who presumes to doubt the eternal damnation of the doubter. Verily, 'as troops of robbers wait for a man, so the company of priests murder in the way by consent.' Thus far the Papal anathemas apply only to the realm of opinion; did they stop here the civil powers would continue to look on with placid indifference. But these far-reaching curses consign to perdition every man who dares to accept the evidence of his senses that civil society *can exist apart from the Roman Catholic Church*. They invade the rights of nations, and pre-eminently of France, by aiming at the subversion of Concordats, the only safeguards of Catholic governments against priestly encroachments.

We see, to-day, the Catholic governments of Europe conceding liberal institutions, in the hope of directing, as the only alternative of being subverted by, the advancing and irresistible tide of democracy. Will they, will France, concede the claim of Rome to propound laws upon which no lay sovereign may trespass save at the peril of eternal damnation? 'Thy people are as they who strive with the priest,' was the bitter taunt with which Hosea demonstrated the hopelessness of Israel's controversy with Jehovah. But the day is past when it shall be said, 'There shall be like people, like priest.' Priestcraft is dead; it remains only to be buried. The Council which is to proclaim the infallibility of the chief priest of Rome, has well inaugurated its discussions by this wild utterance of Papal self-inflation, exhibiting in its true character the corpse which it is now the business of civil society decently to inter.

The definition of Infallibility to which the Council will be invited to attach the seal of authority, has been recently published as an additional article to the *Schema* to which I have referred. It is in the following terms:—

'Chapter to be added to the decree upon the primacy of the Roman Pontiff, to the effect that the Roman Pontiff cannot err in the definition of matters of faith or morals.

'The Holy Roman Church possesses the supreme and complete primacy and principality over the Universal Catholic Church, which it verily and humbly acknowledges to have received, with the plenitude of the power of the Lord himself, in the person of St. Peter, the Prince of Apostles, of whom the Roman Pontiff is the successor.

'And as, above all things, it behoves it to make clear the truth of the faith, all questions which may arise upon matters of faith must be determined by its judgment, seeing that otherwise the words of the Lord Jesus Christ (*Tu es Petrus*, &c.) would be disregarded.

'That which has been set forth upon this point has been proved by the results as in the Apostolic See. The Catholic religion has always been preserved immaculate, and its doctrine has always been maintained at its fulness (*celebrata*).

'Consequently, we inculcate, with the concurrence of the Holy Council, and we define as a dogma of faith that, thanks to the divine assistance, it is that the Roman Pontiff, of whom it was said in the person of St. Peter by our same Lord Jesus Christ, "I have prayed for thee," &c. cannot err when, acting in his quality as supreme teacher of all Christians, he defines what the Universal Church must hold in matters of faith and morals, and that the prerogative of inerrancy or infallibility extends over the same matters to which the infallibility of the Church is applicable. But if any one should dare—which may God forbid!—to controvert our present definition, let him know that he departs from the truth of the faith.'

It is easy to comprehend the overwhelming interest which the court of Rome must take in the authoritative definition of Papal Infallibility. If, they contend, the Church be an organic body possessing infallibility, that infallibility must reside in its head. In the pretension itself there is nothing new. It is the world, and not the Pope, that changes; and to this is assignable the now recognized absurdity of claims, blindly accepted during the middle ages, and only necessary to vindicate and enforce by the decisions of a Council when the advance of freedom and intelligence, the revelations of science[1], and the consequent elevation of opinion, has snapped the fetters of priestcraft, and proclaimed the divorce of civil society from that old order of things to which the Church of Rome tenaciously clings.

By the entire Ultramontane press of Europe the question of Infallibility is regarded as one altogether fundamental—touching the essential constitution of the Church itself. In the *Tablet*, of the 12th of March, we read:—' As far as it concerns their immunity from errors in matters of faith, by providing them with an

---

[1] The first proposition on 'rationalism' submitted to the Council, and which has elicited such a storm of condemnatory eloquence from many of its most eminent members, is said to be this:—' That the human mind, unassisted by Divine light, is unable to arrive at truth, and therefore that the conclusions drawn from history, science, and experiment, if not in accordance with the dogmas of the Church, are to be rejected and condemned.'

infallible guide, it is a purely spiritual question, affecting the truths of revelation, and our own certainty with respect to them. But in its bearings on the general constitution of the Church it has also a politico-religious aspect which deserves separate attention, *and of which the gravity is apparent* even to non-Catholics.' It is in this politico-religious aspect that the decisions of the Council upon this and other matters claim consideration here.

To an ordinary understanding it would seem that the alleged necessity of a Council to propound dogmas, and to solve doubts, involves the deliberate acknowledgment of FALLIBILITY. And this view is consistent with the history of the Church—not indeed with the popular creed throughout the darkest period of the middle ages, but with the repeated decisions of Councils regarded by Rome herself as Œcumenical, and their decrees consequently binding upon the conscience of Christendom.

With infallibility is intimately associated *the principle of absolute supremacy*. The tendency of Rome towards absolutism we have seen to be of ancient date. But the dogmatic definition of the Personal Infallibility of the Pontiff, and by induction of his superiority over Councils, in the face of repeated decisions of Œcumenical Councils in a contrary sense, involves the absurdity of demonstrating *the fallibility* of *infallible* Popes and Councils. Either the Council of Constance was infallible or it was not. If it was not, then on the Ultramontane theory of the Pope's sole infallibility, all preceding Councils were also fallible, and the Council of the Vatican cannot be held to constitute an exception. But Rome has always held that the Council of

Constance *was infallible*; the Pope, therefore, who dares to question the binding power of its decisions incurs the sin of schism, and the resulting penalty of deposition.

> 'When Popes damn Popes, and Councils damn them all,
> And Popes damn Councils, what must Christians do?
> When they each other's laws damn and recall,
> How shall we know whose power then was true[1]?'

But this question of infallibility has also wider bearings. It will inevitably—in point of fact it does already—awaken the jealous susceptibilities of governments from which Rome cannot afford to be alienated. The recent changes in the home policy of the Emperor of the French, necessitate his reverting to the original condition—that of good government—upon which the French protectorate in Rome was undertaken. It is impossible for him to promote in France those civil institutions which, supported by the protection of French troops, the Pope is trampling under foot in Rome, without raising suspicions as to the sincerity of his liberal intentions. The Emperor of Austria is equally pledged to oppose the fanatical pretensions of the Pope's Ultramontane advisers, whilst other powers, both Catholic and Protestant, concur in protesting against these extravagances. 'These governments,' says the *Times*, 'would be all more or less anxious to prevent the Pope from being invested with an unlimited and uncontrolled spiritual authority which he might possibly make use of to create embarrassments in their respective dominions. The new dogma would offend a large proportion of Latin Catholics, as introducing a profound change in the constitution of the

---

[1] Richard Baxter.

Church, and because, in our times, absolutism in religion is not more relished than in politics. Oriental Catholics would take immediate alarm at a dogma which is directly opposed to their unbounded veneration for Œcumenical Councils, and would render those solemn assemblies useless in future.'

The position in which Pius IX will find himself, through the reassertion of the mediæval pretensions, is that of his own choosing. Italy waits for her capital, and the world's plaudits would attend the magnanimity of the ruler who should say—IT IS HERS!

The supremacy involved in the recognition of infallibility would be complete over the material as over the spiritual world. It would stamp out the last remnant of the Gallican school, and of the liberal and constitutional party in the Church of Rome, all over Christendom, and secure the uncontrolled triumph of the Ultramontanes, animated by their old proclivities to tyrannize over the rulers and peoples of the earth. The result might be fittingly embodied in a formulary which we humbly submit to the consideration of H. E. Cardinal Antonelli:—

> 'This is the Pope,
> That rules the Council,
> That rules the Church,
> That rules the world.'

'The great object of the Council,' remarks an eminent ecclesiastical historian[1], 'is to place society and the Church on what Rome regards as their true basis.

[1] *British Quarterly Review*, April, 1870. Article, 'The Council of the Vatican.' We can hardly be in error in attributing this able and interesting article to the pen of the distinguished author of 'The Church of the Restoration.'

This basis for the State is a theocracy; for the Church, the Pope's infallibility. Thus to confirm the Syllabus, to proclaim Papal infallibility, to complete the glorification of Mary, is the programme elaborated at Rome.' Throughout the world a conflict between Church and State will be precipitated, and its issue is not uncertain. The prescience of Rome descries 'terrible revolutions' as the penalty of civil laws 'contrary to the decrees of the Council.' But Rome has no longer the power to accomplish the fulfilment of her own prophecies. 'For these "terrible revolutions," indeed, it is difficult to say who ought to be most anxious to prepare; for, although during these last eighty years revolutions have been only too frequent, we cannot recall one that has arisen out of zeal for the Papacy, or in defence of Concordats, or out of resentment for the disregarded decrees and regulations of a Council. Rather the reverse has generally been the case. The thread of tyranny snapped when it was pressed too tightly in obedience to Papal ascendancy. If the *Civiltà Cattolica* doubt the fact, let it look at the fallen dynasties, victims of "terrible revolutions"—those Tuscan, Neapolitan, and other royal families now crowding the Royal Tribune at the Council Hall in the Vatican—those dynasties who cast in their lot with the Pope, and whose lot the Pope himself partially shared. In this matter of "terrible revolutions," it will be well if the warning which Rome addresses to her neighbours be not lost upon herself [1].'

But this dogma, to be defined out of consideration for 'the greater glory of God,' is also fraught with danger to the Church as a spiritual corporation. There

---

[1] The *Times*.

is a limit—and Rome must learn the fact—to the passive susceptibility whose impotence of resistance has allowed the definition of the dogma of the Immaculate Conception; whilst the spectacle of the civil governments arrayed in self-defence against the reviving encroachments of a spiritual power in avowed antagonism with all that is liberal and progressive in modern ideas, is little calculated to retard the advance of rationalism and infidelity which it is the mission of the Church to arrest.

The discussions of the past sessions of the Council, wherein language, to which Rome is little accustomed to listen, has fallen from the lips of prelates of high degree, may induce the managers of the Council yet more effectually to seal the lips of the refractory bishops. But what if Catholics outside, profoundly believing in the direct superintendence of the Holy Ghost over the deliberations of the Council, should be perverse enough to regard such tactics in the light of an impious attempt to control the mouth of inspiration? What if indignant Catholics, in Germany, Hungary, Switzerland—even in priest-ridden Spain and Italy—should clamour for *the establishment of National Churches*, enjoying, at the least, the liberty which France extorted as the condition of tolerating the Roman Catholic religion? These are not visionary dangers. From Madrid we learn that the Government abstain from sending a special envoy to the Council on the ground of the intolerant spirit which prevails at Rome. This is consistent with the rapid spread of a diametrically opposite principle in Spain, where complete liberty of conscience is now recognized as the divine right of man.

The consequences, as regards the Roman Catholic laity of Switzerland, of the attempts to check all free discussion in the Council, are thus described by an intelligent observer :—'There is some reason to think that the Roman Catholic laity of Switzerland will set an example of resistance to the pretensions of the Ultramontane clergy, which may probably be imitated in other countries. The position taken up by the Swiss prelates at the Council, with only one exception, has been deeply resented by their countrymen. An address issued by the Catholics of Aargan represents the opinion of the public with considerable accuracy. Its authors denounce the views now in favour at Rome as contradictory to the teachings of history and science, and describe the attribution of supernatural powers to the Pope as a return to the blindness of heathenism. They hold that the only true remedy must be sought in a searching reform of the Church, and the complete subordination of the clergy to the State, with the institution of diocesan synods, in which the laity must be largely represented. Their demand, in short, practically amounts to complete independence of Rome. The opposition of intelligent laymen is a disturbing element which as yet has not been sufficiently taken into account. In Switzerland it is probable that Rome will provoke a secession. In Southern Germany, where Austria has lost a golden opportunity of placing herself at the head of liberal Catholicism, the Jesuits, it is now seen, have been playing into the hands of Bismarck, and forcing the ablest thinkers in the Southern States to look to Prussia as the ultimate safeguard of the independent Church of Germany.'

An eminent German bishop has declared his conviction that one effect of the decree of Papal infallibility would be to make all Germany Protestant. The German press teems with contemptuous ridicule of the programme of the Jesuits. The *Neue Freie Presse*, an Austrian journal, says:—'The Pope has at length resolved to make a bold stroke on the question of Infallibility. On the 25th inst., the Feast of the Annunciation, we are told that the Œcumenical Council will, in a public sitting, proclaim "the additional article of the *Schema*," the Infallibility of the Pope. Christ, according to the Scriptures,' it continues, 'became man and dwelt among us. Pius IX and his successors are to become God from the 25th of March, during the short time of their pilgrimage upon earth. But,' it adds, 'the Pope, adorned with his new infallibility, may learn that there are certain things the nineteenth century will tolerate just as little as the sixteenth.'

As an illustration of the boldness of the language in which zealous Catholics do not hesitate to denounce the projects of the Roman *Curia*, the following quotation from an address, 'to the Vatican Council,' by Dr. Sepp, quoted from the *North German Correspondent*, is interesting and significant:—'The supreme authority in the Church will be always respected by Catholics so long as we hear nothing beyond authority, but the word "infallibility" is a stumbling-stone and an offence, and woe to him by whom offences come. "You shall be as Gods," was not a celestial but a demoniacal suggestion. The deification of the Roman emperors conduced neither to the welfare of the world nor to that of the Cæsars, and what advantage is to accrue to humanity from this new and significant dogma of Infallibility? It is surprising how often in history ecclesiastical dignitaries, especially among the Latin nations, have been the promoters of temporal despotism. The supreme Head of the Church must never degenerate into the Dalai Lama of the West. Never must we recognize in the Pope a new incarnation of the Logos, an additional revelation and ecclesiastical oracle. Christ alone, and not his high priest, must personally be the object of our faith and trust. The thunders of the Vatican may be tried to subject the world to the claims of this overweening ambition, but a recognition of such pretensions cannot be obtained by force. When brought fairly face to face with the difficulties of the position, the most devoted adherents of Rome will hesitate and conscientiously refuse to proceed farther. Such an act of self-glorification inspires the reflecting Catholic with horror, and it reminds non-Catholics of some parts of the book of Revelation. By the virtual institution of an exclusively Italian Church government, by the assumption of one infallible Head of the Church, deciding dogmatically in disputed questions, the formation of independent national Churches is provoked, and in addition to a Gallican and an Anglican a German Church may, by the force of circumstances, be brought into existence. It is not an error to assert that even a hierarchy cannot rule without a certain popularity. In the course of a thousand years so many dogmas have not been proclaimed as in our times during a single Pontificate, and no one felt the least longing for them with the exception of certain gentlemen in Rome. The proclamation of the new dogma would be the first signal for a new conflict with the Jesuits, and the first step to their second overthrow.'

In France the memorable letter of Father Hyacinthe to the General of the Barefooted Carmelites at Rome, revealing as it did, 'a pure element of religion aiming at emancipation from Roman tyranny,' will not soon be forgotten. Denouncing 'the divorce, as impious as it is senseless, which Rome seeks to bring about between the Church, which is our mother according to eternity, and the society of the nineteenth century, of which we are the sons in a temporal sense, and towards which we also have duties and sympathies,' he declares himself— knowing well that he carries with him the sympathies of millions—'at war with those doctrines and practices which are called Roman;' with that false Catholicism to which he attributes the social, moral, and religious anarchy, into which France is plunged.

In the same sense, and within a fortnight of his death, we have a kindred protest from the distinguished historian and statesman to whose letter I have already had occasion to refer. 'A few hysterical words,' says the *Tablet*; but they are words carrying the emphasis which we instinctively attach to all 'last words,' whose echoes will outlive the pretensions they denounce. Their significance was at least recognized by the Pontiff, who, if report speaks truly—though afterwards expressing the pious hope that the Count had recanted his errors, and ordering a mass to be said for the repose of his soul— exclaimed on hearing of the distinguished patriot's death, 'Oh, what good fortune [1]!' Here are the words of this

---

[1] The *Tablet* would have blushed to attribute to the Pope a sentiment which even a man capable of feeling it would be ashamed to avow. But the statement of the generally well-informed correspondent of the *Pall Mall Gazette*, is not less complimentary to the good sense and refined feeling of the Pontiff,

most prominent champion of liberal views:—'Never, thank Heaven, have I thought, said, or written anything favourable to the personal and separate infallibility of the Pope, such as it is sought to impose upon us; nor to the theocracy, the dictatorship of the Church, which I did my best to reprobate in that history of the "Monks of the West," of which you are pleased to appreciate the laborious fabric; nor to that "Absolutism of Rome," of which the speech that you quote disputed the existence, even in the Middle Ages, but which to-day forms the symbol and the programme of the faction dominant among us ..... Therefore, without having either the will or the power to discuss the question now debating in the Council, I hail with the most grateful admiration, first, the great and generous Bishop of Orleans, then the eloquent and intrepid priests who have had the courage to place themselves across the path of the torrent of adulation, imposture, and servility by which we risk being swallowed up. Thanks to them, Catholic France will not have remained too much below Germany, Hungary, and America. I publicly pride myself, and more than I can express by words, to have them for friends and for brother academicians. I have but one regret, that of being prevented by illness from descending into the arena in their suite, not, certainly, on the ground of theology, but on that of history and of the social and political consequences of the system they contend against. Thus should I deserve my

than the account of this incident given by his monitor. 'What he (Pius IX) did say,' says the *Tablet*, 'was that Montalembert was one of those liberal Catholics who are only half Catholics. Here the manner of Pius IX *indicated very emphatically* a feeling of disgust.'

share (and it is the only ambition remaining to me) in those litanies of abuse daily launched against my illustrious friends by a too numerous portion of that poor clergy which prepares for itself so sad a destiny, and which I formerly loved, defended, and honoured as it had not yet been by any in modern France.'

There is no doubt that, to a certain class of mind, the doctrine of Papal Infallibility possesses a powerful fascination. It terminates once and for ever those perplexing questionings to which few reflective minds are strangers, and which will wear the heart and brain until they are resolved by hard, earnest, and honest thought; or by that which is of infinitely less trouble, an appeal to infallible authority.

Rome counts, no doubt, upon the implicit acceptance by all the faithful of whatever decrees the Council may promulgate. I have already referred to the improbability of a successful schism, and to the prevailing disposition of the laity in most Roman Catholic countries to accept, without enquiry, whatever may be prescribed by the head of the Church. 'It is a comfort,' says the *Tablet* of the 19th of March, 'to anticipate that our accusers, as soon as the definition is made, will not only cease from the strife and clamour, but accept it with *as cordial submission of heart and mind* as if it had always been the object of their wishes and prayers.' But Rome has given a mighty impulse to the spirit of enquiry, and has demonstrated more effectually than all the learned arguments of Protestant controversialists which have been launched against her pretensions, that her vaunted unity is a grand myth—her uniformity, even, a thing of the past. It remains to be seen whether in these days, intelligent and liberal Catholics will bow down their reason with the blind submission of the dark ages—whether, having unfurled the banner of Christian freedom, they will lower it under the abject pretext of submission, and thus 'lend their influence towards confounding the Gospel of Christ with a system of oppression which disgusts all upright consciences[1].'

The independent and antagonistic attitude assumed by so many of the Fathers in the Council, has encouraged independent thought amongst their flocks; and the demonstration of the fallibility of Councils held to have been infallible, by the reversal of their decisions in the promulgation of the dogma of the Infallibility of the Pontiff, will assuredly create greater consternation amongst the faithful in the nineteenth century, than did the declarations of Popes contradicting the doctrines of the Church, and their mutually destructive enunciations, in the Middle Ages. It will not be forgotten that the very last General Council imposed limits on the personal Infallibility of the Pontiff, and declared the voice of the whole Church, and not the voice of the Pontiff, to be supreme.

The world has now heard more than enough about one Infallible undoing and denouncing the acts of preceding Infallibles. The *Times* has recently remarked:—

'Pius IX has said "Let there be light," and light there cannot fail to be. Let the upshot of the Council be what it may, it will require no great effort for mankind to arrive at the conclusion that the Papal Infallibility, which so many took for granted, is a point on which the Church never agreed, and never can be brought to agree—a point which implied the

---

[1] 'British Quarterly Review,' April, 1870, Art. 'The Council of the Vatican.'

subjection of the Church to the Pope, and the discussion of which is by no means unlikely to break up Papal supremacy and accomplish ecclesiastical emancipation.'

The Church makes no new decrees, say the Ultramontanes; she does but place in a clearer light an ancient and primordial truth in opposition to a later error. The 'later error,' now to be exploded by the refulgence of light thrown upon it by the decision of the Council, is the supremacy of Councils over Popes. But the demonstration of this 'error' is the demonstration of the Fallibility of Popes and Councils alike who have decreed and enforced it. The well-known canon of St. Vincent, '*Quod semper, quod ubique, quod ab omnibus,*' the very charter of the unity of faith and practice in the Catholic Church—is abrogated.

Remembering how irrational, inconsistent, and even heretical, some of the Popes have been—and this vast prerogative, if now declared, must be held to have applied to all such—it is at least within the region of hypothesis to imagine a future Pontiff emulating the religious aptitudes of the first Napoleon, and justifying, on the ground of expediency, his profession of Islamism. By a stroke of his pen such an Infallible may substitute Mahomet for Christ in the creed of the Roman Catholic Church. His decision being infallible, would constitute an unimpeachable arret; the Christianity recognized at Rome, and from which already Christ is well-nigh ostracized by the greater honour rendered to the Virgin, would be blotted out of existence. Whether or not the world and *the Catholic Church* would be gainers by the process, is a subject of discussion not within our province.

It is impossible to escape the conviction that the attempt to cripple all intellectual movement and scientific activity in the Church by establishing the doctrine of the personal Infallibility of the Pontiff, and the still more absurd dogma of the corporeal assumption of Mary and her husband—the principal objects of the Council, to which the Pope will resist all opposition—will try the fabric of the Roman Catholic Church as nothing has tried it for centuries. It will arrest that sympathy with Roman Catholicism which has developed into an unreasoning passion with Liberals in Protestant countries. Protestants may take pride in contrasting the fearless honesty with which Protestant narrowness and bigotry have been denounced in England and Germany, with the extreme severity visited upon every form of Protestantism in Catholic countries[1]. Surely, however, adopting the language of the *Pall Mall Gazette*, the time has now come for a rather different policy:—

'Popery has in all directions become so vivacious of late years, and so many circumstances combine to help it on as a whole, and to give it favour in the eyes of large classes of our countrymen and countrywomen, that it is very desirable from time to time to insist upon the fact that a large part of what it teaches is paltry and effeminate nonsense, utterly destitute of the slightest pretensions to the consideration of any serious man, and deserving of the same sort of unqualified contempt and disgust with which reasonable people regard fortune-telling or any other gross delusion. But

---

[1] If the Council declares the propositions of the Syllabus to be Articles of Faith, religious persecution will become a sacred duty, obligatory upon every member of the Roman Communion.

it is difficult to imagine a more offensive or degrading spectacle than that of a number of men, mostly old men too, meeting together to affirm in the most solemn way the truth of a matter of fact about which they neither do nor can know anything at all. If they do make the affirmation in question, it will be neither more nor less than a gross falsehood, for what falsehood can be grosser than that of a person who solemnly affirms the truth of a matter of fact which he does not and cannot know to be true? The falsehood, moreover, will neither be less false nor less immoral because it will be told in a deeply religious spirit by very pious men. It is, indeed, obvious enough that to tell some such falsehood as this, the more monstrous and baseless the better, is the very object for which the Council is convened. The object is to affront and protest against human reason and the results to which it inevitably leads, and to set up other standards of truth than those which all men acknowledge in all other affairs. It is a conspiracy to force down the real truth by setting up a sham clerical truth based on mere assertion and sanctioned by anathemas instead of evidence; and this appears to us a proceeding as immoral as it is contemptible. It is a relief to turn to the vast though confused answer to the challenge which rises in different accents from every part of the world. We, say the Pope and his lieutenants, are the sole organs of moral and spiritual truth. We can announce to mankind at large all that they ought to know and believe on all great subjects *ex cathedrâ* and without giving any sort of grounds for our opinions. The answer is indirect and multifarious, but not the less impressive. Religion, says the Parliament of England, is matter of opinion. We will have free trade in it, and will make our laws upon all subjects with less and less reference to theological principles. The principles of 1789, say the French, express our real belief, and if we can but settle our political difficulties, you shall see how much we love you. The Spaniards convey their criticism through a revolution. The Italians look forward to the possession of Rome. Southern Germany is shaking off the Concordat and all its works. Northern Germany treats the Pope with civil contempt, and North America leaves very little Popery even in the Irish of the second generation. All this does not look as if the world at large believed that the Pope knew very much even about the Virgin Mary and her bodily assumption. To be sure he knows just as much about it as any one else, and a great deal more than the author of the fourth gospel knew, or, at all events, chose to tell. This writer—though, according to his own account, he "took her unto his own home," and ought, therefore, to have been well informed on the whole subject—says not one word about her except that she was present at the crucifixion, and was reproved at the marriage at Cana in Galilee.'

A General Council, says Dean Milman, is 'unnecessary, and could hardly be convoked but on extraordinary occasions, to settle some questions which have already violently disorganized the peace of Christendom.' But from the highest dignitary of the Church to the meanest *curé*, there is not one that fails to recognize the insufficiency of the reasons assigned in the Syllabus of June, 1867, for the convening of an Œcumenical Council. No new heresy exists to be combated, no schism to be anathematized. But whilst the apprehensions of numerous ecclesiastics respecting the real objects of the Council are shared by the secular Catholic powers, whose representatives are excluded from its deliberations, their distrust hardly ventures upon remonstrance or enquiry. Indeed it is easy to perceive that enquiry respecting the true aim and the practical regulation of the Council, would be silenced by the retort that it is impossible to predict the proceedings of men acting under the direct inspiration of the Holy Ghost.

Those who have watched the proceedings of the court of Rome since the close of the Italian war, must have observed in how marked a degree the instability of purpose by which, for a decade, Pius IX had been characterized, has given place to that constancy which was an eminent characteristic of his early life. Constancy in love, unrequited by the fair object of his affections, converted the youthful soldier into a priest. Constancy in the duties of his sacred calling rendered him one of the brightest ornaments of the Church, both in the mission-field abroad, and in more responsible offices at home. Constancy to liberal principles in an era of corruption and of political disquiet, secured his election to the Papal throne. Constancy in friendship, both before and after that event, is the brightest trait in a character altogether estimable.

'Rare is true love; true friendship is still rarer[1]!'

Constancy of purpose enabled him to confront the most powerful and determined opposition, and to inaugurate his reign by that great act of grace, the political amnesty, to which allusion has been made,

[1] La Fontaine.

and afterwards to attempt the dangerous experiment of constitutional rule.

From that period the reins of government have been held by Antonelli, in whose hands the Pontiff long remained but a vacillating tool. But the Cardinal who, if the wisest, is no longer the most influential of the Pope's advisers, is in disfavour; and in the same ratio as his influence declines, the Pontiff's firmness of purpose appears to revive.

In the revival, and the unfettered exercise of this distinguishing characteristic, we see a guarantee for the accomplishment of the cherished project of Pius IX; and anticipate that concurrently with the pretentious assumptions with which the so-called Œcumenical Council shall declare him personally the organ of the unseen Ruler of the world, we may witness the commencement of the last vital struggle for the maintenance of the Temporal Sovereignty;—the beginning of the end of that august power which, for fifteen centuries, has committed itself to an internecine contest with human intelligence and freedom.

The world has long been familiar with the pretensions of Rome, but it is not often that they are stated with greater candour and conciseness, or by one better entitled to speak with authority, than in the following sentences from the important address recently delivered by Archbishop Manning at Kensington :—

'What was the meaning of modern civilization? The state of political society founded upon divorce, secular education, infinite divisions, and contradictions in matters of religion, and the absolute renunciation of the supreme authority of the Christian Church. Could it, then, be matter of wonder that when the Roman

Pontiff published the Syllabus all those who were in love with modern civilization should have risen in uproar against it? Or could it be wondered that when the world, with great courtesy sometimes, with great superciliousness at another time, and great menace always, invites the Roman Pontiff to reconcile himself to Liberalism, progress, and modern civilization, he should say, "No, I will not and cannot. Your progress means divorce; I maintain Christian marriage. Your progress means secular education; I maintain that education is intrinsically and necessarily Christian. You maintain that it is a good thing that men should think as they like, talk as they like, preach as they like, and propagate what errors they please. I say that it is sowing error broadcast over the world. You say I have no authority over the Christian world, that I am not the Vicar of the Good Shepherd, that I am not the supreme interpreter of the Christian Faith. I am all these. You ask me to abdicate, to renounce my supreme authority. You tell me I ought to submit to the civil power, that I am the subject of the King of Italy, and from him I am to receive instructions as to the way I should exercise the civil power. I say I am liberated from all civil subjection, that my Lord made me the subject of no one on earth, king or otherwise, that in His right I am sovereign. I acknowledge no civil superior, I am the subject of no prince, and I claim more than this—I claim to be the Supreme Judge and director of the consciences of men; of the peasant that tills the field and the prince that sits on the throne; of the household that lives in the shade of privacy and the Legislature that makes laws for kingdoms—I am the sole last Supreme Judge of what is right and wrong."'

We need not pause to criticize the Archbishop's definition of 'modern civilization.' Whether or not it will, as alleged, fall to the lot of this English prelate to become the mouthpiece of his fraternity in praying the Pontiff to elevate the propositions of the Syllabus into Articles of Faith, this is certain—that he is in entire accord with that notorious document which closes with these words, 'They are in damnable error who regard the reconciliation of the Pope with modern civilization as possible or desirable.'

The principles of authority, and of the right of private judgment—in conflict for three centuries—are now seen preparing for a struggle which, it is admitted by the advocates of both, must be decisive and final. The issue cannot be uncertain. That ancient and crumbling theocracy which, arrogating to itself the voice of prophecy, 'I will make him my first-born, higher than the kings of the earth,' has asserted a supreme authority, in the regions both of the spiritual and the secular, and still, with unabated presumption, sets itself in opposition to the tide of progress and of civilization, whilst poisoning Christianity at its source, must give place to that light which it has striven to quench in the blood of martyrs—and by atrocities always on a par with its arrogance—even 'the true Light which lighteth every man that cometh into the world.'

> 'O that the free would stamp the impious name
>   Of Pope into the dust! or write it there,
> So that this blot upon the page of fame
>   Were as a serpent's path, which the light air

Erases, and the flat sands close behind!
  Ye the oracle have heard;
  Lift the victory-flashing sword,
And cut the snaky knots of this foul Gordian word,
Which, weak itself as stubble, yet can bind
  Into a mass, irrefragably firm,
The axes and the rods which awe mankind.
  The sound has poison in it—'tis the sperm
Of what makes life foul, cank'rous, and abhorr'd:
  Disdain not, then, at thine appointed term,
  To set thine armèd heel on this reluctant worm[1]!'

[1] Shelley.

APPENDIX.

THE important events which characterized the Pontificates immediately preceding that of Pius IX cannot be rightly apprehended without some degree of acquaintance with the history of those secret societies in the Peninsula through whose agency they were brought about.

The history of Italy in the first half of the nineteenth century is not that of a united people; for, notwithstanding its unity of language, the unmistakable similarity of national character which pervades its whole population, its singularly advantageous geographical position, the universal aspiration after liberty, and many abortive attempts to shake off the yoke of foreign oppression, it had failed to recognize, or at least to bring into healthy activity, the first elements of national strength.

The curse of Italy from the twelfth century to the present time has been the number, the power, and the antagonism of the 'sects.' From the time of Conrad III, when the rival sects of Guelphs and Ghibellines were established, the chief element of discord, the most fatal hindrance to progress, has been the power of secret societies, of political and politico-religious *sects*—the natural offshoots of despotic governments—which have diverted patriotism and the energy of the nation from their legitimate aims, and proved the handmaid to tyranny, division, and irreligion. In Italy, if anywhere, such associations were justifiable; for here, a people possessing those qualities—physical, intellectual, and moral—which fitted them to become a great and independent nation, had, through long ages, been held in check by despotic governments; until the impossibility of realizing the high aims to which they aspired, left them a prey to paltry disputes, and to the *finesse* of the promoters of secret societies, which, however, have worked nothing but ill; and, when associated with the ruling powers, have brought governments into contempt, subverted the very principle of authority, and intensified the alienation of the disaffected.

The most distinguished of these secret societies which have had their birth within the present century, was that of the *Carbonari*. The object of this association was the overthrow of existing governments, for the accomplishment of which it relied mainly upon foreign aid, and was ready to ally itself with any power, French, English, or sub-Alpine, which would take the initiative; beyond that it was content to leave to the future to arrange and harmonize the diverse aims and opinions of its members, who entertained every possible variety of political opinion, but the great majority of whom were believed to be Republicans. The oath which was administered on initiation said nothing as to the aims to be reached; it simply enjoined *implicit obedience* to the executive, and, if necessary, the sacrifice of self for the good of the order.

Carbonarism may be said to have had its rise in the perfidy of the Archduke John, who, in the year 1809, had promised independence to the Italians.

The name of the society was derived from the woodland and mountainous districts of Calabria, whither many refugees had resorted, and where their chief occupation was the manufacture of *charcoal*. The secret meetings of their order were called *Vendite*, or charcoal sales. In its early career the association received the support of many distinguished men who aspired after Italian unity. Its establishment in the kingdom of the Two Sicilies, in 1811, had the approbation both of Murat and of the Minister of Police; Murat sagaciously recognizing, in its extensive and powerful organization, a valuable auxiliary in carrying out his own ambitious design of establishing a great independent Italian kingdom. A year later, Count Nugent, the commander of the Austrian forces in Italy, with a perfidy which, alas! England may not censure, played upon the imprudent credulity of the Italians by issuing a proclamation from Ravenna, on the 10th of December, 1812, in which he promised independence and union. Two years later the sympathetic voice of England encouraged the same delusive hopes. Lord William Bentinck favoured the movement which the Carbonari had originated, promising the assistance of British arms to restore Italy to the position she occupied in her most brilliant epochs. On the 29th of March, 1814, he landed at Spezzia with 12,000 men, unfurled his banners bearing the inscription 'Independence of Italy,' and issued a proclamation summoning the Italians to arms; whilst, probably impelled by the apprehension of Austrian intervention, immediately upon hearing of the abdication of Napoleon, he despatched a messenger to Victor Emanuel I requesting him at once to take possession of his dominions.

In 1815, the insincerity of Murat had been demonstrated. The infatuated and ambitious king, believing that the moment had arrived for the realization of his bold design of bringing the whole Peninsula under his sway, was now in open alliance with Napoleon; and, chagrined at the loss of the English alliance, and his inability to command that support in Italy upon which his credulity had led him to rely, he staked the success of his mad enterprise upon the patriotism of the Carbonari, and excited them to rise and assert their country's freedom. The allies, however, had resolved upon the restoration of the Sicilian family to the throne of Naples; the Duke of Wellington in an interview at Ghent with the exile king, Louis XVIII, having declared that he regarded the restoration of the Bourbons as essential to the equilibrium of Europe [1].

At this time Carbonarism had become the ruling power throughout Sicily and Corsica, and had penetrated into the Roman States. Its role of members increased with astounding rapidity, and its influence was so far acknowledged that the adherence and support of the society was courted by the competitors for power. The promptings which it received from foreign governments confirmed the inherent weakness of the association,—its absence of faith in the Italians, and its consequent subserviency to foreign impulses.

In 1821, Charles Albert, the heir-apparent to the Sardinian throne, enrolled himself a member of the association; a circumstance which, though it inspired great hopes of conducing to the early and complete realization of the objects of the society, was in reality a fatal blow to its success. In 1821, Charles Albert, *the Prince*, was a conspirator; but in 1831, Charles Albert, *the King*, had no liking for a society which aimed at subverting the principle of monarchy; and his former complicity with the revolutionary association rendered him, as King, its most powerful and effective antagonist. At this time, Mazzini imforms us, ' the society had reached a degree of numerical strength unknown to any of the societies by which it was succeeded. But the Carbonari did not know how to turn their strength to account. Although the doctrines of Carbonarism were widely diffused, its leaders had no confidence in the people, and appealed to them rather to attain an appearance of force likely to attract those men of rank and station in whom alone they put their trust, than from any idea of leading them to immediate action. Hence the ardour and energy of the youth of the order—of those who dreamed only of country, the republic, war and glory in the eyes of Europe—

---

[1] Alison, vol. xix.

was entrusted to the direction of men, not only old in years, but imbued with the ideas of the Empire—cold precisionists who had neither faith nor future, and who, instead of fostering, repressed all daring and enthusiasm. At a later date, when the immense mass of Carbonari already affiliated, and the consequent impossibility of preserving secrecy convinced the leaders of the necessity for action, they felt the want of some stronger bond of unity, and not having a *principle* on which to found it, they set themselves to find it in a *man—a prince*. This was the ruin of Carbonarism.'

The insurrections of the Carbonari were successful, but were invariably followed by intestine discords. In religion, as in politics, they lacked a definite programme. Republicans in principle, they hailed and supported monarchy for the sake of associating a royal name with the insurrection, and openly recognized Charles Albert as a leader—a man whom they hated and despised. Hating Murat, and disgusted both with the form and the severity of his government, they madly threw themselves into his enterprise against Austria, heedless of the appeals of Nügent[1], of the declared purposes of the brave but unprincipled and despotic king, and of the condemnation, because of the inevitable failure of the enterprise, by Napoleon, who prognosticated that his brother-in-law incurred greater risk in making war in 1815 than he had done in abstaining from war in 1814.

Two million of Italians were ready to rise at the call of their leaders; but though the necessity of war with Austria had been foreseen, and even hailed, no preparations had been made; and the arms which the people demanded were refused them. Deserted by Charles Albert, and betrayed by Murat, 'they fell,' says Mazzini, 'not vanquished by superior

[1] Count Nugent, who was in command of the Austrian forces in Italy, energetically warned the Carbonari of the danger of being ensnared by the specious promises of Murat.

forces, which would have left them the honour of combat, but overthrown by a sophism which they introduced into their revolutionary programme.' The Pope formally condemned and anathematized them, and sanctioned the formation of the rival sect of SANFEDISTS.

The professed object of the association, which enjoyed the patronage of a Holy Father, and of all the despotic governments of Italy, was to defend the Roman Catholic religion, and the temporal dominion and prerogatives of the Papacy, both from the plots of the Carbonari and the aggressions of Austria. An unmitigated hatred between the two sects ensued, and on the pretext of a detected conspiracy, the Papal Government commenced an organized system of persecution to which many of the leading Carbonari in the Papal States fell victims. The number of the proscriptions, including men in every province, and of every social class—priests, nobles, soldiers, and peasants—revealed the extent to which the sect had spread its ramifications, and inspired new hopes of eventual success. Secret inquisitions were established by the Government; politics took the place of religion in the pulpits; the punishment of death was not too severe for those who were even *suspected* of Carbonarism. The result of this Sanfedist persecution was that Leo XII died in 1829 execrated by the great body of his people, whilst many of the wealthy and educated classes had emigrated to Lombardy and Tuscany, where they contributed to help forward the liberal movement which was soon to prove the Nemesis of Sanfedist malevolence.

In early life Mazzini had enrolled himself a Carbonaro. 'While studying the events of 1820 and 1821,' he says, 'I had learned much of Carbonarism, and I did not much admire the complex symbolism, the hierarchical mysteries, nor the political faith—or rather the absence of all political faith—I discovered in that institution. But I was at that time unable to attempt to form any association of my own, and in the Carbonari I found a body of men in whom, however inferior they were to the idea they represented, thought and action, faith and works were identical. Here were men who, defying alike excommunication and capital punishment, had the persistent energy ever to persevere and to weave a fresh web each time the old one was broken. And this was enough to induce me to join my name and my labours to theirs.' Within a few months of his initiation he was betrayed by a certain Major Cotton, to whom he was deputed to minister the oath for the second rank of Carbonari. Rifle-bullets, the formula of the oath, and other treasonable papers being found upon him, he was at once arrested, and was confined for some months in the fortress of Savona. Here it was that, reflecting on the defective aims and organization of Carbonarism, he conceived the plan of the association of *La Giovine Italia*.

On the accession of Charles Albert to the Sardinian throne in 1831, Mazzini resolved to address him through the press. His address, which has been appropriately described as 'a flash of divine eloquence, such as never before shone over Italy,' recalled the hopes awakened in the minds of Italians by the accession of a prince who had been a Carbonaro in 1821, and exhorted the king to undertake the liberation of Italy. In a preface to the republication of this letter in 1847, Mazzini says: 'I do not believe that the salvation of Italy can be achieved now or at any future time by Prince, Pope, or King.' And he adds, '*I held these convictions even at the time when I wrote that letter.*'

An order for the arrest of Mazzini, should he attempt to return to Italy, followed the publication of his letter to the king; and abandoning the hope, which his own words show that he never honestly entertained, of help coming from Sardinia, he betook himself to the development of his projected association, the *Giovine Italia*, or 'Young Italy;' and for the better prosecution of his plans he removed to Marseilles.

In the association of 'Young Italy' Mazzini aimed at the development and completion of the fundamental ideas of Carbonarism. That association concerned itself chiefly with the work of destruction, and relied upon the harmony, induced by united effort, for the successful guidance of the *revolution* which should succeed the *insurrection*. Mazzini, on the contrary, believed that the success of the revolution depended upon its having *a practical aim*. The new society, therefore, presented a definite programme, and publicly announced it to their fellow countrymen. That aim was *revolution;* but profiting by the experiences of Carbonarism, which had taught the importance of union in the critical moments which follow success in action, they would inculcate beforehand the steps by which the attainment of their aims must be accomplished. Young Italy was boldly proclaimed to be *Republican* and *Unitarian*, whilst it further sought to secure unity of religious faith. What this faith was is not very clear, but it was adverse to the Papacy. Mazzini affirms in his writings at this period that 'liberty and the Papacy are in direct contradiction and opposed to each other,' and that 'the Papacy is extinct and Catholicism a corpse.'

Instead of admitting heterogeneous elements, as did Carbonarism, the society was confined to those who accepted and believed in its avowed creed, for the elucidation and dissemination of which a special literature sprang into existence, and a journal bearing the name of the association was started towards the close of 1831, and was conducted with amazing vigour and ability, Mazzini and his Genoese friends being the principal contributors.

The means which the *Giovine Italia* proposed to itself for the accomplishment of its aims were *education* and *instruction;*

by education was understood the teaching by example, word, and pen, of the necessity of insurrection. It proposed to carry on the insurrection by means of guerilla bands, which should render it universal throughout Italy, and so consecrate every foot of native soil by the memory of some great exploit: 'the soil once free, every authority will bow down before the national Council, the sole source of authority in the State[1].' The one thing wanting to twenty millions of Italians desirous of emancipating themselves, was affirmed to be not *power*, but FAITH. 'Young Italy will endeavour to inspire this faith, first by its teachings and afterwards by an energetic initiative;' and it repudiated alike the assistance and pity of foreign governments. The government during the insurrection was to be vested in a provisional dictatorial power, concentrated in the hands of a small number of tried and trusted men. The banner of Young Italy, displaying the colours white, red, and green, was to bear on one side the words 'LIBERTY, EQUALITY, HUMANITY,' and on the other 'UNITY AND INDEPENDENCE.' Rejecting the complicated symbols and hierarchical mysteries of Carbonarism, the members were divided simply into two classes—the Initiators and the Initiated, and the form of oath, administered upon initiation, distinctly declared the objects of the society and the means to be employed for their accomplishment.

Mazzini placed himself at the head of the movement, which was to have its centre out of Italy, and devoted himself, safe in exile, to the framing of plots, and to the work of forming committees of the association throughout Italy. In the Pontifical States he found many ready accomplices, through the vindictive spirit which Papal misgovernment, and the malignant operations of the Sanfedist faction had provoked. The sect spread rapidly, enlisting the sympathies of multitudes who were not enrolled as members, and re-

[1] 'Life and Writings of Mazzini,' vol. i.

ceiving into its ranks Italian patriots, Polish refugees, and French Republicans.

The publication of the journal *Young Italy* had been preceded by a manifesto, clandestinely circulated, in which the objects of the association were set forth, and the history of 1821 and 1831 was proclaimed to have consummated and concluded the separation of Young Italy from the men of the past; and therein to have taught a better lesson to the rising generation than whole volumes of theories. These publications were designed to supply the place of personal influence, and, for a while, were easily smuggled into Italy. But when the attention of the authorities had been thoroughly roused, and large rewards offered for the seizure of the papers of the association—whilst non-informants who were privy to their introduction into Italy were threatened with a heavy fine and two years' imprisonment—much caution and ingenuity were requisite to accomplish this end. The members of Young Italy, however, outwitted the Government spies, who dogged them continually; their writings found their way into Italy as freely as before, and were reproduced by means of clandestine presses established in various central places.

Thus in one year the *Giovine Italia* became the dominant secret society throughout the whole of Italy, whilst 'a central committee existed abroad, whose duties consisted in holding aloft, as it were, the flag of the association, forging as many links as possible between the Italian and foreign democratic element, and generally directing and superintending the working of the association[1].' Before the year had closed Mazzini had become the heart and soul of the Italian movement, the recognized 'King of Young Italy,' the undisputed ruler of a State of his own creation.

Attempts were made, through the medium of agents of the

[1] Mazzini.

Italian Governments, to suppress the publication of *Young Italy* in France, and in August, 1832, a decree was issued by which Mazzini was exiled from the country. He contrived, nevertheless, to continue to reside, and to superintend the publication of his journal at Marseilles, for a whole year, cleverly eluding the unremitting search of the police. On one occasion, when his asylum was at last discovered, he persuaded the prefect to send him away quietly *under the escort of his own agents*, and succeeded in substituting and sending to Geneva in his place, a friend, who bore a strong personal resemblance to him, whilst he walked quietly through the whole row of the police officers, dressed in the uniform of a National Guard! Banished from France, proscribed in Piedmont and Switzerland, he sought refuge from political persecution where alone it was to be found, in the free soil of old England.

At this period much odium was brought upon the *Giovine Italia* by the atrocious calumnies launched against Mazzini, charging him not only with sanctioning the odious practice of assassination, but with the actual personal guilt of the crime—a charge from which the accused triumphantly vindicated himself. 'I abhor,' he says, 'and all those who know me well know that I abhor, bloodshed, and every species of terror erected into a system, as remedies equally ferocious, unjust, and inefficacious against evils that can only be cured by the diffusion of liberal ideas.' And again, in his pamphlet, entitled 'Italy, Austria, and the Pope,' published in London in 1844, he says, 'I firmly believe in the immorality of the punishment of death; and it seems to assume a colour yet more degrading to our age, when visited on political offences.'

This association, then, whatever view we take of its claim to consideration on the ground of moral, social, or political expediency, or of its appropriateness to the circumstances and the character of the Italian people, was in advance of those secret societies by which it was preceded, and particularly of Carbonarism, out of which it sprang, and which it had sufficient vitality to absorb and transform, in these particulars.

It suppressed all condemnations to death, and in the punishment of treachery and insubordination substituted simple expulsion from its ranks for the stiletto of the assassin.

By announcing *a definite programme* and *political faith*, it afforded *a test* which enabled its members to rely upon union in the pursuit of a common object, when the insurrection should be accomplished.

By *its widely-circulated writings* it kept the great fundamental objects at which it aimed constantly before its members, thus educating them to unity of purpose.

By insisting upon *unity of religion* on a broad basis, it closed the door at once to ill-timed religious discussion and to the infidelity which had proved a source of much weakness to Carbonarism.

By *limiting the association to the youth of Italy*, and excluding all above forty years of age, it secured a degree of enthusiasm which was invaluable; and if this were purchased by the loss of the wisdom and experience which belong to age, the limitation further excluded many dangerous men, deeply imbued with Carbonarism, and hostile to the Republican form of government. And lastly,

By boldly proclaiming that Italy was strong enough to effect her own deliverance without the aid of foreign governments, it struck at the root of that pusillanimous fear which, pointing to foreign alliances as Italy's only hope, had enervated and eventually destroyed Carbonarism.

But it had also this radical weakness,—its centre of authority was placed *abroad*. The refugees were to be the real soul of the movement. 'This,' says Farini, 'was a recurrence to the times and customs of the Middle Ages, when as often as citizens were banished by their opponents, who had gained the ascendancy, from those turbulent republics, they used to apply themselves in exile to raise money and troops in rival cities, or in intriguing courts, and then attempted the conquest of their country by stirring up the factions at home.' And it must be confessed that in the face of powerful standing armies, and the secure alliances under which all the Italian Governments, and particularly that of the Pope, reposed, the tactics of Young Italy appear quixotic, and ill-adapted to the attainment of the objects of its lofty and patriotic ambition.

Another important politico-religious association demands a reference, on account of the influence which it exercised in the north of Italy, and particularly in Piedmont. *La Catollica* was essentially an institution of the Jesuits; it took its rise during the French occupation of Italy at the close of the eighteenth century, and became affiliated with the government of the princes of Savoy, whose territory was then confined to the island of Sardinia. Its avowed objects were the maintenance of the privileges of the Church, and of the principles of absolute government; hence the tenacity with which it retained its influence over the court and the clergy. Councillors of State, bishops, and clergy were generally chosen from its ranks; whilst the powerful engine of education was employed for extending its ramifications throughout Piedmont, where, at the commencement of the reign of Charles Albert, its power was practically unlimited, and secured for prince and people the distrust of the Liberals in the other Italian States.

APPENDIX B.

The printed scheme of the dogma of Infallibility has been distributed. It contains five canons:—

I. If any one should say that the episcopal chair of the Roman Church is not the true and real infallible chair of Blessed Peter, or that it has not been divinely chosen by God as the most solid, indefectible, and incorruptible rock of the whole Christian Church, let him be anathema.

II. If any one should say that there exists in the world another infallible chair of the truth of the Gospel of Christ our Lord, distinct and separate from the chair of Blessed Peter, let him be anathema.

III. If any one should deny that the divine *magisterium* of the chair of Blessed Peter is necessary to the true way of eternal salvation for all men, whether unfaithful or faithful, whether laymen or bishops, let him be anathema.

IV. If any one should say that each Roman Pontiff, legitimately elected, is not by Divine right the successor of Blessed Peter, even in the gift of the infallibility of *magisterium*, and should deny to any one of them the prerogative of infallibility for teaching the Church the Word of God, pure from all corruption and error, let him be anathema.

V. If any one should say that General Councils are established by God in the Church as a power of feeding the Divine flock in the word of faith superior to the Roman Pontiff, or equal to him, or necessary by Divine institution, in order that the *magisterium* of the Roman Bishop should be preserved infallible, let him be anathema.

www.ingramcontent.com/pod-product-compliance
Lightning Source LLC
Chambersburg PA
CBHW021209230426
43667CB00006B/619